Cherishing the Earth – Nourishing the Spirit

Edited by Maria Curtis

The Lindsey Press
London

the unitarians

Published by The Lindsey Press on behalf of
The General Assembly of Unitarian and Free Christian Churches
Essex Hall, 1–6 Essex Street, London WC2R 3HY, UK

www.unitarian.org.uk

© The General Assembly of Unitarian and Free Christian Churches 2023

ISBN 978-0-85319-098-1

Designed and typeset by Garth Stewart

Contents

Preface
Maria Curtis

Cherishing the Earth – Nourishing the Spirit is written exclusively by Unitarians, but it is not exclusively for Unitarians: this book is for anyone searching for a spiritual response to the current ecological crisis. The contributors consider what it might mean to live in right relationship with the Earth. Clearly, urgent action is needed to reduce emissions of greenhouse gases, but we ask what changes we all need to make *in ourselves* to work towards healing the Earth and restoring balance to the global ecosystem. We, as a species, need a change in consciousness.

The Unitarian perspectives here view the ecological crisis that confronts all of us as a spiritual crisis. These values are shared by our Quaker friend, environmental activist Alastair McIntosh, whom we thank for his stimulating Foreword. We ask ourselves how we humans have got to the point where our behaviour has upset the balance of nature to such an extent that we are facing the sixth mass extinction event in the history of life on Earth – the only one caused by human activity. What does it say about us that for the last thirty years, or more, the damaging effects of carbon emissions on the climate have been understood, yet we have carried on cutting down forests (which absorb carbon and provide us with oxygen) and burning even more fossil fuels at an even faster rate? We continue to replace biodiverse habitats with monocultures. We continue to pollute water, land, and air. This is ecocide and suicide.

This book questions our identity as human beings – who *are* we to have let this happen? We are so clever, yet so stupid. Unitarians generally take a benign view of human nature – favouring original blessing over original sin – but perhaps now is the time to acknowledge our human frailty. Are we intrinsically selfish? Are we condemned to short-term thinking? Are there limits to the extent of our compassion? Or can we rise above competitive individualism to embrace a genuinely universal concern for the welfare of all humanity, the Earth, and all her creatures? We believe that our salvation lies in stepping down from our self-assigned place at the pinnacle of creation and accepting, with due humility, that we are not only interconnected with all other life forms, but also interdependent. We cannot, must not, stand apart from the web of life.

For too long – a blink of an eye on the geological time scale, but long enough to cause untold damage – we humans have engaged in an exploitative relationship with the Earth. Many of us from industrialised societies have become disconnected from the Earth, which renders us indifferent to her plight. The contributors to this book all give voice to the need for humankind to reconnect with the Earth – to literally get back in touch – and embrace our animal nature. Perhaps by paying attention, with all our faculties, to the bounty of the Earth, we will fully comprehend the gift that we are squandering. Perhaps gratitude for the gift of life will bring us back to our senses.

As a species, humans are young upstarts. We need to grow up fast if we are to save the Earth. We celebrate our human consciousness, ingenuity, and capacity for intimacy. Acknowledging our unique responsibility as the species that caused the decline, we must now co-operate to find creative solutions so that we and the Earth may flourish once again.

Our liberal faith

Unitarianism is a liberal faith which has evolved out of the Judaeo-Christian tradition (and continues to evolve). Because it is a faith free of dogma and rigidly held beliefs, you will find a rich kaleidoscope of views presented here. We look to our individual consciences to discern what is of highest worth. Our truth is rooted in personal experience rather than external authority. As a dissenting denomination, we value our hard-won freedoms, but the freedom to choose what we believe does not imply that anything goes. Paradoxically, the absence of a creed strengthens our commitment to what is right, along with our determination to pursue truth and justice. We are not captive to any orthodoxy; rather, we maintain an openness of heart and mind which is, in itself, a discipline.

We respect many different faith traditions and philosophies, gleaning from them insights that accord with our fundamental values. We find wisdom and inspiration in the world of the arts and sciences. We respect the scientific method and are ready to change our opinions when they are challenged by the evidence.

Unitarians may not share a single theology, but we all take life seriously, with a focus on what really matters. Some speak of a transcendent God, others of the Divine, or our Higher Self, to refer to what is of ultimate value. We feel gratitude for the gift of life. We offer our love and compassion to all human beings, acknowledging their inherent worth regardless of differences such as those of race, religion, gender, and sexual orientation. We also extend our concern and compassion towards all living things and the Earth-system itself.

Members of a liberal faith tend to be reluctant to take up a prophetic stance, lest it be construed as evangelism; we do not believe that we have a monopoly on truth, nor do we wish to impose our beliefs on others, but perhaps now is the time to "reclaim prophetic witness".[1] There are some strong prophetic voices to be heard among the contributors to this book, and not only in Part One. At this critical juncture in human history we feel the need to speak out, to challenge some basic societal assumptions of the 'affluent West' in a counter-cultural way. In particular, you will hear a rejection of the quasi-religious dogma of neoliberalism, with its nationalistic, competitive growth agenda.

---

[1]   Paul Rasor, *Reclaiming Prophetic Witness — Liberal Religion in the Public Square* (Skinner House Books, Boston, MA, 2012).

Our Unitarian spiritual communities have been called "laboratories of faith",[2] places where our values are strengthened by tradition, but are tempered by worshipping alongside others with whom we co-create new visions of reality. In our congregations we can share our joys and sorrows, our hopes and fears. In silence and meditation, through prayer and ritual, with music and song, we open ourselves to the Divine Spirit and ask for strength to enable ourselves and others to flourish in this glorious but challenging world.

There are tensions inherent in following a liberal faith. Several of the writers in this volume challenge the individualism that might be seen to be integral to Unitarianism. Perhaps now is the time to suppress our individualistic tendencies in the light of the need to work together, both in our spiritual communities and the communities in which we live. Ultimately our concern is for the wider sacred community of the Earth herself.

Having set a high value on rationality, we are beginning to realise that we need head and heart working in harmony to confront the current ecological crisis. And so, in "the Unitarian dance",[3] our writers weave paths between thinking and feeling; individual and community; tradition and freedom; tolerance and commitment; pluralism and conviction, as we consider how to cherish the Earth. We hope that the creative tension that this generates will be enlightening and inspiring.

About the book

The chapters are arranged in five parts (interspersed with short poems, prayers, and rituals). However, all the contributions acknowledge our unique responsibility as human beings for having caused the current

----

2   David Usher, *Life Spirit* (The Lindsey Press, London, 2015).
3   Phillip Hewett, *The Unitarian Way* (Canadian Unitarian Council, 1985).

ecological crisis. We take it as our duty to work towards cherishing the Earth and enabling her to flourish. We come from a place of reverence and gratitude for the sheer joy of existence.

Running through these chapters is an awareness that the environmental crisis is a multi-faceted justice issue in which poverty, racial injustice, and gender discrimination intersect. We are all embedded in a global political and economic system which operates like a dogmatic religion, but not one of our choosing. We in the 'Global North' continue to reap the benefits of our colonial past. In considering how to change the world, the contributors to this book focus on the need to start by changing ourselves, by growing up as human beings, being honest, acknowledging our privileges and our prejudices, and taking responsibility for trying to make the world a more just and equitable place for all.

The first three parts are loosely themed (although the allocation of the pieces is somewhat arbitrary, as similar concerns wind their way through all of them).

The pieces in Part One, **Prophetic Voices**, look at the bigger picture, considering our need, as spiritual beings, to speak truth to power, to name the powers – a challenge in our world of faceless multi-national corporations. The writers unveil, beneath the ecological crisis, stories of social injustice; both within our own country and across the world, huge disparities of wealth and opportunity prevail. They challenge the orthodoxy of neoliberalism, with its celebration of growth and exploitation. The dominant nations have exploited the Earth and vulnerable peoples on the Earth, and continue to do so. Our writers stress the importance of acknowledging our complicity as a species in the demise of the Earth .They consider the question of what sort of action we need to take to challenge the 'business as usual' model; all agree that each of us merely 'doing our bit' will not suffice to avert the unfolding global catastrophe.

Part Two, *Honouring the Earth,* is concerned with our relationship with the Earth – the land, the air, rivers, oceans, and all creatures. And our own bodies. We celebrate with joy and gratitude the stunning diversity and beauty that we perceive on Earth. Contributors all agree that we must abandon notions of dominion over the rest of creation and take our place *alongside* the myriad other species on Earth, acknowledging not only our interconnectedness but also our interdependence, in showing respect for all life forms.

We ask to what extent humans are honouring the Earth with industrial farming of plants and animals. What is the impact of our way of life on the natural world? Do we have a right to sacrifice the lives of other beings in our own interests? What would a more respectful relationship with other living things look like? Our writers consider overlapping Panentheist, Eco-feminist, and Pagan theologies, all of them perspectives whereby the natural world is seen as sacred and not merely as a provider of resources, or a backdrop to our existence. We have much to learn from Indigenous peoples all over the world who have long embraced the importance of a reciprocal relationship with the Earth and all her creatures. Western philosophy has traditionally separated mind or soul from the body; these chapters reject this dualistic perspective, offering a more integrated view of humankind – as bodies embedded in a spiritual milieu; in the words of John O'Donohue,[4] "*The body is in the soul*".

Part Three, *Changing Hearts and Minds,* acknowledges that neither heart nor mind alone will change human behaviour. The Prologue celebrates the openness of heart and mind characteristic of Unitarianism – its commitment to the pursuit of truth; to looking dispassionately at the evidence; to listening to marginalised and disenfranchised voices; above all, to "hearing the cry of the Earth", in the words of Thich Nhat Hanh. Contributors consider the importance of education in developing

----

4   John O'Donohue, *Anam Cara: Spiritual Wisdom from the Celtic World* (Bantam Books, 1997).

sensitive people who can respond in a caring, empathetic way to the plight of the Earth. We acknowledge our anxiety, guilt, and discomfort, as we seek a way through to Hope. We look at processes whereby we, in the Global North, can pass beyond denial and face up to our complicity, our privilege, as an essential stage in changing our own hearts and minds and enabling others to do the same. We can rethink our behaviour as consumers and experiment with a different relationship with 'stuff'. But we always start from a place of celebration of the Earth as sacred.

Part Four, **Active Hope** (edited by Claire MacDonald), is fairly self-contained. The Prologue unpacks Joanna Macy's concept of Active Hope[5] as a spiritual path between Denial on the one hand and Despair on the other, to promote the "Great Turning". We do not have to keep doing things in the same destructive way. We can learn to mobilise our resources in creative ways, working co-operatively alongside others in community. This section includes personal testimony of practical interventions, exploring the relationship between ourselves and the natural world, demonstrating how cherishing the Earth can at the same time nourish our spirits; the writers show how *doing* something for the Earth, with the Earth, is also doing something for ourselves in a relationship that is reciprocal.

In the final section, **Young Voices**, we hear the heartfelt words of the young, who must inherit the problems that older generations have caused in our reckless plundering of the Earth's resources. They are poignant voices who tell their truth without dissembling. It is saddening that they must carry our burden into the future. We are grateful to these brave eco-warriors.

---

5   Joanna Macy and Chris Johnstone, *Active Hope: How to Face the Mess We're In with Unexpected Resilience and Creative Power* (New World Library, San Francisco, 2022).

How to use this book

The book can simply be read from cover to cover on your own. However, you will probably gain more from it through discussion with others. You will see that there are questions for discussion at the end of each chapter. We recommend creating small, facilitated study groups. And why not invite people from other faith groups (or none) to join you? Focusing on the ecological crisis, an important issue in which we are all stakeholders, may help to open lines of communication with others outside your usual community.

You may wish to focus on a theme, like *Celebration* or *Grief*, including poetry and prayer and ritual in your sessions as well as discussion. Or you may want to focus on local initiatives, examples of hope in action. Or perhaps you would like a more philosophical session, asking questions about human nature, for example. Or all of the above. The topics addressed in this book are important. I am confident that whatever you choose to read, you will find it stimulating and significant.

Revd Dr Maria Curtis

Maria is a Unitarian minister who served the Horsham congregation before retiring in 2019. She discovered Unitarianism quite late in life, at the end of a career as a teacher and educational psychologist; her doctorate is in cognitive development. She feels privileged to be part of the open-hearted and open-minded liberal Unitarian community – a community in which she is free to celebrate her wide-ranging interests in science, philosophy, literature (especially poetry), and music.

Foreword

Alastair McIntosh

One sentence from this book lingers longest with me: the last sentence in the last chapter. Sophie Emm, one of the Unitarian children who have contributed to the volume, expresses a concern that could speak for so many of us. She suggests that even if we do switch to electric vehicles, and even if we otherwise edge towards greener ways of living, so much will have been lost. You can't bring back what's gone extinct. You can't unmelt the glaciers, she says. And in a tone of understated, searing honesty, she leaves us with the stark question: "*What if it's already too late?*"

That question encapsulates the importance of this book. We can start by acknowledging that, for some species, it is indeed already too late. For the two thousand people who died and the two million made homeless in the Pakistan floods of 2022, it is already too late. Elsewhere, for those driven off their lands by drought, or coastal peoples watching theirs yield slowly to the waves, it is already too late.

Some will ask: "What use is spirituality now? What is the practical use of a book like this?" My short answer is: because we need to reconsider how to live. My longer answer is more complicated. Prophetic work (and many of the chapters in this book are prophetic) involves a relationship with time, especially when we are working towards a stepped vision for the future, and practical steps in public policy along the way.

In any highly charged political field, powerful forces will try to capture our attention, energy, and resources in directions that suit their interests. Most of us will be very well aware of the kinds of forces that have driven climate-change 'denialism', claiming that it's not happening, or, if it is, it's not caused by the emissions of greenhouse gas for which human impact is responsible. Less expected are the forces of 'alarmism' on the other side, which exaggerate the science either as a public expression of their own anxiety, or in the hope of boosting political action. One problem with such 'alarmism' is that it edges over into 'doomism', which in turn risks encouraging recklessness, wasted energies, or despair. Both polarities misdirect our energies.

I name these tendencies because exponents of both positions attend my talks, and it is the alarmism that most bothers me, because that feels like friendly fire. I mean forecasts made by people who may set themselves up as experts, but who lack a reputation in the science that is worth not losing. I mean climate-futures prophecies such as six or seven billion people dead by the end of this century, the 'inevitable' near-term social collapse of many or most countries in the world by 2028, or even human extinction by 2026. At least the retired American ecology professor who pumps the latter date to his cult-like following has now granted an extension. As he blogged last year: "*I stand firm on my prediction that there will be no humans on Earth in 2030.*"[1]

For the most part, we only know what we think we know about climate science because of the climate science. If we claim to know better, if we either ignore the consensus of expert science or exaggerate it, we had better have credentials that are credible, otherwise we are deluded and deluding at best, and charlatans at worst. Religious studies can offer important insights here. Such studies understand, better than most academic fields, the psychology of end-of-world millenarianism. Moreover, they understand the vacuum in authentic spirituality that such narratives can be sucked into.

For my part, I give credence to the work of the scientists who serve, in their many thousands, such organisations as the UN's Intergovernmental Panel on Climate Change (IPCC). Critics accuse them of being conservative and compromised. But in science, if you play a compromised

---

1   Guy McPherson, 'Transcript: Why Are We Here?', *Nature Bats Last* blog, 20 February 2021, https://guymcpherson.com/transcript-why-are-we-here/

game for long, you get found out. The scientists whom I respect point out that the mainstream science is already alarming enough to require no added alarmism to hammer on the door of politicians, even if they are amenable to listening. As summarised in one of the most recent IPCC reports at the time of writing:[2]

> It is unequivocal that human influence has warmed the atmosphere, ocean and land ... The scale of recent changes across the climate system as a whole ... are unprecedented. Human-induced climate change is already affecting many weather and climate extremes in every region across the globe.

* * * * *

If we follow the siren voices of denialism, then we do nothing. That may protect us from the imposition of carbon taxes and immediate lifestyle changes, but it sends the planet to hell in a handcart. But equally, if we follow the voices of alarmism, we risk betraying public trust in science if our exaggerations get found out. As with the IPCC's famous error in 2007, where bad referencing caused it to predict the demise of Himalayan glaciers by 2035, such slippages of rigour provide an endlessly recycled stream of bullets which the climate-change deniers then deploy to discredit science itself.

Moreover, if all we do is drive panic, without a vision that can stack up in a democracy to suggest what an alternative future could look like, then our agitation is but music to the ears of reactionary politicians who raise the spectre of climate refugees in order to clamp down on asylum seekers, and music also to the ears of developers, investors, and lobby groups pushing for geo-engineering as an alternative to cutting emissions. Notions such as dimming the amount of sunlight

---

2   https://www.ipcc.ch/report/ar6/wg1/downloads/report/IPCC_AR6_WG1_
     Headline_Statements.pdf

reaching Earth, while superficially attractive, would have unpredictable weather effects and consequent political effects; they would do nothing to slow down ocean acidification caused by the relentless build-up of CO_2; and they would provide cover for consumerist business-as-usual carbon emissions, leaving posterity to deal with 'termination shock' if such hi-tech interventions were ever ceased, or otherwise knocked out, causing abrupt planetary re-heating to unprecedented levels.

In science, there is no substitute for 'tell the truth', and that is why responsible bodies such as the IPCC make careful and defined use of such everyday language as 'high agreement', 'limited evidence', or 'about as likely as not'. For example, the latter implies a probability ranging from 33 per cent to 66 per cent, while acknowledging that such qualitative language has 'fuzzy' boundaries.[3]

We need to act now, but unless such action intends to bypass democracy, we need to carry others with us. I hear those who cry, "But that'll leave it too late!", to whom I am forced to reply: "Well, I hope you'll do authoritarianism better than whoever else will take the lead if you let that one out of the bag." And to say so feels awful, because I have seen the looks of trapped panic on the faces of faithful, passionate activists. On the one hand, the reality that climate change is closing in on us. On the other hand: what more can we be doing to head it off within the disciplined approach of democratic politics? Even if they choose to lead, politicians can only lead so far ahead of the electorate and still get voted back in. Here, then, is our stark conundrum. If we are alive to what gives life, where do we turn? For haste, indeed, "is of the devil". But what of God? What of those mills that turn so slowly? Have they anything to offer but the panacea phantasms of opium?

$$* * * * *$$

---

3   IPCC, *Guidance Note on ... Consistent Treatment of Uncertainties*, Geneva, 2010, https://www.ipcc.ch/site/assets/uploads/2017/08/AR5_Uncertainty_Guidance_Note.pdf.

Leading climate scientists insist that there is still time to save the Earth, or much of what we love, but that requires action not just on the short temporal horizon, but also with medium- and long-term thinking. If we focus only on what can be done immediately, we foreclose on the future. There are pathways to a sane future, and in my view these need to be better understood. One set of such pathways are the technical-emissions scenarios laid out by the IPCC in its Special Report in 2018 on limiting global warming to around 1.5°C. This massive study is prefaced with a quote, in French, from Antoine de Saint Exupéry, who wrote *The Little Prince*. Translated, it reads: "*As for the future, it is not a question of foreseeing it, but of making it possible.*"[4] However, as the report is careful to acknowledge, it is one thing to say what it is possible to do within the bounds of physical science; quite another to translate that into politics, policy, and practical action. At this juncture, at what has been called "the physics–politics gap", most of the mainstream discourse gets stuck. Ergo, the angst of climate-change campaigners, and their sense of being trapped.

Personally, I think that there are ways forward. They mean setting aside such quasi-conspiratorial notions as human extinction by the year 20-whenever, or whatever, and planning action not just in the short term, but simultaneously for the medium and long terms (by which I mean before and after the turn of this century). Put simply, *total greenhouse-gas emissions equal population multiplied by consumption*. Some would add *technology* into that equation, but my simplification assumes it to be integrated into emissions caused by material consumption.

Accordingly, if either human population numbers or the levels of material consumption fall, then we are on the right path. In my book *Riders on the Storm*[5] I have asserted that the population agenda must not

---

4   IPCC, *Special Report: Global Warming of 1.5 °C*, Geneva, 2018, https://www.ipcc.ch/sr15/
5   Alastair McIntosh, *Riders on the Storm: The Climate Crisis and the Survival of Being* (Birlinn, 2020).

be conflated with authoritarian notions of 'population control'. Rather, there is abundant demographic evidence that fertility rates fall naturally, and rapidly, when two main conditions are satisfied: a secure and just society (call it 'social security' for short) and women's emancipation. In the words of the poet Adrienne Rich:[6]

> The decision to feed the world
> is the real decision. No revolution
> has chosen it. For that choice requires
> that women shall be free.

Furthermore, the UN's 17 Sustainable Development Goals (SDGs), adopted by all member states in 2015, provide a roadmap towards such objectives. These include such driving themes as zero hunger, gender equality, responsible consumption, climate action, and peace, justice, and strong institutions.[7] When people ask, "What can I do?", I reply: "Work as best you can on pretty much any of the UN's SDGs". Translate concern to care; the creation of a care society. But there is an even bigger picture, and this is where theology and its application in spirituality kick in.

* * * * *

In October 2022, the European Unitarian Universalists invited me to speak at their annual conference in Mittelwihr, Alsace. Somebody said beforehand, with what I hoped was a wry but jocund nod, "Don't give them too much Christianity". So I gave them lots! But in counterpoint I preached the Sunday sermon from the Bhagavad Gita, the most sacred text of Hinduism, and specifically from Juan Mascaró's beautiful Penguin Classics translation of the first half of the first verse of the first chapter.

---

6   Adrienne Rich, 'Hunger (for Audre Lorde)', *The Dream of a Common Language*, W.W. Norton, NY, 1978, p. 13.
7   UN, *Sustainable Development Goals*, 2015, https://sdgs.un.org/goals.

It reads: "*On the field of Truth, on the battle-field of life, what came to pass, Sanjaya ...*",[8] employing three Sanskrit words (*Dharmakshétre ... Kurukshétra ... Sanjaya*) which encapsulate for me three key ontological perspectives. Each of them is nested within the others, and it is my experience that with them we can spiritually fortify the effectiveness of our engagement with climate change. I will take them in reverse order. That way, we can view them from a human standpoint.

First, who is Sanjaya? Sanjaya is the eagle-eyed charioteer of the blind king, Dhritarashtra. Blind, because political power is blind. That is why it needs an eagle-eyed charioteer. This is the level of immanent action in the world, in the present moment, when, as Extinction Rebellion urges, we must "act now!". Let that be our immediate calling, and let us remember also the expression of a French Jesuit priest, Jean-Pierre de Caussade: "*the sacrament of the present moment*".[9] If our activism calls us to break laws, then let us break them as we might break bread: sacramentally.

Juan Mascaró, whose sensitive translation was praised by Rabindranath Tagore, renders *Kurukshétra* as "*the battlefield of life*": the realm of all our inner and outer conflicts. This is the second level, where we glimpse intimations that individual spiritual life is not detached from the life of the world. Our locus of agency as activists widens.

The third, and ultimate, level is that of *Dharmakshétre*, the field of Truth, of *Dharma*, of "*the way, the truth, and the life*", as Jesus put it. That is the level that reminds us that the whole shebang is held in God's hands. We can live our lives, we can engage in the hand-to-hand 'fight' of daily action, but never forget, as the Moody Blues' 'Om' lyric has it, that "*far away, the distant sound/ is with us every day*".[10]

---

8   *The Bhagavad Gita* (trans. Juan Mascaró) (Penguin Classics, Harmondsworth, 1962, p. 43).
9   Jean-Pierre de Caussade, *The Sacrament of the Present Moment* (Fount Classics, London, 1996).
10 The Moody Blues, 'The Word / Om', *In Search of the Lost Chord* (Deram, 1968), YouTube: https://www.youtube.com/watch?v=wRGJbk4XpYs&t=28s.

Here we see the roots of the kind of American Transcendentalism that Ralph Waldo Emerson, with his Unitarian associations, wrote about. But the transcendent walks hand in hand with the immanent. Such is the significance of 'incarnate' Christian theology, where the living 'blood' of the Spirit interpenetrates the 'bread' that is the fabric of the universe. And that is deeply challenging. From this deepest level, our calling may be as expressed by the Orthodox tradition of Eastern Christianity, which maintains that St Silouan of Mount Athos heard Christ say: "*Keep your soul in hell and do not despair*".[11]

To quote Sheila Stewart, the tradition bearer of Scotland's ('Gypsy') Travelling People, writing of her people's hard times and cruel persecutions, especially of the past: "*God's no' sleeping*".[12]

* * * * *

It is here that the work of faith groups is so important in our times. I speak to many such groups, and my constant message to them is this. Ours is not to replicate the work of secular groups like Greenpeace, WWF, or Friends Of The Earth. Ours is to be salt of the earth, leaven to the bread, light to the world. Consider again the equation that *greenhouse-gas emissions = population x consumption*. Today the greater part of that equation is played by consumption. In my lifetime alone, since 1955, world population has roughly trebled, but greenhouse-gas emissions from consumption have increased around sixfold. I define consumerism as *consumption in excess of what is needed for a dignified sufficiency of life*. But dignified sufficiency is both quantitative and qualitative, and to achieve more satisfaction out of less material input, and therefore lower emissions, is more a question of psychology and spirituality than of economics and technology. What faith groups can bring to the climate crisis is, therefore, a deepening understanding of how to live life: as Jesus put it in one of my favourite Bible translations, "*that they might*

11   Paul Evdokimov, *In the World, of the Church* (St Vladimir's Seminary Press, New York, 2001, p. 193).
12   Sheila Stewart, *Pilgrims of the Mist* (Birlinn, Edinburgh, 2008, p. 19).

have not just any sodding old life, but promised life abundantly".[13] That's about our inner work, but spiritual qualities also play out into our outer lives, our work for justice and peace, our hands-in-the-soil work, as one of the chapters in this collection has it, of *"redeeming a rubbish dump"*.

We must be humble. Each of us is but one eight billionth of the human race. Ours is to participate in the work of God, but to remember that we are not God. Ours is to do what we can, and then remember, whether literally or metaphorically, the Sabbath, the time of rest, and that it was *"made for man, not man for the Sabbath"*.[14] But that eight billionth can, before the lens of God, be magnified. *"My soul doth magnify the Lord"*, said Mary,[15] and the Greek word *megalynei*, as in our word 'mega', literally means to make great. How? Through such acts as witness, prayer, and prophecy. Through asking inwardly to be held in God, to hold one another in God, and the matters that we feel passionate about. *"Members of a liberal faith tend to be reluctant to take up a prophetic stance, lest it be construed as evangelism"*, concedes Maria Curtis in her Preface to this book. But then, and with resurgent energy, she adds: *"perhaps now is the time to reclaim prophetic witness"*.

Yes, indeed, Maria and your fellow writers and the wider Unitarian movement! Within this book are both roadmaps and social legitimation for so doing. I am a Quaker, not a Unitarian, but in those of your services that I have attended I have seen an open and even interfaith theology, more outward structure than a Quaker meeting, and an approach to 'worship' – etymologically, a 'worthship' – that will speak to the need of many people for ritual, music, warm local presence, and even 'a damned good sermon'!

The prophetic, as a social expression of the mystical, opens the inner eye. How do we open such vision? Jesus said: *"Blessed are the pure in heart, for they shall see God."* [16] The Chandogya Upanishad of the Vedic traditions

---

13   John 10:10, MOT (My Own Translation).
14   Mark 2:27, New Internationalist Version. In which respect, note the Green Sabbath Project: https://www.greensabbathproject.net/.
15   Luke 1:46, King James Version.
16   Matthew 5:8, King James Version.

says: "*There is a bridge between time and Eternity; and this bridge is Atman, the spirit of man.*" [17] There we glimpse the 'over-soul'[18] as expressed by Emerson, himself of a Unitarian family, ordained in Unitarian ministry, and influenced by his reading of the Bhagavad Gita and other Vedic thought. To make this connection between the transcendent and the immanent, heaven and earth, the inner and the outer, is the great work for which our times call. It is the work of reconnecting Nature and our human nature, whereby, as the ending of the New Testament echoes the prophet Ezekiel, "*the leaves of the tree are for the healing of the nations*".[19] The passage from the Chandogya Upanishad quoted above goes on to spell out the consequences of such bridging very clearly:

> Evil or sin cannot cross that bridge, because the world of the Spirit is pure. This is why when this bridge has been crossed, the eyes of the blind can see, the wounds of the wounded are healed, and the sick man becomes whole from his sickness.

Finally, back to Sophie's question: "*What if it's already too late?*" It is already too late for so much, Sophie. And yet you are here, and I am here, and we are all together. As long as you can plant a seed in the soil, and as long as it grows, it's not too late in any final sense. "*We are stardust/ We are golden/ And we've got to get ourselves/ Back to the garden.*"[20] Let us study this book, rejoice, and dig from where we stand.

Alastair McIntosh

Social and environmental activist, human ecologist, writer, and Quaker.

17 *The Upanishads* (trans. Juan Mascaró), Penguin Classics, 1965, p. 121.
18 Ralph Waldo Emerson, 'The Over-Soul', *Essays, First Series*, American Transcendentalism Web, originally 1841, https://archive.vcu.edu/english/engweb/transcendentalism/authors/emerson/essays/oversoul.html
19 Ezekiel 47:12; Revelation 22:2, New Revised Standard Version.
20 Joni Mitchell, 'Woodstock', 1970, https://jonimitchell.com/music/song.cfm?id=75.

Introduction

Introduction

Maria Curtis

The natural world is the larger sacred community to which we belong.
To become alienated from this community is to become destitute in all
that makes us human. To damage this community is to diminish our
own existence.
(Thomas Berry[1])

This book is about the relationship between humanity and the natural world – a relationship that has drifted so far from a caring, cherishing relationship that, in the words of the United Nations *Prayer of Sorrow*, "We have forgotten who we are". In fact, it's looking more like an abusive relationship – although there are little pockets around the world where people are trying, often against the odds, to live in right relationship with the planet. We need to re-imagine what a healthy relationship might look like, one conducive to the flourishing of all beings on Earth.

Our contributors approach this issue from many directions. They write from different theological perspectives, as Unitarianism is a pluralistic faith. But what our writers share is a commitment – for some, a covenant – to engage in loving, caring, respectful relationships with one another, within their immediate communities, and with the wider Earth community, which is seen as sacred. Central to their spiritual perspective is a sense of gratitude for the whole of creation, informed by a stance of humility, as they acknowledge our interconnectedness and interdependence with all living things on Earth. We feel the need to accept this gift with good grace. We should be full of joy when we perceive our glorious environment. And we are conscious beings, able to apprehend beauty and share intimacy with others. We are indeed blessed.

---

1   Thomas Berry, *The Dream of the Earth* (Sierra Club Books, 1990).

We have much to celebrate, while still acknowledging our unique responsibility as thinking creatures – the only species in a position to choose between cherishing or destroying our rich and precious biosphere. But we, especially those of us from the affluent countries, with our history of exploitative imperialism and racism, must acknowledge our culpability, our complicity, in the current ecological crisis. We may not have done it deliberately, but our lifestyles have all contributed to this crisis. Acknowledging our human frailty, now is the time for us to own our shadow and consider how we can get back on an even keel before it's too late. How do we mobilise our better selves and influence those with power to act more responsibly? We have faith (possibly against the evidence) that human beings are fundamentally decent creatures. We therefore need to understand ourselves better. Under what conditions do we become selfish and competitive, or cruel and aggressive? What is needed for empathy and compassion to be felt for all of human kind? What helps us to flourish? Who is our neighbour? Perhaps we should include the whole Earth community? We face a stark choice: compassion for the Earth or indifference. We choose to cherish the Earth.

The problem

"We have a brief and rapidly closing window to secure a liveable future" – so said Hans-Otto Portner, co-chair of a working group of the Intergovernmental Panel on Climate Change (IPCC) in the Panel's report published in March 2022. Climate breakdown is accelerating rapidly, with many of the impacts proving to be more severe than originally predicted. Human activity affecting the climate is already causing dangerous and widespread disruption, threatening devastation to vast areas of the planet, and rendering many places uninhabitable. Droughts, floods, heatwaves, and other extreme weather events are accelerating and wreaking increasing damage.

Allowing global temperatures to increase by more than 1.5°C above pre-industrial levels will result in some irreversible impacts. These include the melting of ice caps and glaciers, and a cascading effect whereby wildfires, the die-off of trees, the drying out of peatlands, and the thawing of permafrost (releasing methane) amplify emissions further. António Guterres, UN Secretary General, described the report as *"an atlas of human suffering and a damning indictment of failed climate leadership"*.

John Kerry, US special envoy for climate, said that in view of the lives and livelihoods already lost, *"The question ... is not whether we can avoid the crisis – it is whether we can avoid the worst consequences."* Although every inhabited area of the planet is affected, about half the global population live in areas "highly vulnerable" to climate change. Millions of people face food and water shortages. Mass die-offs of species, from trees to corals, are already under way. Coastal areas around the globe, and small, low-lying islands, face inundation if temperatures rise more than 1.5°C.

And that's just climate change, one outcome of the way in which we have dishonoured the Earth. This intersects with (or is exacerbated by) the loss of biodiversity as a result of human activity.

Since the IPCC report came out, there have been devastating floods in Pakistan, with one third of the country under water. Homes and livelihoods washed away. Family members lost. We had record-breaking temperatures in the UK in summer 2022. Just 40°C felt unbearable. Imagine 50°C – the norm in some places now. Drought in the Horn of Africa is causing widespread famine, with millions of people at risk of starvation and death.

Concerted global action is needed now to avoid the worst impacts. But we humans are not working together. We live in one world, but there are huge disparities of wealth and opportunity within and between different regions; half of the world's net wealth belongs to the richest one per cent. Our governments cannot, or will not, agree on measures to alleviate disaster, dominated as they are by parochial, short-term thinking. And it is not just governments. There are the vested interests of multinational corporations, too, driven by the profit motive. To quote Green MP

Caroline Lucas, "*We need a bold reimagining of our economy and the power structures that sustain the status quo.*"

If we needed reminding that we live in an interconnected world, the Covid-19 virus showed itself to be no respecter of national boundaries. And in 2022 the shocking and devastating invasion of Ukraine has further reminded us that we live in one world. Ukraine is one of the major 'bread baskets' of the world. Many places in China, the Mediterranean, and the Middle East depend on imports of Ukrainian wheat. But the supply of staples is controlled by a few mega-corporations. With climate change, flooding or famine in just one of the other main wheat-, corn-, or rice-growing areas could mean serious food shortages throughout the world, where many communities already suffer from food insecurity.

The war in Ukraine has shocked the world; it is painful to witness the suffering, especially of the civilian population, and to be powerless to stop this cruel and unjust war. The UN seems impotent. There are parallels with the ecological disaster that we witness unfolding: our political processes have failed to deliver positive solutions to the crisis. Nations and multinational corporations put their own interests first, rather than working together co-operatively for the good of all people on Earth. For too long, we have been immersed in an ideology that propagates injustice, where the only thing that matters is profit. Climate injustice is one facet of this.

At the COP27 conference held in November 2022 in Egypt, the focus was on justice. But the fossil-fuel lobbyists were out in force, outnumbering any single frontline community affected by the climate crisis. COP27 failed to agree targets to reduce emissions. However, there was agreement to establish a 'loss and damage' fund to support the most vulnerable, who produce the smallest volume of emissions but are disproportionately affected by the effects of climate change. We look forward to seeing some hard cash going into the fund! And perhaps some changes to the international banking system whereby, rather than loans, vulnerable communities receive grants to introduce adaptive measures.

Climate change; loss of biodiversity; population increase: all contribute
to the ecological crisis that threatens our very existence. We have to face
it together – or perish.

"The arc of the moral universe is long, but it bends toward justice." This
observation is often attributed to Martin Luther King Jr, but it first
appeared in an 1853 sermon by the Unitarian minister, Theodore Parker,
as a statement of faith based on his experience of working for the abolition
of slavery. But there is nothing inevitable or pre-determined about the
course of justice, no guarantee that moral progress will prevail. It depends
on our own vigilance. As Dr King expressed it, *"Evil may so shape events
that Caesar will occupy a palace and Christ a cross."* We have to make the
world a more just place. The arc won't bend toward justice on its own.

A sense of perspective

Marcia Bjornerud thinks that we need to develop our "time-literacy".
In her book, *Timefulness – How Thinking Like a Geologist Can Help
Save the World*,[2] she claims: "We are navigating recklessly toward our
future using conceptions of time as primitive as a world map from the
fourteenth century". Thinking like a geologist gives us an awareness of
deep time and very slow Earth processes, like the movement of tectonic
plates, and mountain building and the carbon cycle: a perspective
that sees rocks not as nouns but as verbs! We become aware of the
relationship between the biosphere and the atmosphere over millions of
years; it is a delicate balance, which can be easily disrupted to devastating
effect, causing at one time overheating, or, at another, "snowball earth".
We humans should be chastened by the magnitude of our effects on
the planet in the very short time that we have been around. Bjornerud
urges: "Timefulness is vital in the Anthropocene, this human epoch
of accelerating planetary change; we need a more time-literate society."

---

2   Marcia Bjornerud, *Timefulness – How Thinking Like a Geologist Can Help Save the
     World* (Princeton University Press, Princeton NJ, 2018).

So let's go for an imaginary walk in deep time. We will cover 13.8 kilometres in two days, as we walk the story of the cosmos from the Big Bang, when our universe began, to the present. Every two steps represent a million years. The longest part of our journey is lifeless chaos, until mid-morning on the second day, a mere 5 billion years ago, when our solar system began to form. We humans appear in the last few centimetres of the journey.

We have achieved many astonishing things in our little blink of cosmological time: the use of language and writing; the disciplines of mathematics, science, technology, philosophy; the ability to use imagination to envisage different futures; education, human rights, democracy (in some places); the visual arts, literature, and music. But this deep-time perspective should also engender due humility in us. We have placed ourselves at the pinnacle of creation, as if we got here by merit. Now we need to dethrone ourselves and see ourselves as part of Nature, part of an interconnected and interdependent world. We need to change the story of our place in the universe – and our place on Earth.

There is a lot at stake: nothing less than the future of our species (and that of many others). With imperialistic zeal, we have trampled roughshod over the Earth, greedy for her resources. From a tiny band who narrowly escaped extinction, we flourished, then multiplied at an alarming rate until we became the dominant species on the planet. And now we've reached 8 billion! We have colonised nearly every corner of the world. Now we are on the verge of catastrophe. At first unknowingly, our species began to damage the Earth. However, much damage has been done in the full knowledge that we were causing harm. More than half of the carbon dioxide added to the atmosphere from the burning of fossil fuels has been emitted in the last 30 years; that is, since Al Gore published his first warning about climate change in *Earth in the Balance*. More emissions in 30 years than in all the previous millennia of human existence. Somehow the bare facts fail to motivate us to act differently; we need a change of heart.

So this is the sorry tale of the Anthropocene, the era in which human activity has become the dominant influence on climate and the environment. We have disrupted the balance of the ecosystem in so many interconnected ways. The results include the melting of polar ice sheets and glaciers, leading to rising sea levels and further warming as the darker sea water absorbs more sunlight; loss of biodiverse habitats and whole ecosystems – forests, coral reefs, wetlands; acidification of the oceans from increased CO_2 absorption; pollution of water, land, and air with pesticides, plastic, and by-products of combustion; loss of fresh water; loss of good-quality soil. All contributing to the sixth mass extinction event on Earth – and the only one caused by humans. And yet we carry on driving our cars, travelling by air, eating meat, addicted to our wasteful, consumerist lifestyles (which generate clothing waste, food waste, single-use plastics, and built-in obsolescence): buying into the capitalist myth that business as usual will prevail.

Here in the affluent UK, where rampant inflation at the time of writing is causing a cost-of-living crisis, some families are having to choose between heating and eating. Elsewhere in poorer parts of the world the struggle for survival is the norm, a struggle intensified by the effects of climate change. Here people may face even starker choices – between a livelihood from mining or drilling for oil versus no livelihood at all, for example. Faced with such a dilemma, we would surely all opt for gainful employment, however damaging to the planet, rather than leaving our children to starve. We must therefore focus on justice first, aiming for a fairer distribution of wealth which enables people to flourish and live fulfilling lives wherever they are.

It's all connected

Our lives do not proceed in a vacuum, separate from other lives. We need to see ourselves as part of the natural world. It is not just a backdrop for us. We are interconnected with all life on Earth in ways that we are just beginning to understand. For example, in 2019, authors of a major report[3] on insects worldwide concluded: "*If insect species losses cannot be halted, this will have catastrophic consequences for the planet's ecosystems and for the survival of mankind.*" Insects are in serious decline and could die out by the end of the century; and if they die out, we die out too. We are dependent on them to pollinate our food plants; they also recycle nutrients in the soil and are a major food source for other creatures. The analysis points to intensive agriculture as the main driver of the decline, particularly the use of pesticides. Urbanisation and climate change are also significant factors. That is just one illustration of our interdependence with other species.

And yet when this deeply shocking report came out, it was the last item on the news – we in the UK were in the throes of the Brexit drama at the time. It seems that, in the words of T. S. Eliot in *Four Quartets*, "*Human kind cannot bear very much reality*". We cling to our parochial concerns, our short-term outlook, but while we fiddle Rome burns. Our culture – that of the affluent countries of the Global North – seems to be in denial about the disruption that we have caused and continue to cause to the interconnected web of life. We are shamed by the young who feel the urgency of the crisis and are desperately trying to make us act responsibly. If only we could reclaim some of their innocence and righteous anger.

As Thomas Berry, Passionist priest, claims in *The Great Work*,[4]

> Both our religious and our humanist traditions in the West are primarily committed to an anthropocentric exaltation of the human. We have difficulty in accepting the human as an integral part of the Earth community. We see ourselves as a transcendent mode of being.

---

3   Francisco Sanchez-Bayo and Kris Wyckhuys, 'Worldwide Decline of the Entomofauna: A Review of its Drivers', in *Biological Conservation*, 20.01.2019.

4   Thomas Berry, *The Great Work* (Harmony/Bell Tower, New York, 1999).

Our view of ourselves as the pinnacle of creation, or the centre of the universe, has been severely challenged over the centuries (for example, by the heliocentrism of Copernicus and Galileo). But some people still have difficulty accepting that the human race evolved from a common ancestor with chimpanzees – an endangered species with whom we share >98.4 per cent of our DNA. We feel that we deserve a privileged position among living things, as if the Earth and all her creatures were merely a resource for us; but this species imperialism is dangerous and unfounded. In the words of Unitarian Universalist minister Fredric Muir:[5]

> There is no higher or lower, best or worst – the language of hierarchy, inherent value, or anthropocentric categorising does not apply to species or to the evolutionary process. The proximity of a species to human beings does not determine its worth. Take away these false divisions of life, and all that remains is simply difference. Humans are not higher than dogs, just different; chimps are not more valuable than fish, merely different; finches are not better than worms, but different.

With species extinction occurring at an alarming pace, we need to remember that there is no reason why *Homo sapiens* could not be added to the extinction list. Muir again:

> Darwin gave us a liberating gift: He freed us from our demi-god bondage at the centre of the universe, divorced from the web of life. His theory of evolution can help us appreciate the preciousness, fragility and connectedness of all living things. Because of this, we have the knowledge and motivation to save our species and our planet.

---

5   Fredric Muir, ed., *The Whole World Kin: Darwin and the Spirit of Liberal Religion* (Skinner House, Boston, MA, 2010).

The agricultural revolution of 10,000 years ago, when plants and animals became domesticated, heralded great changes in the way people lived. We can speculate about how the increase in control over the environment might have affected our conception of ourselves. Perhaps this is when we began to see ourselves as superior to other species, as "demi-gods", as Fredric Muir puts it. Was this the beginning of our hubristic world view?

The industrial revolution that began a few hundred years ago represented another significant transition. Society began to organise itself in different ways; relationships among people changed, alongside people's relationship with the Earth. We continued to plunder the Earth's resources and use them in more and more ingenious ways, all in the name of progress.

Now we need another revolution if we are to make the transition necessary to save the planet. We need a shift in consciousness, an awareness of a deeper unity connecting us, and we need to climb down off our pedestal. Our duties to future humans, to animals, and to the environment need to come together – as a whole system – in a way that has not been done before. Our trade, investments, and even expressions of opinion can affect all sorts of distant events. With the world-wide web, we can communicate with anyone in the world, but we are beginning to realise the inherent threats to democracy and truth that unregulated social media present. We need to adapt our morality, which was formed for a different world, and extend our compassion beyond the tribe, out towards others who may be very different from us. We need to see everything in global terms, pursuing justice on a global scale. It is hard now for us to accept the facts of environmental destruction and react effectively. And the hope that science and technology will get us out of the problem by themselves is a misplaced fantasy. They may be part of the solution, but first we need a change of heart: we need to care.

Taking responsibility

When a lawyer posed the question, *Who is my neighbour?* (Luke 10:25-37), Jesus of Nazareth responded with the parable of the Samaritan, a member of a despised group who showed compassion to a man left for dead at the roadside, where a priest and a temple official had both passed by on the other side. The Samaritan was the good neighbour; we are encouraged to do likewise. We must be neighbours to those beyond our tribe, our country, our class, our race, our religion, extending our compassion to the whole of humanity and to the whole Earth community.

What are we waiting for? Responding to Psalm 24, Annie Dillard[6] empathises with our reluctance to step up, as we plead special circumstances, but she warns that if we don't do the work, nobody will.

> Who shall ascend into the hill of the Lord? Or who shall stand in
> his holy place? There is no-one but us. There is no-one to send,
> nor a clean hand, nor a pure heart on the face of the earth, nor in
> the earth, but only us, a generation comforting ourselves with the
> notion that we have come at an awkward time ... But there is no-one
> but us. There never has been.

As meaning seekers and meaning makers, what sustaining narratives can we find to guide us through this ecological crisis?

I find comfort and wonder in the Universe Story, especially the idea that the potential for consciousness is inherent in matter. Or, in the words of Thomas Berry,[7] the idea that "*In the end the universe can only be explained in terms of celebration. It is all an exuberant expression of existence itself.*" And I find the story of Evolution on Earth moving and inspiring – the tenacity of life clinging on despite enormous threats to its existence

---

6   Annie Dillard, *Holy the Firm* (Harper & Row, New York, 1977).
7   Thomas Berry, *The Great Work* (Harmony/Bell Tower, New York, 1999).

in the geological past. Life in all its glorious diversity, with all of its symbiotic relationships; life continuing to evolve and express itself in new forms, if we let it.

Joanna Macy, Buddhist eco-warrior, asks what narratives can motivate us in the face of the collapse of ecological systems, climate change, and the mass extinction of species? In her book, *Active Hope*,[8] she outlines three choices. We can adopt a *Business as Usual* mentality, defined by the assumption that there is little need to change the way we live; this amounts to *denial* of the severity of the ecological crisis. Or we can enter the mindset that Macy calls *The Great Unraveling*: a perception of the world as being in terminal decline, which reduces us to *despair*. We may find ourselves adopting either of these narratives at different times. It is possible to be in full consumer mode, making plans for a future that we assume will be much like today. Then something will pull us up short – an image, perhaps, or a sudden insight into how our lifestyles are contributing to the ecological crisis – and we plunge into despair.

But beyond denial or despair, Macy proposes another option, which she calls *The Great Turning*, a narrative whereby our sense of agency is restored as we engage in action committed to the recovery of our world. (See Part Four of our book for some heart-warming stories of hope in action.) *Active Hope* considers how we can tap into our resources and find the strength to contribute fully to this great shift. We are guided on a journey of gratitude, grief, interconnection, and, ultimately, transformation.

The contributors to our book reflect ways in which our Unitarian values might inform our journey towards a healthier, more reverential relationship with the Earth. The Guidelines below, adapted from Joanna

---

8   Joanna Macy and Chris Johnstone, *Active Hope: How to Face the Mess We're in Without Going Crazy* (New World Library, San Francisco, 2012).

Macy's Foreword to *Stories of the Great Turning*,[9] accord well with our fundamental belief in *"respect for the interdependent web of all existence of which we are a part"*.[10] May these Guidelines sustain us and nourish our souls as we engage in the critical process of cherishing the Earth.

Guidelines for the journey

- **We must start from a place of gratitude and celebration.** Macy: "Life is an inestimable gift: to be alive in this wondrous, self-organising universe with senses to perceive it, lungs that breathe it, organs that draw nourishment from it. And how amazing it is to be accorded a human life, with self-reflexive consciousness which allows us to make choices, letting us opt to take part in the healing of our world."

  So we celebrate our gift, but accept it with grace and humility, as unmerited.

- **We need to acknowledge our human frailty.** We need to own the shadow within that is our constant companion. We acknowledge the fragility of civilisation and our need to be vigilant in sharing our values, especially when they are counter-cultural, working co-operatively in our communities in the cause of freedom and justice. We confess our complicity, directly or indirectly, in causing suffering to our fellow human beings, other creatures, plants, and animals, and upsetting the balance of the Earth system. We grieve the loss of extinct and dying species.

  Zen master, Thich Nhat Hanh, was once asked what we need to do to save our world. He replied: "We need to hear within us

---

9   Peter Reason and Melanie Newman, eds., *Stories of the Great Turning* (Vala, London, 2013).

10   *Principles of the Unitarian Universalist Association (USA).*

the sounds of the Earth crying." This is a dark time filled with suffering; grief and lamentation, anger and fear are appropriate responses arising from the depths of our mutual belonging, testimony to our inter-connectedness. Through rituals of prayer and contemplation, we find the strength to face the truth without turning away.

- **We need the courage to imagine a better world.** We have been infantilised into thinking that there is no alternative to the way things are. Never has what Macy calls "the juicy, enlivening power of the imagination" been more desperately needed than now. Curiosity – about the world; how it is interconnected; about others, especially those very different from us; about ourselves – is a virtue to be used in all our encounters. We need to maintain openness of heart and mind and a willingness to listen to the voices of the most vulnerable.

- **Join together with others, building bridges, not walls.** The individualism of competitive industrialised culture has isolated people from each other, but The Great Turning is a joyous team undertaking. It evolves out of countless "spontaneous synergistic interactions as people discover their common goals and their different gifts", in small- and large-scale projects; we can have fun, play and laugh while engaged in co-creating a better world.

And finally:

- **Act your age!** Macy: "Now is the time to clothe ourselves in our true authority. Every particle in every atom of every cell in your body goes back to the primal flaring forth of space and time. In that sense, you are as old as the universe, with an age of about 14 billion years. You have an absolute right to step forward and act on Earth's behalf." And a responsibility. No-one else will. There is only us.

Conclusion

We are apparently three quarters of the way through the window of habitability on the Earth. In about 1.5 billion years from now, the sun will have grown so luminous that the oceans will begin to vaporise; water molecules will be broken down into hydrogen and oxygen and lost to space. Life on Earth will no longer be possible. But meanwhile, we still have more living to do. Why end it all prematurely?

Marcia Bjornerud's book *Timefulness*[11] ends with these words:

> Tomorrow's the Anthropocene. We've all enjoyed the fantasy that we can keep playing our self-absorbed and careless games – that when we choose to come inside, our supper will be waiting for us, and nothing will have changed. But no one is home to take care of us. Now we need to grow up and navigate on our own, doing our best with the Atlas of the Past to make up for so much lost time.

Let us continue to occupy our place in space and time, not as plunderers and exploiters but with gratitude and humility, aware of our interconnectedness and interdependency with the Earth, her land, her rivers and oceans, her air, and all her creatures. Let us preserve the natural world as the primary revelation of the divine. It is our duty as conscious beings to use our gifts wisely and responsibly.

Let us be worthy of the 13.8 billion years that brought us into being.

---

11   See note (2).

PART ONE:
Prophetic Voices

1 Resistance, Repentance, Resilience: a prophetic spirituality for the climate crisis

Stephen Lingwood

Introduction

In October 2018 scientists warned that the world had twelve years left to prevent an unprecedented climate catastrophe.[1] This news was mostly greeted by a deafening silence from governments and the media. But it does seem to have struck a chord in the minds of a great many members of the public (including myself). Something shifted, maybe just a bit, but maybe just enough. Many more of us began saying "We are in a deadly emergency! Why aren't governments acting as if this were true?" Some of us began to act in louder and louder ways to get that message across. This was most visibly seen in the Youth Strike for Climate, and in Extinction Rebellion.

It seems clear to many of us that to prevent imminent climate catastrophe we need to move away from dependence on fossil fuels – oil, gas, and coal – immediately. We need to transition from a carbon-based economy to a non-carbon-based economy as rapidly, and justly, as humanly possible.

---

1   Matt McGrath, 'Final call to save the world from "climate catastrophe"', https://www.bbc.co.uk/news/science-environment-45775309, accessed 23/08/22.

But here's the problem: the carbon economy has created the world as we know it today. The carbon economy is simultaneously the colonial economy, the global finance economy, the global capitalist economy. So moving away from carbon will involve a radical reshaping of the way the world works. But some kind of reshaping is inevitable. The carbon-based capitalist system, if it continues to grow unabated, will cause the collapse of our civilisation. The fact that the system is based on unending growth means that it cannot be sustainable. Perpetual economic growth means that every year we make more things, do more things – every year there is just more stuff. Our economy is based on the idea that every 25 years or so there needs to be double the amount of stuff there was before – that is what is meant by economic growth of 3 per cent a year. But infinite growth is not possible on a finite planet – and that's before we even get to the damage that carbon dioxide does to the atmosphere. The carbon system is doomed, in one way or another, and the only question is: when will it die, and how difficult will that transition be for the world? But one day it will break, and we will have to make a different world.

That, at least in my view, is the problem. So what is the solution? Clearly we all need to contribute to it in our different ways. My own contribution is made here as a theologian asking the question: what kind of spirituality will serve us in this time of crisis? How can a spiritual approach facilitate the death of this old world, assist in the creation of a new world, and help us to weather the storm of change?

The best answer I can offer is the need for three Rs. I want to advocate a spirituality of *resistance, repentance, and resilience*. And so this chapter explains what these three Rs mean, and why I believe that they are vital in this crisis.

But first I need to describe my methodology. I am writing here as a Unitarian Christian attempting to do theology. This is a biblical and Christian piece of theology. In offering it, I do not mean to suggest that this is the only kind of spirituality that will serve us in the crisis that confronts us all. I only mean to suggest that the contribution that I am most qualified to make is a product of my own faith tradition, a tradition shaped and re-shaped over thousands of years of thought and practice.[2]

The spirituality that I am exploring here is a *prophetic* spirituality. This means that I am drawing primarily on the prophets of the Bible (Isaiah, Amos, Jeremiah, and others) and their modern interpretation by thinkers such as Walter Wink, Walter Brueggemann, and James Luther Adams. I am starting with the foundational prophetic insight (built upon by later Jewish, Christian, and Muslim thought) that there is a God who is involved in history; and that this God has a vision of *shalom*, and that that means peace, justice, and wellness for the whole Earth.

The Hebrew prophets had a vocation to tell the truth of the injustices of their society, and to proclaim that this fell short of a vision of God's *shalom*. The Unitarian theologian James Luther Adams built upon this tradition in insisting that this prophetic task is still required today, and is the responsibility of the whole church.[3] It is from these foundations that I want to explore a prophetic spirituality that helps us to answer the question of what we must do in the climate crisis and the wider ecological crisis.

---

2   I also do this out of a conviction that being rooted in a living, evolving tradition
    is the best way to cultivate wisdom, truth, and goodness. See S. Lingwood,
    '"A Definite Plot of Soil": a Unitarian Theology of Tradition', *Faith and Freedom* vol.
    70, part 2, no. 185 (2017), pp. 111-24.
3   "*Our tradition has articulated and emphasized the notion, not only of the priesthood
    of all believers, but also of the prophethood of all believers. This means especially the
    capacity and the right to participate in the shaping of the congregation. This prophethood
    belongs not merely to the clergy: It belongs to the congregation and to the individuals in
    the congregation*" (James Luther Adams, quoted in *The Unitarian Life*, ed. Stephen
    Lingwood, London: Lindsey Press, 2008, p.42).

Cultivating a spirituality of resistance

What kind of spirituality will serve us in this crisis? My first contention is that *in a world run for the gain of the Powers, we need a spirituality of resistance*. That spirituality of resistance needs to tell the truth of what's going on, name the Powers, and actively resist the Powers.

So what or who are the Powers, and why should they be resisted? The simplest way I can express it is that the world is on fire. And we can't deal with that unless we deal with the arsonists who are setting it alight. We can't just throw in a thimbleful of water and say "I've done my bit", while down the road someone is actively pouring petrol on the fire. We have to confront, we have to resist, the ones actively pouring petrol on the fire. The ones pouring petrol on the fire are the Powers.

Who are these Powers? To answer that question we have to ask another one. We have known very clearly about the climate crisis since the 1980s. So why have we not already dealt with this problem? The explanation is to be found in what else was going on at that time. The 1980s was a time when a new powerful ideology was rising in the world: the ideology of neoliberalism. Just when we needed a massive intervention in the global economy (to shift from a carbon-based economy to a non-carbon-based economy), an ideology was on the rise that believed in, preached, and successfully evangelised a doctrine based on vast deregulation of free markets, privatisation, unending economic growth, and consumerism. The doctrine of neoliberalism states that *market forces must be left alone*. So a deliberate intervention to force a transition out of carbon went against the dogmas of neoliberalism. That is why it didn't happen in the 1980s and 1990s, and why it still is not happening today.

Naomi Klein's excellent book *This Changes Everything: Capitalism vs the Climate* meticulously documents this. She puts her finger on exactly what the problem is and shows how the doctrines of neoliberalism, free-market fundamentalism, growth-ism, and the powerful disciples of these ideologies are the real blocks to climate action. This is why we have failed to deal with the climate crisis – because of the think-tanks that promote neoliberalism, the politicians that believe it, the oil companies that profit from it, the financial industries that profit from it, the banks that bankroll it, and the international free-trade agreements that give legal backing to it. These are the arsonists, pouring oil on the fire. These are the Powers that are responsible for blocking climate action, as well as being responsible for a continuing massive transfer of wealth from the poor to an increasingly elite capitalist class.

There is no dealing with this crisis without clearly naming and holding responsible those people and powers that are causing it. There are particular structures of power that are responsible for the climate crisis, as well as much else, and our moral obligation is to resist these Powers, to cultivate a spirituality of resistance.

What excites me about a prophetic approach is that, even though it is derived from prophets of thousands of years ago, it provides us with a language and a practice for doing just that: the language of naming, unmasking, and engaging the Powers. Ethicist and theologian Walter Wink has drawn upon biblical language to describe structures of power – such as neoliberalism – in theological terms. He writes:

> Every power tends to have a visible pole, an outer form – be it a
> church, a nation, or an economy – and an invisible pole, an inner
> spirit or driving force that animates, legitimates, and regulates its
> physical manifestation in the world. Neither pole is the cause of the
> other. Both come into existence together and cease to exist together.
> When a particular Power becomes idolatrous, placing itself above
> God's purposes for the good of the whole, then that Power becomes
> demonic. The church's task is to unmask this idolatry and recall the
> Powers to their created purposes in the world.[4]

---

4   W. Wink, *Naming the Powers: The Language of Power in the New Testament* (Philadelphia: Fortress Press, 1984), p.5.

This language enables us to consider how a Power such as neoliberalism is both structural and spiritual, both economic and psychological. The realisation and unmasking of that reality is necessary to defeat it.

Naming is the first part of this process. For example, why do you think we name hurricanes, and even winter storms now in the UK? It is because our psychology means that we understand and take seriously that which is named. So if I tell you "It's going to be very wet and windy tomorrow", this does not have the same effect as saying "Storm Dennis is coming tomorrow". When something is named, even personified, we are more likely to take action in response to it.

So we must name neoliberalism as a Power. We name the think-tanks that influence government policy. But we also need to understand their deeper impacts, and we will explore those more below.

Once we have named the Power, we must unmask it. This task of unmasking is now most urgent in the work of climate justice. Indeed it is the failure to name and unmask the Powers effectively that is the source of much ineffectiveness in climate campaigning. We desperately declare "Somebody needs to do something!", but we struggle to answer questions such as "Who?", "Who needs to do what?", and "Why aren't they doing it?"

The ineffective, and frankly wrong, answer is that "We all need to do something". So much of the climate conversation concentrates on changes to our lifestyle: eat less meat, switch to a greener energy supplier, drive a little less. The dogma of neoliberalism has so dominated our culture that we try to solve the climate crisis only by controlling our *individual* consumption. But consumerism (one aspect of neoliberalism) is one of the *causes* of the crisis. We cannot solve a problem with the same logic that created it. Nevertheless this consumerist response remains dominant in much of the climate conversation. The answer that we are given (on TV documentary programmes, for example) is that "we all have to do our bit", and if we do it, the cumulative effort will make a difference.

But it won't. It simply won't. If we all, individually, did our bit, it would not solve the climate crisis. The climate crisis is caused by our global economic systems, and it can only be changed by a massive overhaul of those systems, and this will only come about by us naming and actively resisting them. This is the truth that the Powers do their best to hide from us. This is what leads oil companies to encourage consumers to calculate their personal 'carbon footprint' – thus deliberately shifting the responsibility for the climate crisis away from the systems of high-carbon capitalism (and the richest one per cent of the population) and on to individual citizens. It is a deliberate campaign of distraction.

Even climate activists fail to name the Powers clearly. This applies too often to Extinction Rebellion, with their activities of general disruption and undirected protest. When Extinction Rebellion block a road,[5] the protest gives the impression that they are against motorists, or against the general public for not doing enough in their lives to fight climate change. That is the message perceived by the general public: that Extinction Rebellion are protesting against *them*. The messaging is not clear enough. The Powers have not been named clearly enough.

There is also a naivety in Extinction Rebellion's belief that one parliamentary bill or one Citizens' Assembly will provide the solutions to the climate crisis that will then be enacted by government. This underestimates the insidious strength of the Powers. They will fight with all the power at their disposal to prevent that. And they have a lot of power and huge amounts of money. Only a mass people's movement that names and condemns these Powers will counter their strength.

The religious, prophetic task is to name the Powers in louder and louder ways. Once we know that these are the Powers, we can begin to fight

---

5   Full disclosure: I have done this. I have taken part in mass cycle rides with Extinction Rebellion that deliberately slowed down traffic, and I have taken part in protests on blocked roads. My thinking on all of this is always evolving.

against them. Their unmasking is their undoing, as darkness is their greatest weapon.[6]

The political shift that would happen if we truly recognised that these Powers are the source of the world's problems is immense. And so the constant work of these Powers is to keep themselves in the shadows and encourage us to look elsewhere for the source of our problems – not just the climate crisis, but poverty, inequality, austerity, and racism.

On the one hand, politicians on the Right try their hardest to convince people that the sources of their problems are immigrants, ethnic minorities, and 'liberal elites'; on the other hand, liberals mistakenly believe that the sources of the problems are religious fundamentalists, right-wing 'crazy people' like Donald Trump, backward-looking conservatives. These are the things that keep us trapped in culture-wars, which suits the Powers because we are blinded from seeing them and really addressing the structural economic systems that are the root cause of our problems.

Often we protest about the climate crisis, as so many of us protested against the Iraq War in 2003, but are we unmasking the Powers behind such injustices – revealing the story that links them all together? Do we understand that the Iraq War was driven by the carbon economy's need for more oil reserves? Do we understand how the same Powers undermine our efforts to move away from carbon? Can we understand that the Iraq War, the climate crisis, the cost-of-living crisis, and workers dying in factories in Bangladesh to make our cheap clothes are all part of the same story, all rooted in the same Power?

Once we understand this truth, and once millions of people in our world understand this truth, our attention becomes sharply focused on

---

6   The *"anonymity of neoliberalism is fiercely guarded"* (George Monbiot, quoted in S. Weintrobe, *Psychological Roots of the Climate Crisis*, New York: Bloomsbury, 2021, p.37).

unmasking and defeating these Powers, and their days become numbered. We will see that this economic model is not serving us, and that we must turn away from it. That is the critical moment, when we begin to be part of a revolution that moves the world in a different direction.

A spirituality of resistance actively resists the powers of the carbon-neoliberal economic order. How do we do that? We *tell the truth*, consistently and repeatedly: that this Power is responsible for the climate crisis, as well as global economic inequality, violence against Indigenous peoples, and regimes of austerity. We actively join with coalitions of people telling this truth and calling for climate justice and transformational change in our world. We continue to educate ourselves and raise our awareness of it all. We listen to Indigenous peoples and those most directly affected by environmental destruction, and we follow their leadership.

A prophetic approach tells this truth with the tools of a particular biblical language. So if I am asked, for example, to give a speech at a protest, I really see no point in saying something that any trade union leader or political campaigner could say. My gift, my vocation as a minister in the world, is to tell a story through the languages and practices of my faith. As a person of faith, rooted in a particular language, I can sing that song, I can express that poetic language, I can tell the story with a biblical perspective, inspired by those prophets of thousands of years ago. Now people may be drawn to that language, or they may just take it as a gift in that moment. But I think it is a gift and an insight to say "*Isaiah struggled under the tyranny of the Babylonian Empire, and Jesus struggled under the tyranny of the Roman Empire, and now we struggle under the tyranny of an empire of neoliberalism, and we're continuing in this struggle for God's justice. We are dealing with a struggle that has always existed: the struggle between the powers of empire, and the powers of the God of liberation.*" This gives us a historical consciousness that locates our struggle with those who struggled in the past, as well as the vision of a future of justice that beckons us forward.

This is not about promoting or growing our own religious institutions. It's not about getting our name in the papers for doing the work. It is about being in coalition with others in the task of facilitating the birth of a new world. The world needs this shift, this revolution, and our mission is to cultivate a spirituality of resistance that can be part of this great turning.

Cultivating a spirituality of repentance

My second contention is that *in a world built on the uncaring self of the ego we need a spirituality of repentance, which acknowledges that these forces of violence and power exist within us, and models how to change from the uncaring self to the caring self.*

Walter Wink's work enables us to understand how the Power of neoliberalism is both structural and spiritual, both economic and psychological. On the structural and economic side, neoliberalism is a set of institutions and people. We could literally name the addresses of think-tanks in London and Washington D.C. that are the Powers of neoliberalism. But neoliberalism is also spiritual and psychological. These are Powers that exist not only in a very material sense in the world, but also in a spiritual sense in your heart and in my heart.

It is true that the neoliberal system increasingly benefits the richest one per cent, but we must also recognise that many of us who are relatively comfortable in the Global North also benefit. And so defeating the Powers requires a robust rejection by those people who are relatively well off in this system.

Neoliberalism is about sixty years old and can be traced to certain economic theorists of the twentieth century.[7] But of course its roots go

---

7   See S. Weintrobe, *Psychological Roots of the Climate Crisis* (New York: Bloomsbury, 2021), pp.33-56.

much deeper: to centuries of colonialism, empire, and extractivism (the unsustainable taking of resources, particularly from poorer countries). It is the latest phase of a historical movement that has seen the exploitation of people (and planet) for the enrichment of others, from an ideology that treats people as a means to an end, rather than an end in themselves.

This goes hand in hand with white supremacy. It requires a belief in the inferiority of non-white people for white people to justify an empire that enslaves or impoverishes them for the good of white people, particular the richest of white and European societies. This has manifested itself of course in slavery and the genocide of Indigenous peoples around the world by white colonial powers. Although today we have gone some way towards limiting this ideology through a language of inherent human rights, we still live in a system that treats people as ultimately disposable, as cogs in a machine, and treats the Earth as a resource to be exploited. It is no coincidence that some of the most effective climate activism around the world has come from Indigenous peoples, who cultivate a different world view and enact resistance based on that world view. As Chief Arvol Looking Horse has said, "*Grandmother earth [is] our source of life, not a resource*".[8]

But the economic system in which we are embedded is built on the opposite world view: that Earth is a resource, and, in many ways, so are people. This has to be built on an ideology, a theology if you like, a psychology that says, "It is OK to treat people as cogs in a machine. It is OK to be selfish. Greed is good. Look out for Number One." It has to be built on an ego-based psychology, a psychology that operates out of an uncaring self.

This has been demonstrated in the excellent book *Psychological Roots of the Climate Crisis* by Sally Weintrobe. She argues that within every person is both an uncaring self and a caring self. We each have the

---

8   https://worldpeaceandprayer.com/wppd-2022.html, accessed 23/08/22.

potential within us to follow both, but in the neoliberal economy and politics an approach has grown that encourages the dominance of the uncaring, narcissistic self. She writes of her own work:

> The book argues that Exceptionalism, a rigid psychological mindset, is largely responsible for the climate crisis. Exceptions, people caught up in this mindset, falsely believe they are entitled to:
> - see themselves in idealized terms;
> - have whatever they want (because they are ideal);
> - dispense with moral and practical limits through omnipotently 'rearranging' reality.[9]

It is this narcissistic self that is the foundation for the theology and politics of neoliberalism. As the environmental lawyer and activist Gus Speth has said,

> I used to think the top global environmental problems were biodiversity loss, ecosystem collapse and climate change. I thought that with thirty years of good science we could address these problems. But I was wrong. The top environmental problems are selfishness, greed and apathy, and to deal with these we need a spiritual and cultural transformation, and we scientists don't know how to do that.[10]

Naming the Power of neoliberalism is a revolutionary act. But to truly defeat neoliberalism we need to address the selfish psychology that undergirds it. We need a cultural and spiritual transformation that addresses selfishness, greed, and apathy, and begins to see the caring self as the foundation for a different world order. How can a spiritual approach help us to do this?

---

9   S. Weintrobe, *Psychological Roots of the Climate Crisis* (New York: Bloomsbury, 2021), p.1.

10 https://en.wikiquote.org/wiki/James_Gustave_Speth.

One answer is by rejecting a spirituality of independence and embracing a spirituality of interdependence. The growth of neoliberalism has coincided with a growth of more and more individualistic approaches to religion and spirituality. Whether expressed by the Evangelical Christian theology of "Jesus is my personal saviour", or the spiritual culture of buying products on the road to self-enlightenment, or even at times the Unitarian language of "building your own theology",[11] the spirituality of our times is often deeply rooted in an individualistic culture.

The sociologist Stephen Hunt describes this consumerist spirituality in this way:

> A veritable 'spiritual marketplace' has emerged which encourages people to pick and choose until they find a religious identity best suited to their individual, rather than collective, experience – a freedom to seek a religious faith which reflects, endorses, and gives symbolic expression to one's lifestyle and social experience. The contemporary religious environment therefore permits individuals the freedom to discover their own spiritual 'truths', their own 'reality', and their own 'experience' according to what is relevant to their lives.[12]

Notice how the dominant metaphor for this is a marketplace – a very neoliberal image. And notice how this parallels Weintrobe's point about rearranging reality – so that you think you are immune from the consequences of your actions. (Is discovering your own reality the same thing as rearranging reality?) Individualist, consumerist religion at best enfeebles our efforts to cultivate a spirituality to meet the needs of our time, and at worst actively works against it.

---

11 A growing number of thinkers now see the culture of individualism not as the essence of Unitarianism, but in fact its biggest problem. The *"persistent, pervasive, disturbing, and disruptive commitment to individualism"*, according to American Unitarian Universalist minister Fredric Muir, *"misguides our ability to engage the changing times"*. (F. Muir, *Turning Point: Essays on a New Unitarian Universalism*, Boston: Skinner House Books, 2016, p.6.)

12 S. Hunt, *The Alpha Enterprise: Evangelism in a Post-Christian Era* (Aldershot: Ashgate, 2004), p.35.

Rather than more individualism, what we need is repentance from operating out of the independent uncaring self, and the ability to root ourselves in the interdependent caring self. The New Testament Greek word for repentance is *metanoia*, understood as a change of direction and a transformation.[13] James Luther Adams saw this transformation as the essential task of the liberal church when he wrote:

> The free church ... when alive ... is the community in which men and women are called to seek fulfilment by the surrender of their lives to the control of the commanding, sustaining, transforming reality. It is the community in which women and men are called to recognise and abandon their ever-recurrent reliance on the unreliable.[14]

This approach sees our religious task as recognising and abandoning the false. What is it that we need to abandon? The reliance on the uncaring self, the ego. In relation to the climate crisis, this repentance has been written about by Unitarian Universalist minister Ian White Maher. In the same vein as the work of Sally Weintrobe, White Maher sees the ultimate source of the climate crisis as our spiritual condition:

> The effects we are facing today (and tomorrow) are determined by our actions, but our actions are the products of our decisions. The quality and condition of our decisions derive from our thinking. And our thinking is determined by our spiritual condition. To say the impending collapse is the consequence of our actions conveniently avoids our responsibility for our spiritual condition, which is the source of the cascade of all that follows.[15]

---

13   James Luther Adams wrote that "*Metanoia* ... is to be understood as a change of heart, mind, soul – *total* personal orientation" (J. C. Leach, "'Something like Conversion is Essential": The Concept of *Metanoia* in the Writings of James Luther Adams', *The Journal of Liberal Religion* Vol. 4, Number 1, Winter 2003, p. 9).

14   Leach, p.16.

15   I. White Maher, 'A Transformative Spiritual Relationship with the Divine' in *Turning Point: Essays on a New Unitarian Universalism* (Boston: Skinner House Books, 2016), edited by Fredric Muir, p.134.

He goes on:

> The first step toward a solution is to admit that we are beyond the point of avoiding calamitous climate change. We cannot begin our process of transformation into healing beings without admitting that our spiritual estrangement has created an environment that will soon be unliveable for many creatures and, potentially, humans. The second step is admitting we need help. Specifically (I believe) humanity needs help from the divine and creative life force that is greater than the selfish interests of our individual egos. Anything shy of this confession will leave us with the illusion that we will somehow, through our own will power and ingenuity, solve this problem. But we cannot solve a spiritual problem with intellectual solutions.[16]

The repentance required to address the climate crisis involves a shift from the uncaring self to the caring self, or we could say from the ego-self to what in Christian terms we might recognise as *the true self as a child of God*. The mode of thinking that has created the climate crisis believes that there is no limit to human ego power: that we can keep advancing technologically, achieving more, making more, buying more, *being* more as exceptional people who deserve it, regardless of the consequences for others, in total independence and in our own power. White Maher suggests that we need to repent of this thought process and recognise our limits, responsibilities, and dependence on something greater than ourselves. In Adams' terms: recognise and abandon what is unreliable, and surrender to reality.

White Maher, in drawing on Twelve Step spirituality (such as that practised by Alcoholics Anonymous), insists that humanity needs to recognise that our communal life has become unmanageable (Step One – in which we recognise the problems that our ego self has got us into) and that we need to turn to a power greater than ourselves that can restore us to sanity (Step Two – in which we begin to operate out of a caring self that recognises its dependence on a higher power).

---

16   White Maher, p. 135.

Twelve Step spirituality provides a mechanism, a practice that shows what transformation, or repentance, can look like. Crucially this means a rejection of an ego-driven individualism that sees independence and self-assertion as the highest good. Prophetic spirituality, while of course affirming the need for individual and communal well-being, especially of those most oppressed in our current systems of power, constantly practises repentance from the illusions of the ego. It is the practice of constantly rejecting these illusions: that I am the centre of the universe, that I am independent from all else, that the pursuit of my path is all that matters, that I am better than other people (which ironically can mean that I am constantly anxious that I am worse than other people). That is the ego self, and when we constantly prick these illusions we are left with the truth: that I am part of the universe, that I require help from powers greater than myself, that I have a responsibility to care for others, that my inherent worth does not depend on my achievements or my possessions.

How do we do this? The answer of prophetic spirituality is prayer. What do I mean by prayer? Essentially any deep practice, skilfully shaped by generations of practitioners, that helps us to learn to reject the programming of the ego and operate out of the true self, not an isolated self, but a self dependent on, and in relationship with, what I would call God. In the words of the Buddhist teacher angel Kyodo williams:

> We cannot have a healed society, we cannot have change, we cannot have justice, if we do not reclaim and repair the human spirit ... that's the stuff that bringing down systems of oppression is made of. And so capitalism in its current form couldn't survive. Patriarchy couldn't survive. White supremacy couldn't survive if enough of us set about the work of reclaiming the human spirit.[17]

---

17 'The World is Our Field of Practice', angel Kyodo williams, *On Being*, https://onbeing.org/programs/the-world-is-our-field-of-practice-apr2018/, accessed 23/08/22.

Prayer is the doing of this work through regular sustained spiritual practice. It is *"repairing and reclaiming the human spirit"* (williams). It is *"recognising and abandoning your reliance on the unreliable"* (Adams). It is *"admitting you need help"* (White Maher). These are not just ideas to agree with: they are actual practices that happen daily in the act of sitting, or chanting, or breathing, or singing, or dancing, or speaking to God. Every time we move past a distracting thought and consciously surrender into the presence of God, we are creating actual psychological change that shifts us away from the uncaring self. In Christian language, these practices allow you to operate out of your true self, the Christ-self, dependent upon the power of God.

The climate crisis is caused by the economic system in which we live, and the economic system we live in depends on the uncaring self (largely of the billionaire class, but to some extent of the relatively privileged people in the Global North), and prayer is a tool that allows transformation from the uncaring to the caring self. So prayer is a tool of transformation. Prayer is revolutionary.

That means that the role of religious communities is not merely to lobby Parliament and attend protests (religious people can certainly do this, and should, but so can everyone else). The unique gift that religious communities can offer the world right now is to sit down and offer to teach these amazing practices of prayer that have had this transforming effect for thousands of years.

I find that a very powerful thought, because it means that religious and spiritual traditions have a vital role to play in creating this transformation in the world. Scientists don't know how to create this shift, and it's not their job to know it: it's the job of religion, it's my job, it's our job. We have a vital role to play in being part of this movement by offering this spirituality of repentance, this transformative spirituality.

Cultivating a spirituality of resilience

My third contention is that *in a world where the Powers are winning, and will continue to do much more damage to people and to the Earth, we need a spirituality of resilience that gives us some hope and some sustenance, even in the darkest times.*

There is no doubt that things will get worse before they get better. We may reach the significant point of an extra 1.5 degrees of warming as soon as 2025.[18] The climate crisis is here, it is happening, and all we can do is make it less bad. What will this mean? That is hard to answer. But I feel that the COVID crisis is a taste of many more crises that will soon be upon us – different crises, which will affect us in different ways, but serious crises.

Life will become harder in ways that we may not even have begun to realise, primarily for people in equatorial regions, but increasingly for everyone on the planet, including in the UK. I think those of us in the UK and similar countries who were born after the Second World War have a sense that our civilisation is stable and inevitable and will never stop functioning and growing, whatever happens, but I just don't think that's the case. We can't imagine that there will be a day when the stock market just collapses, but it is probably going to happen. We can't imagine that there will be a day when electricity doesn't come out of our sockets, and water doesn't come out of our taps, but these things are all dependent on systems that will be put under more strain than ever before. We cannot continue to take them for granted.

In a twenty-first century that is less stable than the twentieth, what are the world's needs? One is *community resilience*. In climate-disaster events, such as Hurricane Sandy in the United States in 2012, the most

18   Weintrobe, p. 216.

at-risk people were those who didn't know their neighbours, or who were afraid of them.[19] When the floods hit, as they probably will do where I live in Riverside in Cardiff, we're going to need to know our neighbours. I need to know which house in my street has an old man who can't walk well, and which one has a new-born baby. We're going to need to live in streets where people look out for each other. Those are the kinds of place that are going to be resilient when the electricity stops, or the floods hit. So we need to start doing this now. We need to know our neighbours, we need to build community where we are. We need to find local ways of living that can make that happen.

Community building, street by street, neighbourhood by neighbourhood, is an essential part of building our resilience, an essential part of our mission in this time of crisis. I believe in the hyper-local – as adrienne maree brown advocates, not mile-wide, inch-deep, but inch-wide, mile-deep.[20] That is one of the principles that guides the work of Gentle/Radical, the community arts organisation with whom I work.

I believe that God has called me to work in literally thirty streets in Cardiff – that's it. That's enough. Enough for one person and one lifetime: hyper-local work to create resilience. I am lucky in that I have connected with Gentle/Radical, which operates out of exactly those values. One of the projects to which I have contributed with Gentle/Radical is a community podcast about life in the COVID pandemic. And in a sense the end product of a podcast doesn't matter as much as the fact that, with teams of my colleagues, I have knocked on hundreds of doors in the streets where I live, and I have asked people how they are. It is painstakingly slow, painstakingly gradual, inch-by-inch community work, but it is necessary to create community resilience.

---

19   N. Klein, *This Changes Everything: Capitalism vs the Climate* (Penguin Books, 2014), p.106.
20   brown, a. m., *Emergent Strategy* (Chicago: AK Press, 2017), p.20.

But as well as community resilience, I want to argue for a *spirituality of resilience* that provides hope and sustenance in these times. Such a spirituality, I suggest, will need to be robust. It will require more than consumerist dabbling in a variety of practices, more than superficially investigating a number of perspectives, more than intellectually exploring questions that never produce answers. These things are simply not up to the task of resisting the Powers and surviving this time of crisis. We need something much more powerful, more sustaining, and much more capable of giving us a deeper and enduring sense of hope.

How do people in hopeless situations maintain sustaining spiritualities of hope? One answer is found in listening to Indigenous peoples. If you look to Indigenous peoples around the world, you will see people who have already faced a crisis in which their lands were invaded, their environment dramatically changed, their cultures and their bodies destroyed. And yet they are still here, fighting for their traditions, their languages, their lands, their rituals, their faith. Although of course these crises were caused by systems of colonialism, white supremacy, and capitalism that created wealth still enjoyed by people in the Global North, today that Power has grown and mutated, and we all find ourselves victims of it. And so those peoples who have been resisting it for longer can provide some examples and leadership from which the rest of us can learn.

How do we learn from them? I am not suggesting appropriating rituals and practices of other peoples, as this is often another act of colonial violence. But we are going to need to find those sorts of deep-rooted attitudes, practices, and rituals that will sustain us all.

I am inspired by these stories; but, as a Unitarian who wants to engage with the depths of the biblical stories that have shaped this faith for centuries, I want to turn with renewed vigour to these stories of prophetic hope. I am helped in this task by such thinkers as biblical scholar and theologian Walter Brueggemann. Brueggemann has argued that the prophetic task, while fully and openly telling the truth of our desperate situation, and grieving for it, still resists complete despair, and dreams of hope. He writes:

The despair is countered in prophetic parlance by acts of vigorous hope. The prophets articulate what God has yet promised on which the faithful rely. Such hope is voiced, for example, by Martin Luther King in his mantra, "I have a dream." The dream he dreams is the promise of God; such prophetic hope insists that the circumstance of social failure has not defeated God's capacity to generate new social possibility.[21]

Prophetic spirituality cultivates a historic consciousness, a sense of being part of something bigger that echoes into the past, and something better that echoes into the future; a sense that we are part of a story of hope, a story of hope that we will continue to tell, even through hopeless times.

The story of hope told by Jesus was *"The kingdom of God is at hand"*. When we understand Jesus as a colonised person resisting empire, among a peasant class whose food and financial security were threatened by an imperial economic system,[22] we can see he was telling a story of hope in a situation of hopelessness too. *"The kingdom of God is at hand"* was a prophetic statement meaning *"the kingdom of Caesar is coming to an end"*. And so the prophetic story of hope that this spirituality of resilience can tell in this moment is *"The paradise of God, an Earth healed and abundant, is nearby"*, which means *"The empire of neoliberalism is coming to an end"*. Even, and especially, when it seems that this is an impossible dream, we must tell it. That is the practice of hope.

My personal sense of hope may no doubt wax and wane. But I *choose* to put myself in a tradition of hope, in a story of hope; that is what a prophetic faith offers as a spirituality of resilience: the choice to put oneself into a story of hope. That spirituality, and that choice for hope, is practised in the singing of songs. In a hymn adapted from Isaiah and Amos, we sing:

---

21 https://eerdword.com/three-urgent-prophetic-tasks-walter-brueggemann-on-reality-grief-hope/.

22 See R. Aslan, *Zealot: The Life and Times of Jesus of Nazareth* (London: Westbourne Press, 2013), pp.17-18.

> Come build a land where sisters and brothers,
> anointed by God, may then create peace:
> where justice shall roll down like waters,
> and peace like an ever flowing stream.[23]

This invites us to be part of this building of hope. But a prophetic spirituality also sings songs that remind us that it is not simply *we* that build this promised land, *it is God:*

> Isaiah the prophet has written of old
> how God's new creation *shall* come...
> that wisdom and justice shall reign in the land
> and your people *shall* go forth in joy, in joy,
> your people shall go forth in joy.[24]

It is this final insistence that God *shall* bring about a new creation (defeating the Powers) that creates the deepest sense of hope. It is expressed in poetry and song because it would not seem sustainable, or believable, simply to say it. It is too delicate, too contradicted by facts on the ground, to be simply stated. It is *sung* as an act of defiance in the face of contradictory realities, not to make us think that our own action is unnecessary, but to give us enough hope to fuel our action without falling into despair.

Our action is needed now more than ever. There is a need for a spiritual and cultural revolution that names and resists neoliberalism and the culture of the uncaring ego. There is a need for spiritual practices that cultivate the growth of the caring true self. There is a need for stories and songs of hope and nourishing spiritualities that will hold us in our times of despair.

---

23 'We'll Build a Land' by Barbara Zanotti (adapted from Isaiah and Amos): Hymn 198 in *Sing Your Faith* (London: Lindsey Press, 2009).

24 'Isaiah the Prophet has Written' by Joy F. Patterson (emphasis added): Hymn 80 in *Sing Your Faith* (London: Lindsey Press, 2009)

A faith rooted in the sense of the prophetic offers one kind of spirituality of resistance, repentance, and resilience. A prophetic faith names neoliberalism as a Power that is in contradiction to God's *shalom* for the world. It understands that the Power also exists within every ego, and it offers practices of prayer that rejects egotistic individualism and cultivates a sense of dependence on the power of God. And it cultivates resilience by singing songs of hope that boldly proclaim that justice shall roll down like waters, and peace like an ever-flowing stream.

Questions for reflection and discussion

1. Do you agree that it is vital to move from a spirituality of independence to a spirituality of interdependence? What would that mean for you, or for your community?

2. What would it mean to do activism "inch-wide, mile-deep" in your local community?

3. In the context of the climate crisis, what does God's *shalom* – a vision of peace, justice, and wellness for the whole Earth – mean to you?

The author

Stephen Lingwood is a Cardiff-based writer, activist, pioneer minister, and Creative Associate of the community arts organisation *Gentle/Radical*. He moved to Cardiff in 2017 after working for nine years as minister of a Unitarian church in Bolton. Stephen practises contemplative prayer, creates spaces for deep conversations, writes, and hangs about in Cardiff pubs and cafés. He is interested in how spiritual practice can lead us to the healing justice needed in response to the climate crisis. He is the Editor of *The Unitarian Life* and the author of *Seeking Paradise: A Unitarian Mission for Our Times* (both published by the Lindsey Press).

Prayer

Maria Curtis

Divine Spirit of Compassion,

We humbly open ourselves to your loving grace.

Fill our hearts and minds with your wisdom.

Help us to see the right path, and to choose it.

May our daily needs be met so that we are

Free to love without boundaries.

May we be grateful for the gifts of the Earth

And responsible for her care.

May we forgive ourselves and others

When we constrain our love or cause harm.

Acknowledging our human frailty,

We ask for strength at testing times.

May the power of love reign supreme.

(A version of the Prayer of Jesus written in the Lord's Prayer Study Group at Bank Street Unitarian Chapel, Bolton, in 2013)

2 Intersectionality and Environmentalism

Winnie Gordon

> *There is neither Jew nor Gentile, neither slave nor free, nor is there male and female, for you are all one.*[1]

In the *Dune* science-fiction series written by Frank Herbert, the population of Arrakis live in a desert wasteland, as ecological changes have made it barely habitable for on-planet living. These desert people (working-class, downtrodden, forgotten folk, known as Fremen) live *in* the planet, in underground tunnels and cavern dwellings. To move across the planet, to hunt, to salvage, they wear suits that cover them from head to toe, protecting them from the dry, hot terrain, and the harsh winds that cause sandstorms vicious enough to rip the skin from their bodies, or bury them alive. This brilliant futuristic epic, written in the 1960s and made into a movie in 1984 and again in 2021, may have been only the product of the imagination of one man, but it feels frighteningly relevant to our times.

Personally I cannot call myself an environmentalist, even though I am concerned enough to campaign for action to deal with the ecological collapse that humans have brought about on our planet. Planet Earth is warming, with parts of Britain reaching their hottest-ever temperature, of more than 40°C, in July 2022. Species are becoming extinct through loss of habitat. People are suffering from extreme weather events that cause floods, fires, and famine. Landscapes are changing from lush greenery to dry, desert land – yet we continue to behave as if Frank Herbert's vision of severe climate change and scarcity of resources (gas, water, oil, clean air) is a dream. We have failed to act to prevent this nightmare from happening.

---

1   *Galatians* 3:28.

The reason why I cannot call myself an environmentalist is that environmentalism is not a single issue. Enmeshed with climate justice are other justice issues – of class, race, and gender, to name just a few. There is an intersectionality of inequalities playing out behind the challenge of how we can best cherish the Earth. I call myself simply *a justice activist*.

We in the affluent West assume that our privileges are rights: clean running water on demand; fresh fruit and vegetables throughout the year; motorised public and private transport; a roof over our heads; heating when it's cold, air con when it's hot; a system of social welfare; a public health service; free education. While acknowledging that there are those suffering on the margins within our own culture, we often fail to recognise those on the other side of the world who are suffering as a consequence of our Western excesses: suffering because of our excessive appetites, and the global financial system.

In addition to popular demands for a lifestyle change – reduced excess, or cleaner consumerism – true justice-seeking environmentalism requires a much wider perspective. We need a solution-based approach which encompasses the complexities of inter-related lives and power structures across the planet, taking into account human and other animal experience. Our Westernised environmentalism, as a single-issue agenda, often fails to appreciate the interconnections between those other lives and what we ourselves actively (and maybe unconsciously) do every day. For instance, take waste: we dutifully sort our household rubbish and put it out for recycling, not caring that it will be exported for others to deal with, resulting in negative impacts on other lives across the globe.

For me, Herbert's 'Dune' is now. Just think about a shortage of fresh water; as trees are cut down, soil is eroded and acidic rainwater ends up in the sea. Are we living on the brink of that time when the water that we sweat from our bodies, or release as waste, will have to be recycled in special bodysuits back into drinking water? Oh, what a tangled web we weave when we deceive ourselves and ignore the warnings, turning away from devastation across oceans; when we reap, reap, reap, and rarely sow.

If, as it says in *Ecclesiastes* chapter 3, there is a time for everything, then what season are we living in? Maybe our vanity of vanities is our blatant blindness to our over-consumption in all spheres of life: from clothing, food, housing, transport, fossil fuels, water, and production of farmed foods to excessive use of natural hair extensions, often sourced from marginalised people in many countries. Maybe our vanity of vanities has been our blatant disregard of human over-population: our impact on animal and plant life to the extent of causing species extinctions. Even our bee population, which we desperately need for pollination and the production of honey, is under threat. Maybe, in the spirit of the passage from *Ecclesiastes*, our time to live has passed, and now is our time to die.

Sobering thought! A privileged one too. Living in England, I can be quite philosophical about my mortality. I have had a comfortable life, supported by free education (up to a point), social housing, school-uniform grants, free school meals. I have benefited from central heating in every home I have lived in, a running water supply in the kitchen and bathroom, and indoor sanitation. I have luxuriated in free public libraries, regular public transport, eBooks, and overseas holidays, and I have enjoyed the benefits of the digital age. While there have been times of struggle in my life, of working harder than I imagined would be necessary in order to achieve my goals, still my life has been one of relative ease – because of where I was born. So what if now is the time for our species to die? I have had a life filled with privileges.

I can philosophise about the demise of humanity, but across other lands there are people who have seen only devastating changes that have brought them hardship: people whose traditional way of life has been destroyed; whose trees have been ripped from the land for foreign export or to create space to grow cash crops; whose climate is becoming too hot to be habitable; whose once-lush environment is now barren; whose once-sustainable way of life is no longer an option. They are experiencing stronger storms, more uncontrollable wildfires, more devastating hurricanes, glacial melting, ever-rising sea levels. These victims of ecocide do not have the luxury of ruminating on the idea of the death of humanity. For them, every day is a battle for survival in an increasingly hostile environment. Some of their homelands have already drowned under rising waters.

For our children, the time to keep silent is gone; now it is their time to speak! Around the world, the children are speaking with their voices (and with their feet) in eco-activism. They have shamed us adults in their attempts to make peace with the land, with resources, and with each other. They want to reconnect to the spirit of Nature and live in peace, without fear and without wants; to move away from self-indulgent vanity. Young people are asking what use are more blue jeans and lycra leggings, when the making of these items causes hardships to others and destruction of landscapes? Their manufacture requires vast volumes of water for dyeing, and tens of thousands of hands that receive a pittance for their labour. These two items of clothing connect enslaved labour, water poverty, child labour, and starvation to the Western history of colonialism, industrialisation, and our present system of capitalism which repeats our historic exploitation of people and resources again and again. Young people have more readily embraced the intersection of environmentalism with issues of class, gender, and race. What we do here, what we want here, in our green and pleasant land, interconnects with what goes on over there, in the many lands that we have, in the past, colonised. The life of one affects the life of the other. The hunger of one feeds the vanity of the other.

Climate racism

When I view climate-change activism and protest through the lens of media coverage, I often see a sea of white faces. The person chosen to be the spokesperson is white, more often than not. The stories told are often presented in terms of a white-centred fear of being deprived, at some point in the future, of the goods, services, or lifestyle that protestors presently enjoy. The impact of climate change, in this world view, is more often focused on the future, rather than on the present damage being done to underdeveloped nations of majority black/ brown bodies. I don't often hear the voices of People of Colour or Indigenous nations. Yet Indigenous people and People of Colour are active in environmental campaigns, from China, India, and Indonesia to South America, Australia, Africa, and even Great Britain.

Recently I have been drawn to the work of the artist Fabrice Monteiro, and his depiction of our waste products as we dispatch them to developing nations of the world to be buried. His photograph 'Untitled 1', from his series 'The Prophecy',[2] depicts a giant West African *jinn*, wearing a costume fashioned from waste. This spiritual being – perhaps the spirit of Nature, or our planet – is viewing a landscape where toxic fumes rise in the air from a black pool, surrounded by dead earth, with no sign of life, littered with our human waste. The consequence of our over-consumption and plundering of the planet's resources starkly confronts us in this work of art, portraying as it does the impact of over-consumption on black bodies, on black-majority environments, as opposed to the Western environments where the waste originated. It is a stark vision of those on the other side, whose resources have been stripped from their land. For me, it also depicts the interconnectivity of the existing economic struggles of poverty; the inequality of education and health-care services; and civil wars, historic and present, in some of the West African countries. These vulnerable countries are doubly affected, coping as they must with the current environmental issues of our day, alongside the legacy of exploitation by those old colonialists. It is hard to believe that Western society's environmental activists take seriously the concerns of People of Colour, when the voices of People of Colour are ignored, despite the fact that the consequences of climate change make a more direct and unequal impact on poor communities.

All over the world, at the intersection of race and poverty, vulnerable groups – People of Colour, women and children, renters, the homeless,

---

2   https://www.artsy.net/artwork/fabrice-monteiro-untitled-number-1-1.

nomadic travellers, and refugees – are disproportionately affected by environmental change. They bear the brunt of disasters arising from climate change: floods and droughts, forest fires, dried-up rivers. They suffer the ravages of war on their land, but have fewer opportunities to change their lives. They receive less help, especially in terms of governmental support, both nationally and internationally (for example, the UK government's recent cuts to the foreign aid budget), and they benefit from fewer emergency supplies, often facing evacuation and relocation. Those fleeing end up in refugee camps that are overpopulated and underfunded, becoming environmental nightmares. In attempts to change their own economic status, developing countries often follow the model of the West and are then lambasted for being environmental polluters as they take the road to industrialisation. Yet we, in the affluent West, forget our own complicity and offer no support to help developing countries take a greener, more environment-friendly route in their industrial development. These factors reflect a societal system that unintentionally, or unconsciously, creates a racist structure that disadvantages black and brown bodies. Environmental racism!

Research suggests that in affluent countries People of Colour, compared with white people, are more exposed and vulnerable to environmental hazards through the intersection of poorer access to economic resources, poorer neighbourhoods with higher levels of air pollution and less green space, poorer access to health services, and poorer exposure to educational opportunities. Remember the fate of Ella Kissi-Debrah, the nine-year-old black girl who lived next to the South Circular Road in London and died in 2013 from chronic asthma brought on by toxic air quality? It is not that white children are not exposed to air pollution that affects their breathing and exacerbates asthma to the point of death. It is the fact that, at the intersection of poverty and race, for black children exposed to such an environment there are fewer opportunities to receive adequate health care, to move to live in another area, to prevent illness. We can witness the way in which run-down neighbourhoods with higher climate-related risks become 'white flight' areas: intensely built-up areas with high concentrations of ethnic minorities, with fewer parks, and fewer good schools and shops. These areas are further examples of environmental injustice.

In the constituency of Ladywood, Birmingham, where Unitarian New Meeting is located, the 2011 census indicated that 72.7 per cent of residents are from Black, Asian, and Minority Ethnic groups, compared with 42 per cent for the whole of Birmingham. Birmingham as a whole has the highest infant-mortality rate in England, and in the Ladywood constituency it is even higher. Birmingham has the highest child-obesity rate, and again the rate in Ladywood is higher. Statistics from 2017/18 show the Ladywood constituency to have one of the highest hospital-admission rates for alcoholism and drug misuse resulting in death. It ranks high in deaths from chronic obstructive pulmonary diseases, and high in the prevalence of cancer, diabetes, heart failure, hypertension, and stroke, to name but a few common causes of morbidity. Furthermore, Ladywood, on average, has low educational attainment rates and ranks high as one of the most deprived environments in the country; the community has a lower-than-average life expectancy, and is exposed to poor air quality that will contribute to ill health and early death.[3]

What emerges are patterns of structural disadvantage revealing that people with higher incomes are less affected by challenges to health and welfare caused by environmental issues, such as air pollution, or global warming. The higher the income, the higher the carbon footprint (more flights, more material goods, more use of energy) – but the lower the impact of climatic change; whereas those with lower disposable incomes have a smaller ecological carbon footprint but experience more damaging consequences. This invisible aspect of inequality in our global system operates without the interventions of perpetrators of intentional racism (as argued by Eduardo Bonilla-Silva[4]), but nevertheless reinforces

---

3   Statistics sourced from *Birmingham Health Profile: Ladywood Constituency 2019* (Birmingham City Council, www.birmingham.gov.uk/publichealth).
4   E. Bonilla-Silva, *Racism without Racists: Color-blind Racism and the Persistence of Racial Inequality in America*, 5th edn (Rowman & Littlefield Publishers, 2017).

racial inequality, economic division, and privilege. We need a paradigm shift. Giving voice to those who already face the worst crises and effects of climate change is something that we don't do well in this country.

Kathleen McTigue[5] reminds us that *"we must be willing to privilege the voices, choices, and needs of these frontline communities most affected"*. From the inner-city urban dwellers at risk of chronic asthma, and disproportionately at risk due to their race, class, and poverty, to the people in economically deprived countries, we must work in partnership to repair environmental devastation and injustices. The one cannot be achieved without the other. We cannot advocate the restoration of the Earth and leave populations in poverty and devastation. We cannot repair the greenhouse effect over Britain, nor the pollution of the seas, nor the dumping of waste, without recognising our historic responsibility as one of the biggest contributors to pollution from the early industrial age. In our rush to develop machinery, to burn fossil fuel, to manufacture and sell goods, we lost our relationship with the spirit of Nature, and an awareness of our interconnection and interdependence. We need each other.

Ecospirituality and activism

"We do not inherit the earth from our ancestors, we borrow it from our children" says a Native American proverb. Big corporations have always bemoaned the inconvenient bond that Indigenous communities have with planet Earth. Indigenous communities often speak truth to power, insisting that raping the planet for its resources has caused harm, created drought, killed forests. They often have a more reciprocal relationship with the planet, taking what they need to survive, and no more (and expressing gratitude for the gifts of the Earth). They were often subjected

---

5   K. McTigue, 'Learning to change: Immersion learning and climate justice', in *Justice on Earth: People of Faith Working at the Intersections of Race, Class, and the Environment*, ed. M. Mishra-Marzetti and J. Nordstrom (Boston: Skinner House Books, 2018).

to genocide or forced to assimilate to an alien culture, placed in boarding schools away from their roots, banned from using their own language. All this worked to deny Indigenous bodies their identity, spirituality, and connectivity to the land.

Enormous profits have disrupted our relational way of being with our planet. We have lost the understanding that we are guests on Earth, and (on an evolutionary scale) very recent arrivals. We are responsible for the harm done to the climate – but also for the restoration of the spirit of the planet. That spirit involves more than a mere balancing of the climate or environment; it is a visceral connection with all creatures and a commitment to restoring justice, achieving equity across race, gender, and economic divides for all beings on the planet. In our call to reconnect with the spiritual aspect of our environmental concerns, we need to recognise that our current marginalisation of potential leaders from Indigenous communities and People of Colour imposes a whiteness-centred expectation on those with the smallest carbon footprint, who make the smallest contribution to the crisis. The voices of Indigenous people, urbanised marginalised people, developing nations, and oppressed people everywhere are of paramount importance to the struggle to restore justice, balance, and care to the planet.

A Unitarian spirituality calls us to live out our highest values in the world. A care for the environment calls for awareness of our interconnectivity with the web of life in all its forms: person to person, nation with nation, with the animal kingdom and sea, as particles in the air, and the air itself. For me, an ecospiritual relationship combines all this into a state of activism, where our spiritual and psychological motivation drives our economic, cultural, and societal aspirations in building the beloved community. That beloved community calls for justice for all people, equity for black/ brown and indigenous communities, and the poor and oppressed, wherever they are.

As we confront the many challenges to eco-justice, I call on the Unitarian spiritual community to respect our ancestor-wisdom and embrace the proverbs that speak the truth of our situation. Earth is not ours. We are caretakers only, borrowing the planet for a short time. Our ecospiritual activism must call us to feel the plight of the planet in the depths of our being, hearing the divine (maybe even the spirit of our ancestors) in the natural world around us crying out, calling us to care for it, fight for it, because then it will care for us. Alastair McIntosh and Matt Carmichael, in their book *Spiritual Activism*,[6] quote the Australian rainforest activist, John Seed: "*I thought that I was saving nature, but then I found that nature was saving me.*" An eco-spiritual activism creates a symbiotic relationship between self and the planet whereby we are nurturing one another.

To return to my reflection on *Dune* at the beginning of this chapter: the people living on that desolate fictional planet survived and thrived in a symbiotic relationship with the wilderness around them. They depended on what the planet's resources (silkworms) could provide to enhance their spirituality, and in this their relationship with their environment was one of spiritual activism. There is much that we can learn from this story about living with the natural world around us. If nothing else, we can learn to find the spiritual courage, emerging from an understanding of values and rightness within, to engage with the challenges without. Maybe then, with a better understanding of the natural world and our mutual dependency, we will reach a spiritual understanding that Nature *can* save us, but we *must* save Nature.

---

6   Alastair McIntosh and Matt Carmichael, *Spiritual Activism: Leadership as Service* (Cambridge: Green Books, 2016, p.21).

Questions for reflection and discussion

1. The stark landscape of Frank Herbert's *Dune* is a vivid reminder of what we can expect if change does not happen. What changes in our landscape can you envision in order to attain a world where we live in tune with the planet?

2. From early cave drawings to present-day mixed-media creations, people have always used art to depict our environment and stories of life. Think of all the landscape paintings that you have seen hanging in art galleries. How does the landscape work of black environmentalist artists contrast with your own concept of landscape art?

3. Consider what centres your own eco-spiritual actions, and how intersectionality relates to your eco-activism.

4. A recent report by Greenpeace UK suggests that "*People of Colour suffer disproportionately ... and climate and ecological crisis are the legacy of systemic racism*". Reflect on how Unitarianism can uplift the voices of People of Colour and support an equitable re-balancing that addresses systemic racism.

The author

Winnie Gordon is of the Black British Diaspora, a queer, cisgender minister in the Unitarian faith serving the Birmingham New Meeting congregation. In the wider Unitarian movement she has been a theme speaker and co-facilitator of Summer School programmes, a member of the Unitarian College Academic Board, and Chairperson and mentor for the Worship Studies Course. More recently, Winnie completed a research study investigating the inclusion of People of Colour in the Unitarian worship community. She is also involved with Ladywood Community Project, a local charity that supports families who are experiencing poverty and financial hardship.

Inuksuk

Elizabeth Birtles

(inspired by the Silent Messenger sculpture by Piita Irniq in the British Museum)

A human-sized
stack of limestone pieces,
sculpted blocks from rock
local to London's museum,
where it stands
stock still –
an inuksuk –
born out of,
and dying out of,
Arctic culture,
Arctic climate,
this stark marker of land and ice
calling us: Look!
In the structure's head-height window,
catch a snatch of the way ahead:
listen to the breaking cries
of countless creatures –
this inuksuk –
born out of,
and dying out of,
creaking Arctic air.
Let this Silent Messenger
speak to us, mark our cold hearts,
be a cairn of hope for us.

The author
Elizabeth Birtles is a retired Unitarian minister.

3 Prophecy and Protest
Rob Oulton

Injustice anywhere is a threat to justice everywhere. We are caught in
an inescapable network of mutuality tied in a single garment of destiny.
Whatever affects one directly affects all indirectly.
(Henry David Thoreau[1])

We listen for voices all our lives: voices to make sense of it all, to explain the inner ache and self-doubt that gathers momentum through our childhood and into adulthood. I vividly remember a point, after an adolescent argument with my parents, when I realised, with sadness, that they could not answer my questions or find a way forward for me. It was now up to me to go out into the world and find other voices who might help me to make a rough sketch of a path that might lead towards the answers to the mystery that was now unfolding. The world seemed beautiful and frightening to me, but, conventional and timid as I was, I did not understand how everyone else seemed to believe in the 'givenness' of life, untroubled by what I perceived to be its strange and unknowable aspects. So I searched for the voices that I needed to hear, and I found them, as many do, among writers, painters, poets, religious teachers, philosophers, and musicians: those who never stop trying to diagnose the human condition and who speak to the aching space that we find inside.

Mostly the ache seems to arise from something intrinsic within us, and those voices reassure us that our individuality does have its place in the world, and that what we have to offer has its own validity. But there are other voices – much rarer – who say something a bit different: maybe it isn't all down to us, and the way we seem to have been made. If I don't fit in, maybe it is not because of who I am, but because of

---

[1]   'Civil Disobedience', in *Walden and Other Writings by Henry David Thoreau* (Bantam Classic Edition, 2004).

how the world in which I find myself is set up to work? These voices belong to those whom we might call prophets; those who, in truthfully describing the present, end up showing us how the future might look – both good and bad. They are people who not only feel the anguish of the inner void but make an attempt to explore it, and they explain why often, to quote John Lennon, it is *"the world that's so wrong"*.[2] Theirs is a lonely and vulnerable role, one which often requires great courage. A self-assured and confident prophet is probably a contradiction in terms – someone whose utterances should be treated with caution. Moreover, the vulnerability and isolation of a prophet can easily tip into paranoia, even psychosis. Labels of this sort can be useful for those who wish to shut the prophet up. But, as the old joke says: "Just because I'm paranoid doesn't mean they're not out to get me".

Climate change, with its attendant challenges, has produced its own prophets. The science and its ecological projections have been around for a long time – but part of an increasingly urgent conversation over the past 30 years. It could be argued that science itself has been the vehicle of prophecy. Its disciplines, as well as the honesty and rigour of the academy where truth is nurtured, have been the bed-rock on which the case for action on climate change has been built. But the scientists are often cautious, restrained, reluctant to commit themselves until they are sure – which is as it should be. With a few exceptions, the stand-out prophetic characters have been missing. And there is a problem with the scientific academy. Mostly it is an integral part of the establishment; organically entwined with, and financially dependent on, the complex of government, industry support, wealthy patronage, and privilege within academia. Unfortunately, it shares this space with many of the agencies and voices whose vested interests lie with the status quo. The prophet speaks from beyond the herd and often seems like a misfit: an outsider, or someone prepared to become one, the better to speak out. The risk and vulnerability of this position is clear, but the absence of a sponsor

---

2   'Happy Christmas (War is Over)' by John Lennon and Yoko Ono (1971).

engenders the freedom to 'speak truth to power'. In a world constructed on authority, hierarchy, and exploitation, the voice that addresses fundamental issues of justice is always powerful, however fragile and lonely it may seem.

The climate journalist Amy Westervelt tells a story[3] about a Californian woman – Lori French – whose family crab-fishing business in California was being affected by warming sea temperatures. The family were not big believers in climate catastrophe. What changed their minds and got them involved in a trade-association lawsuit against the big oil companies was their discovery that the fossil-fuel companies had been preparing for global warming since the 1970s, filing patents for special drilling platforms suitable for work in a polar landscape of melting ice caps. It was not the science that got to Lori French, but the injustice of making provision for climate change while telling everyone that there was no risk. Westervelt tells how research has shown that there is very little correlation between public perceptions of climate science and actually taking any action to avert the risks. But when the story is framed as one of injustice or inequality, then people become much more engaged and are prepared to get involved.

The true prophets always appeal to that sense of justice or righteousness. This motivation makes them difficult to buy off, and dangerous to ignore. The overriding concerns of the prophets of the Hebrew Bible are with injustice and the absence of righteousness, rather than the immediate prosperity or comfort of their people. In many ways, they are prototypes for prophecy and direct action down to this day. They often feel powerless and inadequate and are drawn to performative direct action that could be dismissed as histrionic or 'attention seeking', or simply mad. Moses stutters and is terrified of having to speak before Pharaoh; Jeremiah, charged by God with his prophetic mission, says: *"Ah, Lord God, I do not*

---

3   Amy Westervelt, 'Just "following the science" won't deliver climate justice', *Guardian* newspaper, 29/12/2021.

know how to speak; I am only a child"; Ezekiel goes to extraordinary lengths to act out God's displeasure with Israel, including lying on his left side for 390 days to symbolise the 390 years during which the Northern Jewish Kingdom has been unfaithful, and 40 days on his right side – the 40 years of unfaithfulness of the Southern Kingdom.

This kind of 'direct action' by the prophets has been compared to modern performance art. Performance art requires an audience – it needs you to be present to the performer. When your body enters that arena, and you give even a little attention to the performer/prophet, whether you are amused or annoyed, you are certainly involved, and the message begins to tweak your consciousness and possibly your conscience. Similarly, the purpose of ancient Greek theatre was not entertainment, but political education and religious ceremony.

The authorities in Jerusalem were not really worried about Jesus' activities – until he overturned the money-changers' tables in the Temple. Whatever later Christian theology and mysticism have made of the person of Jesus, his followers – and he himself – seemed to have considered him to be a person in the prophetic tradition of Israel. His status as an outsider was clear from the beginning: after he explicitly identified himself with Isaiah while preaching in his home town of Nazareth, outraged locals tried to throw him off a cliff. As Jesus grimly remarked: "*No prophet is accepted in his own country*".

Jesus certainly engaged in controversy and argument, but generally not in direct confrontation with the authorities, seeming to recognise that this is pointless, and that his fellow Israelites were in many ways no better than the occupying Romans in terms of their values and behaviour. But at least some of his healings and exorcisms were arresting 'street events' which manifested the reality of the coming Kingdom of God that Jesus was prophesying about.

When he overturned the money-changers' tables in the Temple, he was not attacking the financial system or mounting an insurrection. His anger was directed at the corruption of the purity of the Temple as a place where, in Jewish thought, God comes close to humankind. Overturning the tables symbolically acted out the cleansing of the religious hearts of the people which Jesus thought necessary for God's Kingdom to come. Nevertheless, as Jesus discovered, forcefully drawing attention to the injustice and corruption at the heart of any power structure is to invite serious push-back. Occupy, Extinction Rebellion (XR), Black Lives Matter, Me Too, and Insulate Britain are just some of the more recent civil disobedience and protest movements that initially caught the authorities flat-footed and uncertain, allowing their message to cut through. Then the push-back began, with heavier policing, the media snarling louder, and the politicians getting to work on the law, clamping down on the right to protest.

But Jesus's career as a truth-telling movement organiser reveals a consistent difficulty for the authorities who often struggle to silence the prophetic voice: you never quite know when or from where the next trouble maker will spring up. After all, even Jesus's first followers had expressed their doubts: "*Has anything good ever come out of Nazareth?*" Even when these characters do appear, most of them come to nothing, so how do you predict the point when the fire is really going to catch?

I am not the first to perceive in Greta Thunberg the figure of a prophet. She is acknowledged as such by Alastair McIntosh in his book about the climate emergency, *Riders on the Storm*[4] – although he is otherwise rather critical of direct-action climate movements such as XR, and firmly of the view that listening to the science is key. The image of this seemingly very vulnerable child on her first solitary 'school strike' for climate action grabbed the world's attention and captured the essence of prophetic power. The vulnerability and solitariness of the prophet is easy to see, but the embodying of protest in her defiant neurodiversity and history of elective mutism, along with her righteous anger, seemed to articulate a

---

4   Alastair McIntosh, *Riders on the Storm: The Climate Crisis and the Survival of Being* (Birlinn, 2020).

parable for our world that soon set a vibration across the globe. Is being on the autism spectrum the only way of living with authenticity in a world of such damaged values? Is remaining mute the only valid language that can be found to address it? 'Acting out' and 'attention seeking' are terms often used pejoratively, but such behaviour may be the only strategy available for the powerless to disclose supressed abuse or injustice. Thunberg's fragile but defiant individuality in some ways seems to be a living myth of the fragility of our common human future, in the face of the abuse that we have levelled at the planet, and its determination to survive, even if it has to be at our own expense. When she found her voice, it was the true voice of the prophet, addressed both to the powerful and to those who defer to them. The adults whose primary task, as she sees it, was to secure the safety and future of herself and her peers were wantonly and selfishly derogating from that responsibility. Where thirty years of respected, though increasingly uncompromising, scientific data had struggled to make an impact, the prophetic voice of uncomfortable righteousness cut through in a major way.

Separated by nearly two centuries from Thunberg, another awkward character who struggled to find a niche in the world wrote what would be the foundation essay that inspired the civil-disobedience movements of the twentieth century. Henry David Thoreau was a New England, Harvard-educated man from a Unitarian family who manifested the character of what today would be called a 'slacker'. Yet his account of a solitary two years spent in a small self-built hut by Walden Pond near Concord, Massachusetts, resulted in one of the best-loved books of all American literature: *Walden*. Its unique blend of ecology, natural history, pioneer narrative, politics, mindfulness, spirituality, and deep (though amused) scepticism about the nascent industrialised consumer society is certainly eerily prescient of the contemporary critics of our twenty-first century way of life.

Thoreau went on to write the basic manifesto for civil disobedience, but his decamping to Walden woods was when he really discovered his prophetic vision – his own 'embodied' protest against the ways of the modern world which he intuited would destroy nature and enslave humankind. His desire for simplicity was not ascetic, but rather deeply celebratory of the world. He had a passion for the experience of being alive, which he held alongside an incomprehension of the values of a world where, as he saw it, instead of 'living', people expended their energy on 'getting a living' purely for the purpose of acquiring superfluous wealth and property. Like so many in the modern ecological movement today, he wondered about the lives of the continent's 'First People', traces of whose lives he found in Walden woods. He describes their way of life – not so different from how he himself was living at that time, simply and in balance with nature – and implicitly contrasts it with the burgeoning industrialised future symbolised by the Boston railway under construction on the other side of the lake. His prophetic doubt again strays to the moral underpinning of this unconstrained industrial expansion, as he reflects that *"we don't ride on the railroad, it rides upon us"*.

In 1849 Thoreau published a short essay entitled 'Civil Disobedience' which would later influence Tolstoy and then Gandhi, who adopted the name and principles for his own liberation movement in India. It is a model adopted by the advocates of many contemporary causes: civil and political rights, land, employment, and union rights. It is a model studied and specifically identified as appropriate by climate campaigns such as Extinction Rebellion. Thoreau's act of civil disobedience was to refuse to pay the poll tax because it funded the federal government which, pre-Civil War, upheld the slavery laws – he was a strong abolitionist. He also objected to the US war with Mexico as unjust and aggressive. He spent one night in Concord Gaol and was rather upset to be released because his embarrassed family paid the tax for him!

In the essay Thoreau reaches the conclusion that however democratic the mandate that a government might have, it cannot overrule individual conscience. He asks:

> Can there not be a government in which majorities do not virtually decide right and wrong, but conscience? – in which majorities

decide only those questions to which the rule of expediency is applicable? Must the citizen ever for a moment, or in the least degree, resign his conscience to the legislator? Why has every person a conscience, then? I think we should be men first, and subjects afterward.

Thoreau thought that democratic majorities may grant authority to a government, but they cannot overrule basic principles of right and wrong. If they do, then the concerned citizen must consider taking direct action. But he was always a realist, and he understood that government could not be perfect. Injustice would always be closely woven into the machine; but nevertheless, if it was *"of a nature that requires you to be the agent of injustice to another, then I say, break the law"*. And significantly for those many people concerned about climate change today: *"What I have to do is to see, at any rate, that I do not lend myself to the wrong which I condemn."*

Thoreau quite understood that we all have many preoccupations and interests: he did himself – he was the opposite of the fanatic. But nevertheless, *"If I devote myself to other pursuits and contemplations, I must first see, at least, that I do not pursue them sitting upon another man's shoulders. I must get off him first, that he may pursue his contemplations too."* This clear issue of justice and fairness, alongside fear for the planet, is what motivates Greta Thunberg, Lori French, and many climate activists. The developed countries, their powerful fossil-fuel corporations, and the post-war generation have built their prosperity on the shoulders of the developing world and the Global South, as well as on the safe and sustainable future of their children and grandchildren. We need to climb down off their shoulders, so that they can equitably pursue their "contemplations too".

Thoreau's method of 'climbing down off the shoulders of the victims of injustice' was to stop complying with the forces that promoted and fostered that injustice. In his case, he stood out against the war in Mexico by refusing to pay the tax that he deemed would be used to support that war: "*If a thousand men were not to pay their tax bills this year, that would not be a violent and bloody measure, as it would be to pay them and enable the State to commit violence and to shed innocent blood*". And he articulated the central practical principle of non-violent civil disobedience, which has guided its practitioners to this day:

> A minority is powerless while it conforms to the majority; it is not even a minority then; but it is irresistible when it clogs by its whole weight. If the alternative is to keep all just men in prison, or give up war and slavery, the State will not hesitate which to choose.

'Clogging by its whole weight' was the tactic adopted by Extinction Rebellion (XR) when it emerged as a new player in the environmental struggle in Autumn 2018. Alastair McIntosh has questioned the claim (based only on one study, and specific to civil-rights struggles) that the figure of 3.5 per cent of the population rebelling is sufficient to compel a capitulation by the authorities. Of course, it pays no regard to the situation in many parts of the world where security services are armed and will use those arms against protestors. Nevertheless, there can be no doubt that XR's big London-based actions of 2019 caught the authorities off guard. The sheer weight of numbers of citizens apparently prepared to risk arrest, their character and demographic, and their very explicit commitment not only to non-violence but also to non-aggression seem to have wrong-footed the police. Thunberg's prophetic voice seems to have stirred something in the consciences of many older people: the 'baby-boomers' born in the 1950s and 1960s who felt that they had had the best of the post-war world of peace and prosperity and that now it was pay-back time. But that generation also remembers a quieter world where there were more green spaces, more wildlife, and fewer cars. David Attenborough finally began to stop pulling his punches and show clearly what humankind was inflicting on the world's natural habitats.

When I got involved in the XR direct action of October 2019, it was my battered copy of Henry Thoreau's works that I took with me, and the desk sergeant at Lewisham police station kindly allowed me to take it into the cell. Thoreau described the method in 'Civil Disobedience', but it was *Walden*, with its description of life in tune with nature, not in dominance over it, that spoke to my heart. My decision to be 'arrestable' was partly made on the basis that I am one of the older 'boomers' who are in 'climate debt' to the younger generation. I am also someone with the least to lose from incurring a criminal record, and I have the financial wherewithal to hire a lawyer and pay a fine. The courage and dedication of the younger generations is something else entirely, for whom getting arrested may put finances, career aspirations, and travel plans in jeopardy.

I have participated in demonstrations from time to time and experienced the thrill of the big noisy crowd, but to sit down in Whitehall on a Monday morning, block the road, and begin to form a camp which shortly becomes a community is to carry protest into the area of prophecy. Not of course that I am in any way a prophet, but to be part of a group that, in its deliberately provocative action, is self-consciously 'acting out' a different model of society is to be involved in embodying a prophetic vision. With its food sharing, its spontaneous 'citizens' assemblies', its artwork and performance, its carefully curated ethos of non-aggression, its celebration of nature and creativity, alongside an intergenerational ethos of kindness and mutual respect, the XR camp may be easily derided as idealistic. But a world in which climate justice can be possible, so that humankind can survive, has to be built on a foundation that incorporates at least some of these basics of kindness, mutuality, and equality. The modern world's economic and political model – a pyramid scheme of exploitation, competition, and coercion – has become so unstable that it threatens to topple and bury us all, even before it poisons the natural world that it so greedily ransacks.

Embodying prophecy in protest affects not only the on-looker but also the participant. By stepping outside the law, beyond the safe perimeter of conformity, the protester feels the fear of the prophet, but also the daring energy of what could be possible; of what human community could become. Expecting arrest on Tuesday evening after the police largely cleared the camp, a small group of us instead became isolated and cordoned-off outside the Cabinet Office. Free to leave, but not to return, in an act of solidarity we stayed, sustained by food, blankets, hot drinks, and the unwavering enthusiasm of the XR teams. As dawn came, we witnessed a trickle of people coming to work in the Cabinet Office – the earliest probably just the ordinary staff, but later the more powerful individuals. Carrying on their phone conversations, and striding purposefully into the command centre of the British Government, they studiously ignored the shabby squatters outside their workplace. The dutiful London constabulary would soon be back to rid them of these embarrassing 'old crusties'; it wasn't anything to concern them – they had more important things to get on with. It was all very well protesting about climate change, but without a functioning 'economy' where would all these simpletons be?

The writer Malcolm Muggeridge used to insist that we ultimately have to make a choice in life about which path to follow: the path of love or the path of power. On that bleary, cold, and damp Wednesday morning in October, waiting in trepidation for my first experience of being arrested and put in a police cell, I felt the reality of that choice. Perhaps the fear, fatigue, and defencelessness made it more vivid, but I could feel the harshness and indifference of power: power which I may not have wielded myself, but which I have nevertheless hidden behind and used for my comfort all my life. This is the power against which Thoreau protested, which had compelled and ordered the human shoulders to carry me and my generation through our privileged lives; the shoulders of the people of the despoiled rainforests and dried-up savannahs, the polluted oceans, precarious lowlands and islands, the thawing tundra – but most of all the frail shoulders of the world's children and grandchildren; so many, already on the move, fleeing war and despoilation.

As grown-ups we are taught to reject black and white thinking: grey is the adult way. But sometimes a stark choice has to be made: power or love? It is our call now. I just hope that I have the courage to call it right.

Questions for reflection and discussion

1. When Henry Thoreau asks: "*Must the citizen ever for a moment, or in the least degree, resign his conscience to the legislator?*", he is implying that there are some issues so ethically important that a simple democratic majority cannot be sufficient reason to overrule a person's sense of right and wrong. Do you agree? What are the pros and cons of this argument?

2. The most notable mass actions of non-violent civil disobedience have been concerned with civil and human rights. Does civil disobedience in pursuit of climate action attain an equivalent level of validity?

3. Prophecy is not only about how bad the future looks; it also speaks about a vision of a better world. What might a Unitarian vision of a better world look like?

4. Is it ever justifiable to disrupt ordinary people's lives by using civil-disobedience tactics? What are the reasons for your opinion?

The author

Robert Oulton is a retired general practitioner in the NHS, and a member of Godalming Unitarians. As an active member of Extinction Rebellion he has been arrested several times at their actions in London. He is a trustee of the local Climate Emergency Centre in Godalming: 'What Next, Earth?'. He facilitates mindfulness meditation groups with his wife, Unitarian minister Sheena Gabriel, and is a member of the Healing Trust, chairing their South-East England group. As well as XR, he is actively involved in campaigning against privatisation in the NHS.

PART TWO:
Honouring the Earth

Honouring the Earth: Prologue
Maria Curtis

The natural world is the primary revelation of the divine.
(Thomas Berry)

If the Earth is the primary revelation of the divine, as Thomas Berry asserts; if God is immanent in the natural world, as Panentheist theologians claim; if we regard Earth as our sacred Mother, along with many pagan and Indigenous peoples; if the world is *"charged with the grandeur of God"*, in the words of Gerard Manley Hopkins – our attitude should be one of reverence. The gift of life comes unmerited, undeserved. We should be delirious with joy and gratitude for this bounty. We have our senses to perceive the riot of colour, scent, and sound; we have the joys of touch and taste; we have minds that can apprehend beauty. We should celebrate the diversity of all forms of life on Earth. Miraculous, the creativity inherent in matter!

For Hopkins, God is manifest in nature. The poet expresses the ecstatic joy that we should all feel in the presence of such glory. In *Spring*, he describes with passionate intensity the energy and beauty of burgeoning life, asking:

What is all this juice and all this joy?
    A strain of the earth's sweet being in the beginning
In Eden garden.

The natural world is an innocent world. We need to fall in love with the Earth with some of Hopkins' passionate intensity. Then we will care. Then we will cherish.

What would it mean to honour the Earth? To be in right relationship with the Earth – her land, oceans, rivers, air, and all her plants and animals? I think we know what an unholy relationship looks like. On our shores in the British Isles, privatised water companies are pouring untreated sewage straight into the sea – not great for swimmers and surfers, but not much good for the fish either. Even the Moon cannot escape this abuse; I cannot get out of my mind the image of used nappies abandoned by astronauts on its surface. That is not reverence.

Hopkins again, from *God's Grandeur:*

> Generations have trod, have trod, have trod;
>   And all is seared with trade; bleared, smeared with toil;
> And wears man's smudge and shares man's smell: the soil
>   Is bare now, nor can foot feel, being shod.

We humans have sullied the Earth. We have fouled our own nest. Our exploitation of the Earth's resources has despoiled the planet. We have treated living things, plants and animals, whole ecosystems, as if they were just stuff, rather than beings; we have shown no respect for the millions of years that went into creating them. Yet Hopkins, writing in the Victorian era, insists:

> ... nature is never spent;
>   There lives the dearest freshness deep down things

But now in the twenty-first century we have to face the prospect that nature may indeed become "spent"; we are in the midst of the sixth major extinction event in the history of the planet, the only one caused by humans. We cannot keep on plundering natural resources as if there were an inexhaustible supply. We cannot keep on polluting air, land, and water and assuming that life in all its current forms will survive. We exercise species imperialism, whereby we assume that our lives are of greater value than those of other species. We are destroying ecosystems – networks of symbiotic relationships and interdependencies – at an alarming rate, while still not appreciating how everything is related.

But increasingly we are presented with new discoveries which should make us reappraise these relationships. Richard Powers' astonishing tree novel, *The Overstory*,[1] is teeming with startling examples: how trees communicate with chemical messages to convey that a dangerous disease is approaching. How the mushrooms that we see on the surface are just the fruiting bodies of fungi bursting out from huge underground networks of mycelia which are nourished by, and at the same time nourish, the trees whose roots they surround. They are more important than leaves in manufacturing food for trees. One of the characters in the novel, attending a conference that is expecting technology to solve the problems of global warming, thinks to herself:

> She could tell them about a simple machine needing no fuel and little maintenance, one that steadily sequesters carbon, enriches the soil, cools the ground, scrubs the air, and scales easily to any size. A tech that copies itself and even drops food for free. A device so beautiful it's the stuff of poems. If forests were patentable, she'd get an ovation.

Remarkable, indeed! As we don't fully understand all the implications of disturbing the balance within ecosystems, and we remain ignorant of the complex ways in which the different species within them interact, the sensible approach would be to play safe and minimise risk.

What we do know is that all plants absorb carbon dioxide in photosynthesis, releasing oxygen into the atmosphere. Thus, they prepared the way for mammals to exist. Perhaps we should feel gratitude. Cutting down or burning forests that are carbon traps is not only ecocide for all the beings living in that habitat, but suicide for us.

And why are we doing it, anyway? In Borneo, we cut down the rainforest, sacrificing our close relatives, the orangutans, so that we can grow palm oil on vast plantations. Monocultures like these are not healthy for plants,

---

1   Richard Powers, *The Overstory* (W. W. Norton, New York, 2018).

so we need to poison the soil with pesticides to prevent disease. And palm oil is a fat, often used as a bulking agent, with limited nutritional value. It makes no sense, unless, of course, you are only interested in making a profit. The Amazon rainforest continues to lose an area the size of a football pitch every second. Most of the deforested land is used for grazing cattle – a very wasteful use of land – or for monocultures like soybean. Indigenous peoples continue to lose their traditional lands. Activists fighting to preserve the integrity of the forests continue to be murdered.

The earth beneath our feet

Let's think about the earth beneath our feet, the soil. The layer of soil covering the land is getting thinner. It is being washed away. Once it's gone, it's gone. Soil is a major repository of carbon, originating from the atmosphere, absorbed by photosynthesising plants and retained when they die. This vast underground store regulates the global carbon cycle, while contributing to food production, biodiversity, and resilience to drought and flooding. Carbon is released when the soil is ploughed or washed away, or the temperature rises. We need to grow more trees and deep-rooted plants, and engage in sustainable agricultural practices to retain the soil. And stop global temperatures rising. Cherishing the Earth is maintaining soil cover.

We need a sense of humility when thinking about our relationship with the land. How odd it would have seemed to our hominid ancestors to hear us claiming to "own" the land, to own trees in forests, or fish in the sea. We visit the Moon and the first thing we do is put up a national flag. How ridiculous to think that we can own part of the universe! Our hubris knows no bounds. Now we fantasise about colonising Mars (Elon Musk, one of the wealthiest people on Earth, aspires to create nuclear explosions in order to release water on Mars!) when we have depleted resources on our home planet. Surely it's better to spend our money looking after this home.

Biodiversity

We are now in the Anthropocene epoch, when human beings have become the primary agent of change affecting the future of the Earth system. There are very few places of wilderness left on Earth, and very few wild animals remaining. I remember my shock when I heard that humans and our domesticated animals represented 96 per cent of mammals on Earth. Vast ecosystems are being destroyed, for use as farmland. The UN estimates that as many as one million plant and animal species are at risk of extinction.

Synthetic pesticides developed during World War II (especially DDT) were used to prevent the spread of insect-borne diseases such as typhoid and malaria. Then Rachel Carson published *Silent Spring* in 1962, showing how chemicals were damaging ecosystems, killing insects and birds, and reaching humans. She was sued and subjected to character assassination by US-based multinational chemical companies. Similar tactics have been used by oil and gas giants to distort the science on the climate crisis from the 1980s onwards.

Species loss is as much a threat to our well-being as thermonuclear war. Since the 1970s we have been aware that *"the rate of exploitation of the ecosystem which generates economic growth cannot increase indefinitely without overdriving the system and pushing it to the point of collapse"* (US biologist Barry Commoner). The 1982 Brandt Report concluded: *"Few threats to peace and survival of the human community are greater than those posed by the prospects of cumulative and irreversible degradation of the biosphere on which human life depends."*

International goals for the preservation of biodiversity were established for the first time at the Rio Earth Summit Conference 1992. The Dasgupta Review[2] in 2021 examined the economics of biodiversity, concluding that *"Nature is a blind spot in economics that we ignore at our*

---

2   P. Dasgupta, *The Economics of Biodiversity: The Dasgupta Review* (London, HM Treasury, 2021).

peril." The review understood the need to rebalance our demand for goods from nature with nature's capacity to supply them.

We cannot separate the climate crisis from the biodiversity crisis. Floods and fires are very visible; biodiversity loss is harder to register. But some of us are old enough to remember the noisy chatter of urban sparrows; the glorious song of the thrush in back gardens; insects spattered on car windscreens; fields full of butterflies; and wasps spoiling our picnics! Now a quarter of UK bird species – the house martin, greenfinch, and cuckoo, for example – are in serious decline.

Every aspect of industry is entwined with nature's destruction. The whole way in which the world economy operates causes biodiversity loss. From hunting huge mammals to extinction to poisoning birdlife with pesticides, we humans have treated nature as an inexhaustible resource for too long. Environmentalists, Indigenous peoples, and scientists have long been sounding the alarm, yet no meaningful action has been taken.

The natural world is not a romantic backdrop against which we can choose to act out our drama. We need to understand ourselves as part of the natural world, embedded in a delicate network of relationships that needs to be conserved.

Animals and us

The division between the human and non-human permeates our western philosophy and thought. Our human identity is traditionally seen as superior to that of the other creatures with whom we share the Earth. But if we define ourselves as not-animals, and *animal* becomes a term of abuse, it is a short step to different and more pernicious forms of 'othering'. The *Animals and Us* exhibition at the Turner Gallery, Margate, in 2019, presented the history of human/non-human boundary making. The artists made the link between 'animalisation' and xenophobia, racism, and the abuse of nature and other animals.

> "Some people talk to animals .... Not many listen, though. That's the problem."
>
> (A. A. Milne, *Winnie the Pooh*)

The exhibition looked at animals: from our closest domestic companions to the food on our plates; from the earliest depictions of wild animals in cave paintings to animals confined in factory farms. There is much to celebrate in our relationships with creatures such as horses and dogs who can be trained to do amazing things (guide dogs for the blind; dogs who can sniff out drugs or cancer, etc.). Yet there were some very upsetting exhibits, too, like the Google Earth images of huge cattle stations, looking like a grid with spots on – which one realised with horror were cows enclosed in pens, surrounded by a vast red lake formed from their slurry. This is hardly treating our fellow creatures with dignity. This sort of industrial farming shows no respect for their natural life style, or for the environment. There were also poignant images of beleaguered species such as polar bears and orangutans, who are losing their habitats as a direct or indirect result of human activity.

The dominant narrative in the 1960s was that humans and apes were different in kind. It was thought that only humans made tools. However, Jane Goodall started with an open mind and a lively curiosity. She simply observed chimpanzees in the wild. She saw them 'fishing' for termites with thin 'straws' chosen for the purpose. She saw them cracking nuts with stones. Moreover, she saw this culture being passed on to infants. As a result of her observations, we had to think differently about chimpanzees. We now know that *Homo sapiens* and *Pan troglodytes* (chimpanzees) descended from a common ancestor – separating approximately 6.3 million years ago. All the great apes – orangutans, gorillas, bonobos, gibbons, and chimpanzees – are declining in numbers because of competition from humans who have encroached into their natural territory in the tropical rainforests of Asia and Africa. Our closest relatives (some of whom, Bonobos, share >99 per cent of our DNA) are threatened with extinction in the next 10–15 years in most places where they range.

Surely this is an insult to the creative force that has supported our development and theirs for the last 6 million years. What gives us the right to obliterate our family members in this way? It should not happen. We need to rethink our relationship with animals, not just with our nearest relatives but with all creatures.

> *The universe is a community of subjects, not a collection of objects.*
> (Thomas Berry)[3]

Many of us choose not to eat meat for ethical reasons, but if we are consuming domesticated animals, let us at least treat them with dignity, as beings worthy of respect; as subjects, not objects; as creatures, not commodities. If we are going to kill them for food, let us honestly acknowledge what we are doing. We might be squeamish about cultures based on hunting (of which there are several in Arctic regions), but it seems to me that these Indigenous people manifest a more honourable relationship with their prey than we do with our industrialised farming of domesticated animals. For example, the economy of the Yupik people of Alaska is based on seal hunting; they acknowledge their dependence on the natural world, expressing gratitude to the creatures whose lives are sacrificed that they might survive; they generate very little waste, using every part of the animal – for food, clothing, heating, etc. Their way of life honours the life of the seal, and the environment is not polluted in the process.

It's a far cry from factory farming. It has to be wrong to rear chickens in crowded conditions, with no possibility of exercise, to be so heavy that their legs cannot bear their weight. They are creatures, not commodities. Some would argue that we should not eat meat at all, but, if we do, surely we should honour the creatures' 'natural' lifestyle and enable them to flourish in their brief lives.

---

3   Thomas Berry with Thomas Clarke, *Befriending the Earth: A Theology of Reconciliation Between Humans and the Earth* (Twenty-Third Publications, Connecticut, 1991).

The same goes for vivisection. Some would rule it out entirely, but if it is the only way to obtain the information that we need, let us do our experiments humanely and not waste lives researching trivial issues; let us be aware that it is lives that we are sacrificing: lives worthy of dignity and respect.

In *Philosophical Investigations,* Wittgenstein wrote: "*If a lion could speak, we could not understand him*". This is because meaning grows out of a way of life. What is significant for a lion is not the same as what is significant for a bird or a human being. It is difficult enough for us to understand another human being, let alone a creature with a totally different life from ours. Let's be curious. We don't know what their experience is.

Consider the octopus – the nearest we will come to encountering an intelligent alien on Earth. They are highly intelligent creatures, yet they are not social beings; they have a short life span and don't rear their young. It is a common assumption that human intellectual capacities developed out of negotiating social relationships. So how come octopuses are so clever? We marvel at their ingenuity – gathering two half coconut shells from the ocean floor, climbing inside them, then rolling away, invulnerable; cutting out the lights in the lab by squirting at the bulbs; showing preference for some members of staff and squirting at those they dislike; playing simply to entertain themselves. In his wonderful book *Other Minds: The Octopus and the Evolution of Intelligent Life,*[4] philosopher and scuba diver Peter Godfrey-Smith describes the thrill of being led by the hand by an octopus. In our ignorance, is not the best approach to be curious when we encounter such a strange creature? What on earth would octopus consciousness be like, with a brain distributed throughout its eight limbs? We can only marvel and celebrate the existence of such a creature who separated from our common ancestor more than 164 million years ago. To be sure, if an

---

4   Peter Godfrey-Smith, *Other Minds: The Octopus and the Evolution of Intelligent Life* (William Collins, 2016).

octopus could talk, we would not understand it, yet we can engage in a relationship and communicate. Our worlds can overlap. It seems a shame to eat them.

Our animal selves

> May we learn to return
> And rest in the beauty
> Of animal being,
> Learn to lean low,
> Leave our locked minds,
> And with freed senses
> Feel the earth
> Breathing with us.[5]

Perhaps if we embraced our own animal nature, we would treat other animals with more respect. Our sedentary lifestyles, our poor eating habits, our constant busyness and anxiety, all contribute to poor physical and mental health. Honouring our bodies would mean spending more time outdoors, not rushing to get from A to B, but stopping to pay attention and delight in the manifold miracles of life.

Reconnecting with the Earth and absorbing her beauty with all our senses is vital for our health and may well be the only way to save her. We need to fall in love with the Earth all over again. Then we will honour and cherish her, nourishing our spirits in the process.

---

5   John O'Donohue, *Benedictus* (Bantam Press, London, 2007).

4 "In Whom We Live and Move and Have Our Being": spirituality, embodiment, and an ecotheology of reverence

Jo James

The ground of all being

The Welsh phrase "*Dechrau wrth dy draed*" – "Start at your feet" – is derived from farm work, but it could be interpreted as meaning "Begin from where you are, use the strategy that is most readily available to you". For those of us who want to begin resisting the current culture of ecocide, this must be our strategy: start at your feet and consider the ground on which you stand.

In Geneva in 1553 the heretical thinker Miguel de Servet (a name Latinised as Michel Servetus) stood trial for heresy for suggesting (among many other heresies) that Deity is consubstantial (of the same substance) with nature. At the trial John Calvin is said to have stamped his foot and cried: "If I stamp on the ground ... I stamp on your God!"[1] Calvin used this mockery to denounce Servetus' idea that God is fully present in the world, but in this chapter I want to consider that our understanding of God might indeed correspond with our understanding of ecological reality. We must remember that God, "in whom we live and move and have our being",[2] is

---

[1] "He [Servetus] held that God was present in and constitutive of all creation. This feature of Servetus's theology was especially obnoxious to Calvin. At the Geneva trial he asked Servetus, 'What, wretch! If one stamps the floor, would one say that one stamped on your God?'" https://uudb.org/articles/michaelservetus.html, accessed 02/02/2022.

[2] *Acts of the Apostles* 17: 28.

all around us, as a "ground of all being",[3] in our lungs, in our blood, and beneath our feet. Like the Rabbi (quoted by Carl Jung[4]) who said that the reason why people no longer see God is that they do not look low enough, we must *dechrau wrth dy draed*, and begin with Earth itself.

Unitarian receptivity to the concept of God as immanent, present in the world, began early, with Servetus, whose work *On the Errors of the Trinity* (1531) so enraged Calvin; but it is also evident in the work of the Unitarian minister Joseph Priestley (1733–1804), a natural scientist whose *Disquisitions Relating to Matter and Spirit* (1777) argues against Cartesian dualism, suggesting that mind and spirit are integral to material being, and that the human soul and the Divine substance are indivisible.

Later Unitarians have been influenced by, and have developed a unique perspective on, the thinking of the German Idealist philosophers.[5] Because of the significant theoretical overlap between Unitarians, German Idealists, English Romantics, and American Transcendentalists, there have existed corresponding areas of shared interest as these streams of thought have developed. Nowhere is this shared development more apparent than in the ready uptake of the related theological concept of Panentheism among contemporary Unitarians.[6]

Panentheism as a theological position differs from both Pantheism (the idea that God is identical with the substance of the cosmos) and Classic Theism (which emphasises God's difference from nature): it constitutes

---

3   The phrase is from Paul Tillich, *Systematic Theology*, Vol. 1, pp. 235–6 (University of Chicago Press, 1973).
4   In *Man and His Symbols* by C. J. Jung (Doubleday, 1964), p.92.
5   Henry Jones, 'The Philosophy of Martineau in Relation to the Idealism of the Present Day', *Nature* 74, 53 (1906), https://doi.org/10.1038/074053b0; and Ruth Watts, *Gender, Power and the Unitarians in England, 1760–1860* (Routledge, 2014), pp. 46, 121–126.
6   For a brilliantly articulated example of this, see http://andrewjbrown.blogspot.com/2009/12/follow-child-and-if-you-look-youll-find.html (accessed 02/02/22), https://danny-crosby.blogspot.com/2017/02/the-essence-of-truth.html, accessed 02/02/2022.

a bridge between them. Panentheism, which literally means '*All within God'-ism*, proposes that, while God and the cosmos are indivisible, it is equally true that God is also transcendent and illimitably 'other'. While God is in all things, so also all things are in God. In one symbolic understanding of Panentheism (inevitably there are many), the cosmos, or the creation, is *the body* of God.[7]

When I discovered the Unitarian church, I found a new way of relating to God and worship. I found a framework with which to dispense with outmoded ideas of God as patriarch or Majesty, and the outmoded cosmologies that accompanied such anthropomorphic theology. I began to see new (to me) ways of understanding God and religion; but along with these critiques of pre-modern views of God, I also began to question many underlying assumptions of modernity too. The mainstream modern narrative (known as 'Materialism' or 'Physicalism') proposes that all the physical reality that we can perceive is composed of the building blocks of matter. These building blocks can be de-constructed, much as you could take apart a machine in order to see how it works. Physical reality can be subdivided and reduced into atomic and sub-atomic particles in an ever-diminishing process. Conversely these infinitely tiny particles combine to construct elements of greater and greater complexity. Materialism admits that its narrative is still incomplete (for example, it does not explain how these elements combine in such a way as to give rise to life or consciousness); but its proponents claim that this is just a matter of time; the scientific progress of knowledge will eventually yield the missing answers. I discovered in a Unitarian chapel other ways of experiencing reality; with a view of God as the underlying principle of material reality, the 'ground of all being', our perspective on material reality, being itself, is transformed: to understand that all that is is within God is to do away with the notion of inert, dead matter and experience the living God as fully present throughout time and space.

----

7   See, for example, Grace Jantzen, *God's World, God's Body* (Philadelphia, The Westminster Press, 1984).

Elargissez Dieu – God at large

I began studying for the Unitarian ministry at Harris Manchester College in Oxford in 2011. As part of my training I researched Unitarian theologies of the Spirit. I was fascinated by interpretations of the second verse of Genesis: *"... And the Spirit of God moved upon the face of the waters"* (Gen. 1:2 KJV). The Orthodox Jewish Bible renders this as: "... And the Ruach Elohim was hovering upon the face of the waters". *Ruach* is a Hebrew word meaning 'spirit' or 'breath'. So we could equally well read the second line of Genesis as "And the breath of God moved on the face of the waters". In Greek the equivalent of *Ruach* is *Pneuma*, and in Latin it is *Anima* or *Spiritus*. Both *Pneuma* in Greek, and *Anima* or *Spiritus* in Latin, evoke the notion of 'spirit' or 'breath'.

In trinitarian Christian theology the Holy Spirit is also co-equally God, and (despite the later trinitarian concept of the Holy Spirit as a distinct persona) *Ruach Elohim/Ruach Hodesh* is indivisible from God in Jewish theology. Spirit always seems to be identified as an animating force, the life of life.

It is important to acknowledge that orthodox theology in the Abrahamic traditions has generally affirmed that God has no body, is incorporeal, and transcends or is beyond physical matter, emotion, and time – thus placing God beyond the forces that affect embodied creatures. Over many centuries, significant controversies and debates have accompanied any attempt to suggest otherwise, as claims for the supremacy of God are usually underpinned by the affirmation that God is of a different order of reality from 'base matter'. The proposition of a spiritual/material duality has grown to represent many theological and philosophical perspectives (the priority given to the notion of a disembodied God allows atheists to propose that invisible is identical to un-real). Yet the etymologies of all the words for Spirit in so many ancient languages – *Ruach; Pneuma; Spiritus; Anima* – forcefully remind us that the spirit is synonymous with breath. And it is impossible to imagine a breath without a body.

In the stained-glass windows[8] that light the north wall of the Chapel of Harris Manchester College, six angels are depicted carrying the Earth through the process of Creation. The motto that accompanies each image is *Elargissez Dieu*. This slightly enigmatic motto can be translated as *Enlarge God*, or perhaps the sense to be gained from Diderot's *Pensées Philosophiques* is 'Broaden your idea of God'.[9] As someone who spent a certain amount of my ministerial formation staring at these windows, I think there is also a sense of liberation, perhaps associated with the contemporary phrase 'at large'. God can be 'at large' in the world and beyond the confines of Classic Theism, so *Elargissez Dieu* can mean 'Set God free'.

The panentheism discovered in Servetus and developed through Unitarian tradition and elsewhere allows us space to explore the moral and ethical implications of God, conceived as embodied by the creation itself, embodied by the cosmos. A felt sense of the reality of God perceived through all five senses allows the worshipper to progress from a disembodied spirituality to an engagement with devotional physicality encountered in various forms of contemplative prayer and ritual: pilgrimage, chanting, dancing, some singing and walking meditations which emphasise the connection between breath and spirit in embodied form. It is a curious anomaly that the popular term 'mindfulness' re-asserts the primacy of the mind, when it could equally be termed 'whole awareness': admittedly not so snappy, but closer, I think, to the intention of Christian contemplation. Panentheism perceives God as both within and simultaneously 'more than' the cosmos, and it provides a grounding from which to reconnect spirituality with ecology.

---

8   Designed by Edward Burne-Jones for the William Morris Co. in 1885.

9   Denis Diderot, "Enlarge God. See him everywhere he exists, or say he doesn't exist at all", from *Pensées Philosophiques* no. 26 (1764).

God's World, God's Body[10]

Nowhere has a holistic religious perspective been more productively explored than in feminist theologies which began in the 1970s to re-examine the patriarchal assumptions of Classic Theism.

Many feminist theologians have shared a view well expressed by Margaret Farley: that the body/spirit dualisms with which religions have struggled since late antiquity are not integral to traditions such as Judaism and Christianity but are instead influences from later doctrinal movements. She points out that a worldview evident in the Christian scriptures seems to sacralise all of the natural cosmos. Nature, she says, is *"valuable according to its concrete reality, which includes an interdependence with embodied humanity"*.[11]

Anyone moderately acquainted with contemporary Unitarian thinking will recognise the resonance of the term 'interdependence', which, since its appearance as the seventh of the Seven Principles[12] adopted by the Unitarian Universalist Association in the USA in 1985, has encapsulated a major hermeneutical perspective in Unitarian theology: a commitment to "Respect for the interdependent web of all existence of which we are a part". This commitment has widening significance in the current century. Like much Unitarian theology, however, the interdependence of all life has remained at an intellectual level and has rarely been intentionally applied or embodied so as to understand our participation in the lively being of an all-pervading, inherent, and transcendent God.

This must urgently change if we are to adjust to the current global crisis of ecocide with a substantial and constructive theological framework.

---

10   The title of Grace Jantzen's book (see note 7).
11   Margaret Farley, 'Feminist Theology and Bioethics' in *Feminist Theology, a Reader*, ed. Ann Loades (SPCK 1993), p.243.
12   https://www.uua.org/beliefs/what-we-believe/principles, accessed 19/06/2022.

Historically Unitarians have been over-dependent on rationalistic intellectualism as our habitual way of understanding; we forget that the word 'understand' is derived from the same etymological root stock as 'inter' (not 'under'); it meant a point of view from within. The 'inte' of 'intestine' is from the same root, and perhaps 'gut-feeling' could sometimes be a more reliable way of understanding. Beverly Wildung Harrison points out that "… *all our knowledge, including our moral knowledge, is body mediated … Ideas are dependent on our sensuality. Feeling is the basic bodily ingredient that mediates our connectedness to the world …*". But she also reminds us that while feeling is the basis of "our relational transaction with the world", religious pietism alone is not sufficient to advance real change: "*The moral question is not 'What do I feel but rather what do I do with what I feel.'*" [13]

For the theological concept of the interdependence of all life to be rooted in a dynamic way within Unitarian theology, worship, and practice, I believe that we must recognise the truth of the feminist precept that our bodies and our selves are one and the same. That we dwell within God's body/God's spirit. And that re-unifying the division created by spirit/body dualism, rejecting any split between the body and the self, and ourselves and our Earth, is also a step towards that liberation which God calls us towards and which we must necessarily embrace in order to avert global catastrophe.

God's fellow workers[14]

Rosemary Radford Ruether, the brilliant theologian who died aged 85 in 2022, explored the social and ethical implications of a Biblical theology of embodiment. In *New Woman, New Earth* (1975) she reminds us that

---

13 Beverly Wildung Harrison, 'The Power of Anger in the Work of Love', in *Feminist Theology, a Reader,* ed. Ann Loades (SPCK 1993), pp. 205–206.

14 "For we are God's fellow workers. You are God's field, God's building" (Paul, *1 Corinthians* 3: 9).

a concept of the interconnection between God and the world is present from the beginnings of the Jewish tradition (and earlier, as Judaism integrated and developed some elements of contemporary Near Eastern religious thought). She describes pre-Exilic Judaism as a religion of "socio-natural renewal", and she underlines the importance of the relational collaboration between God and humanity described as "covenant". As we know, the Hebrew scriptures deeply represent the inherent sacredness of the world, with natural spaces such as wells, fords, mountain tops, caves, and fields bearing witness to God's presence. In one of the most famous episodes of divine self-revelation,[15] God seems to assume the appearance of a bush which burns but is not consumed by fire – an eerie and increasingly resonant image in our age of continual conflagration and spontaneous wildfires.

I would argue that traces of the same naturalistic theology are also recognisably present in Christian scriptures. Many passages express a consciousness of the indwelling nature of God; Jesus mixes earth with his own saliva to heal the blind at the pool of Siloam; he uses earthly proxies of bread and wine as representations of his body and blood; and in the Gospel of Thomas Jesus says: *"Split a piece of wood: I am there. Lift a stone, and you will find me there."*[16] Such Earth-centred spirituality is picked up and transmitted through later developments of Christian spirituality, despite never being representative of mainstream or orthodox Christian authority. The words of Angelus Silesius come to mind in this context: *"To one who realises God, there is no difference between the Spirit and the senses. God is seen, but God is also heard, tasted, felt, and smelled."*[17]

Ruether asserts that the body/spirit duality implicit in mainstream renderings of Christian thought, and western philosophy more generally, serves the dominant, authoritarian political ends of subjugation and

---

15   *Exodus* 3: 2.
16   *Gospel of Thomas*, saying 77.
17   Johann Scheffler/Angelus Silesius, *Der Cherubinische Wandersmann* (1674); *Angelus Silesius: The Cherubinic Wanderer*, translated by Maria Shrady (Paulist Press, 1986).

control, instead of amplifying the relational view of nature that is actually present throughout scripture. She identifies materialistic human demands placed upon our ecosystem as the source of our coming catastrophe: "*infinite demand incarnate in finite nature, in the form of infinite exploitation of the world's resources for production, results in ecological catastrophe*".[18]

Ruether examines the ego-centric religious tendency to identify with the spiritual and transcendent while relegating the body, the material, and the immanent to a lesser status, and she describes the necessity of an entirely new social vision based on her prophetic understanding of the bodily theology of God. "*The centre of such a new society*", she writes, "*would have to be a new social vision, a new soul that would inspire the whole. Society would have to be transfigured by the glimpse of a new humanity appropriate to a new earth.*" She envisions this new state as one of "reciprocal interdependence", an eminently practical vision which critiques the traditional Christian goal of transcendent "self-infinitizing".[19] Instead, she exchanges the prior religious preoccupation with immortality for an entirely new religious sensibility (one which may seem familiar to many Unitarians): a sensibility which prioritises the protection of the Earth and sees the Earth as the ground of being, the body of the transcendent *and* immanent God from which we arise and to which we return.

The ecological economist Professor Julia Steinberger of the Priestley International Centre for Climate, University of Leeds, recently tweeted: "*Climate & ecological crises endanger the possibility of human civilization within this century*",[20] but it is chastening to recognise that Radford Ruether's work, largely (and scandalously) overlooked nowadays, was prophetically warning of the disaster, and providing such a clear analysis of the potential solution fifty years ago.

....

18   Rosemary Radford Ruether, *New Woman, New Earth: Sexist Ideologies and Human Liberation* (Seabury Press, 1975). p 194.
19   Rosemary Radford Ruether, *New Woman, New Earth*, p. 211.
20   https://twitter.com/JKSteinberger/status/1540607081945997312, accessed 19/06/2022.

Newcomers to Unitarianism often assume that rejection of the doctrine of the trinity, or disavowal of the deity of Jesus, must be the unifying principle around which the denomination coheres. I would like to suggest in conclusion that another principle, the theology of universal incarnation, is far more likely to provide motive and inspiration to our movement in its stand against climate catastrophe.

In 1891 the Unitarian philosopher James Martineau wrote: "*The incarnation of Christ is true, not of Christ exclusively, but of Man universally and God everlastingly. He bends into the human to dwell there, and humanity is the susceptible organ of the divine*".[21] Martineau's genius is in recognising the validity of the ancient theology of embodiment, expressed in the Book of Isaiah as *Immanuel, God With Us*,[22] and recasting it to provide a sustaining vision for a reason-based spiritual tradition.

To provide a coherent account of itself in relation to its historical tradition – a tradition of rational dissent which maintains a living relationship with the transcendent – and in relation to the emerging realities of climate change and the pressing need for the ethical realisation of a new society, Unitarians must begin to work towards the religious integration of our own conception of God as universally incarnate. Now, though, we must go further than Martineau did and recognise God manifested in all creation, throughout the interdependent web of all life. We might say: *The incarnation of God is true of humankind universally, and all creation everlastingly*.

To understand creation as God's body is to recognise spirituality as embodied. Humans are not the temporary inhabitants of 'flesh clothes' to be modified or disregarded before they are either discarded or 'self-infinitised', as we are misdirected to believe by both mechanistic

---

21 James Martineau, 'Tracts for Priests and People', in *Essays, Reviews and Addresses* (Longmans, Green & Co, London and New York, 1891) Vol. 2, p. 443.

22 *Isaiah* 7:14.

consumerism on one side and fundamentalist religion on the other. Our urgent spiritual challenge is to realise that our bodies are the sacred sites of connection to the natural world in which we live and move and have our being.

Questions for reflection and discussion

1. Pantheism is the belief that everything is God. Panentheism is the belief that everything is in God: is this a useful distinction for you?

2. What does 'an embodied spirituality' mean to you?

3. What spiritual practices encourage you to remember your physical participation in the life of the Divine?

The author

Born in London to Welsh parents, Reverend Jo James was appointed to the ministry of Mill Hill Chapel, Leeds in 2014. He is a minister on the roll of the General Assembly of Unitarian and Free Christian Churches and currently serves on the Executive Committee. Before ministry, Jo worked for more than twenty years in theatre. He is married to Ann, an artist and designer, and lives in Leeds with their two children, cats, a dog, and some hens.

A Samhain Thanksgiving Prayer for the Elements

Laura Dobson

Spirit of Life, we praise and thank you for the element of Air: Great Wind, who blew our ancestors here from over the sea, bring us your inspiration, that we may know our breath is the same air breathed by our ancestors.

We praise and thank you for the element of Fire: Great Sun, who has sustained all life on Earth since it began, bring us your cleansing warmth, that we may heal the wounds of the past.

We praise and thank you for the element of Water: Great Ocean, who nurtured the first life on Earth and nourishes us all still, bring us your flowing love, that we may show compassion to each other and to all beings.

We praise and thank you for the element of Earth: Great Cradle, Shelter, and Tomb, who births us all, nourishes us and receives us again, keep us grounded and help us to respect and care for you, as we become ancestors for those who will follow us.

Amen and Blessed Be.

The author
Laura Dobson is the minister with Chorlton Unitarians and the Unitarian Transformers project. She is also a member of the Unitarian Earth Spirit Network. Her Samhain prayer was first published in *The Inquirer* on 29 October 2022.

5 An Earth Spirit Perspective

Penelope Quest

Unitarianism is an open-minded and open-hearted faith. For the Unitarian movement in the UK, and its counterpart in the USA, the Unitarian Universalists, there is no defined set of beliefs that people are expected to agree with. Our roots lie in liberal Christianity, but we show respect and tolerance towards other faiths and beliefs, affirming that everyone has the right to seek truth and meaning for themselves, and to discover their own spiritual path.

Perhaps one of the most important aspects of this openness is an acknowledgement of the interconnectedness and interdependence of all life on Earth, and with the planet itself, and that is the focus of this chapter.

Because Unitarian services draw upon the wisdom and insight of all faiths, philosophies, and branches of human knowledge, worship leaders might include readings from the Old and New Testaments of the Bible, and from the Qur'an, Buddhist scriptures, or other sacred or secular texts, as well as inspiration from indigenous peoples around the world such as Native Americans, or the Pagan and Pre-Christian Celts in Britain.

In the early 1990s I trained in the practices of Native American Shamanism, as well as studying Celtic Paganism, so I became more and more connected to Earth-centred spiritual traditions. A few years later I moved to live in Cumbria in the English Lake District. I found spiritual solace in its beautiful landscapes, walking alongside lakes and through woodland, sitting by streams and waterfalls to meditate, celebrating full moons and seasonal changes in individual or shared ceremonies at sacred sites such as the Castlerigg Stone Circle near Keswick.

It was around this time that I also discovered Unitarianism. Until then I had thought that there would be no place for my eclectic beliefs and ideas within any church, but I was delighted when a friend, a Unitarian minister, introduced me to the free-thinking Unitarian movement. I found a place that felt like home to me, where my mostly Pagan beliefs would be welcomed, and where there was an Earth Spirit Network that I could join, linking me with other like-minded seekers.

In our increasingly industrialised and technological modern world we seem to have lost touch with our natural environment, yet everything that we have is provided by our planet Earth, from our food and clothing to our homes and all that we have within them. We plunder the planet for its minerals and metals, its coal and oil and gas, to provide us with electricity to operate ever more complex manufactured devices, as well as providing heat and light and means of transport. And all of this means that we have largely lost our sense of connection with the natural world, and our respect for, and our sense of gratitude to, 'Mother Earth'. We have placed ourselves at the pinnacle of creation, rather than seeing ourselves as simply part of the web of life. It has become even more apparent in recent years that our greed for 'progress', our culture of demanding 'more, more, more', is responsible for degrading the environment and creating the current climate-change crisis. Instead of asserting dominance over the natural world, we need to develop a sense of humility that will lead us towards a more reciprocal relationship with it.

The Earth Spirit Network

The Earth Spirit Network belongs to a Pagan tradition but is also a key element of the Unitarian movement; it links together like-minded Unitarians who feel in their relationship with the natural world a sense of wonder and mystery, and a belief that every living thing is part of something greater. It feels possible to connect with that greater reality, and its associated myths of gods and goddesses, its practices of physical and mental healing, and a sense of serenity that touches the innermost parts of our human lives. As members of the Earth Spirit Network we share our ideas in articles circulated several times a year in *The File* magazine. During the Covid pandemic we met up via Zoom to acknowledge and celebrate Earth's rhythms in the spirit of our Pagan Celtic ancestors.

'Pagan' became a pejorative word once Christianity had established itself, but 'pagan' actually means 'country dweller', and it referred to the way of life practised for centuries by people living in small rural communities whose lives were governed by the seasons. Celtic spirituality was very much centred on earthly rhythms, and the changes in weather patterns, so the year was divided into four sections, based on the journey of the sun through the Winter and Summer solstices, when the sun was at its lowest or highest points, and the Spring and Autumn equinoxes, when the spans of day and night were roughly equal. The other four points coincided with the changes of the seasons, so the Celtic year began in November, the fallow period of Winter, which was called Samhain, followed by Imbolc at the beginning of February, Beltain at the beginning of May, and Lammas at the beginning of August.

Because they were so reliant on what nature could supply, the Celts had a reciprocal, respectful relationship with the Earth, so at each key point in the Earth's cycle they would hold festivals to acknowledge their gratitude, and join together in celebration. These gatherings would often take place at sacred sites, such as stone circles, and would provide opportunities for meeting members of other tribes from further afield for trading in animals or other goods; pairing up to form relationships; and sharing ideas and knowledge. Such gatherings were therefore important for tribal identity and social cohesion. These festivals would last for three days, marked by bonfires, dancing, processions and rituals, drumming and chanting, and feasting, and most would take place at the time of a full moon.

Some of these Celtic celebrations link with events or occasions that are still celebrated in modern times, and that is partly because the early Church tried to replace Pagan festivals with Christian festivals, so that Pagans might be more attracted to the Christian faith. For example, Christmas customs such as feasting and spending time with friends and family, and decorating our homes with holly, ivy, and mistletoe, are traditions whose roots can be traced back to the Celtic Winter Solstice celebrations on the 21st day of December. Similarly the Christian festival of Easter overlaid the celebrations of the Spring Equinox, with its theme of rebirth and resurrection, a time of nature's promise that after death and darkness new life will emerge, new beginnings when the natural world is coming alive again. Easter may even have taken its name from Oestre, the Goddess of Light, often depicted as a Spring Maiden bearing a basket of eggs, to represent the rebirth of nature and the fertility of the earth: hence our modern-day custom of exchanging Easter eggs with our loved ones.

Ceremonies and practices

Shamans, the wise men or women of the tribe, would explore the natural world as a source of spiritual messages. For example, trees have been regarded as sacred by many different cultures, but they have a special place in the world of Native Americans in particular. They call them 'Standing People', and they recognise the trees' unique contribution to the earth as life-givers – providing oxygen for all creatures, just as their trunks, branches, roots, and leaves provide substances with healing properties, as well as homes and food for animals, birds, and insects. Shamans believe that the many years of growth from a sapling to full maturity imbue each tree with wisdom, and that they can intuitively connect with this wisdom by sitting within the tree's energy field and asking the tree to reveal its knowledge and understanding. This is something that I do every year, often on or near the Summer Solstice. You might like to try performing the following Native American Tree Ceremony to gain some personal insight and awareness.

Native American tree ceremony

The best time to seek guidance from trees is in the spring or summer, when their sap has risen and they are at their strongest; but to commune with a tree at any time of the year can be a very special experience. You will need to find a tree that particularly attracts you in some way, perhaps by the shape of its leaves, or the texture of its bark. Entering a tree's 'space' requires great respect, so the following Tree Ceremony should be conducted in the right frame of mind, and in the spirit of seeking your own personal truth. If it doesn't feel right, don't do it!

You will need to establish the orientation of each of the tree's sides, so a compass would be useful; but you could also be guided by the fact that in the northern hemisphere moss usually grows on the north side of a tree, so that will help you to identify the other directions too. You may have some specific questions that you wish to ask, but if you have not done this before, the following suggestions might be helpful.

1. Having found a tree that you would like to work with, you must ask its permission to be used for the tree ceremony. To assess its answer, place your left hand on the trunk. If it feels right, carry on.

2. Circle three times around the tree in a clockwise direction. As you walk around it, be aware that you will enter a special 'place' where you can access the tree's wisdom. Having completed the third circuit, spend a few moments facing the tree, bringing yourself into a quiet and receptive frame of mind, and greet the tree.

3. Then sit and lean your back against the south side of the tree. Ask aloud or silently "**Who am I?**" and wait for the 'whispers'. Use all your senses: look in front and around you for 'messages' from the landscape itself. Notice what 'happens', such as a bird flying across in front of you; feel the temperature, the breeze, the texture of the bark; listen to the birds, the rustle of leaves, or any other sounds. Listen to your inner voice, wait for the words of wisdom from the

tree, received through your Higher Self (spirit), and continue facing south until you sense that it is the right time to move on.

4. Move clockwise and lean your back against the west side of the tree. Ask aloud or silently "*Why am I here?*" and wait for the 'whispers', as above. Be aware of how easy, or difficult, it is to move around your chosen tree.

5. Move clockwise again and lean against the north side. Ask "*Where am I going?*" and wait for the tree's response. Be aware of any feelings that arise from being with this tree and its surroundings.

6. Next lean against the east side and ask "*How do I get there?*". Wait for the whispers and be aware of any sounds or movement nearby.

7. Now circle three times around the tree in an anti-clockwise direction. As you circle, be aware that you are returning to 'normal space'. When you complete the final circuit, turn to face the tree.

8. Thank it, aloud or silently, for sharing its gift of wisdom, and then leave an offering: something of yourself, or something organic that you have brought for the purpose.

9. When the whole ceremony is complete, you may find it useful to write down your experiences, and meditate on any insight that you have received.

The directions and elements

The directions were an important part of any Celtic or Native American ceremonies, alongside the four elements of Fire, Water, Earth, and Air, so if I am leading a Unitarian service on this theme I place something to represent each element on a circular tray or circular cloth on a table as near to the centre of the congregation as possible; this is easy in my church, as there are no fixed pews: we sit on chairs in a circle. Of course, you could also do this at home to create a sacred space for contemplation, prayer, or meditation, and it would work equally well outside, in a garden, woodland, or other open space.

- Fire in the South could be symbolised by a lit candle – such as the Flaming Chalice, which is the emblem of Unitarianism – honouring the sun and its transforming energy.

- Water in the West could be represented by a glass or jug of water, evoking our emotional energy, and honouring the essential part that water plays in supporting our life.

- To honour the element of Earth in the North, we might use a stone or pebble, or a growing plant in a pot, to represent our physicality, and to show respect for the Earth and everything that it provides for us.

- The element of Air in the East could be represented by a lit incense stick or some dried lavender, to honour the vital air that we breathe. This is also the element of thought and intent, so we honour it by breathing deeply and thinking positively.

- In the centre you could place a colourful flower, or a quartz crystal or a smooth stone, to represent the Spirit. Through spirit we are part of all life and all existence, so we can be grateful on all levels – physical, emotional, psychological, and spiritual – for our lives on this beautiful planet Earth.

At the end of the service, or when you have finished your prayer or meditation practice, you can honour each direction again by bowing towards it and saying "Thank you".

Environment and nature in the twenty-first century

We have become much more aware of our environmental responsibilities now that climate change is beginning to have such an impact on our lives, with sometimes disastrous changes in weather patterns. We also recognise that it is not just humans who are being affected by these changes, but that all forms of life, from animals, birds, fish, and the insects that we need for pollination, to plants, crops, and trees, can be affected by droughts and floods, temperature changes, and fires.

But it is human activity, such as burning fossil fuels and destroying rainforests, that has brought about this potentially apocalyptic situation. Collectively, it is our fault. We are responsible for bringing about global warming at an alarming rate. We have destroyed the natural habitats of many of the world's endangered species, and we have polluted rivers, seas, and oceans with chemicals and plastics. It seems that micro-plastics are even finding their way into the bloodstreams of humans. So we are putting our own lives, and potentially the survival of the human race, at risk.

Such is the concern about the loss of biodiversity, as ever-increasing numbers of plants and animals become endangered or extinct, that conserving them for the future has become a priority. The natural world relies on a diversity of organisms to keep it in balance, healthy and thriving, so seed banks are being created to preserve a multitude of plants as an insurance policy against the threats that they may encounter across the world. Also, zoos and conservation groups around the globe have begun collecting and preserving genetic material from thousands of endangered species, because many may not exist in the future, and we do not know what benefits we may lose as a consequence.

But doom and gloom are not the whole story, although as individuals we might feel that there is not much that we can do to change things and bring about any improvement. Earth spirituality can help us to be more attuned to what we need, and to what the planet needs. As Unitarians we respect the interdependent web of existence of which we are a part, and we are encouraged to live in harmony with the rhythms of nature, and to honour and celebrate Earth with all its beauty and abundance.

In recent years there has been a developing interest in growing our own food, and reducing our meat consumption to avoid methane pollution from farmed animals. A vegan diet, consisting only of plant-based food, has become very much more popular. I myself changed to a vegan diet several years ago, and I have found it to be beneficial to my health. Not eating meat, poultry, fish, eggs, or dairy products, and eating more vegetables, also means that no living creatures are killed or harmed in order to supply food for human consumption, which in turn means that at least some of the agricultural land could be used for growing crops, planting trees, and rewilding instead. We can grow some of our own vegetables and fruits, even if we have only a limited area of land. Lots of plants can be grown in pots or tubs, and even a window box can become productive; tomato plants seem to be particularly popular.

There has also been a growth of interest in the health of the soil in which our crops are grown, and that has generated a move towards 'No Dig' gardening and farming. In principle, by avoiding digging or ploughing, plants, fungi, worms, and other micro-organisms can decompose and be incorporated as organic matter into the earth, so the soil's natural ecosystem remains intact, providing better nutrition for the roots of newly sown seeds and young plants.

Nurturing planet Earth and all her creatures, including humans, is a core value for Unitarians. We must do what we can to create a better life for everyone, so we can all make small changes that individually might not make much impact, but if we can each bring about a little improvement, then that will be beneficial for all of us. We need what Earth supplies for us, yet we squander its bounty. However, there are some small things that even individuals can do to care for the planet.

- Water is a precious resource, so we can choose to use less, perhaps by taking showers instead of baths.

- Energy is required to heat our homes, so we should make sure they are energy-efficient, with adequate insulation. Then we can wear an extra sweater and turn down our thermostats by a couple of degrees.

- If possible, we should leave the car at home and walk or cycle, and enjoy the physical and mental health benefits, as well as the satisfaction of knowing that we are not contributing to greenhouse-gas emissions and air pollution.

- For travel further afield, we could use public transport, and perhaps take a 'staycation' instead of flying to far-away places for our holidays.

- We could also become more eco-aware when we are shopping: buy fruits and vegetables in season from local suppliers or farmers' markets, to reduce food miles and our carbon footprint.

- Trees provide essential oxygen, so if possible find somewhere to plant a tree or two.

- Actually, everything that we use as consumers has a carbon footprint, so let's buy only what we need, so that we don't waste food. And we can consider buying second-hand or 'up-cycling': donating to charity anything that we no longer need or use.

During the Covid pandemic many of us learned how being outdoors, spending time in nature, walking in the countryside or our local parks, had a beneficial effect on our mental health, boosting our mood and reducing stress. I hope this is something that we will want to continue. Connecting with nature enhances our well-being and our sense of interconnectedness and interdependence with all life on Earth, and with the planet itself, which soothes us physically, mentally, emotionally, and spiritually – and surely that can only be a good thing!

Let us honour planet Earth and all the beings within it and on it, and live as sustainably as we can, contributing towards a better future for us all.

Questions for reflection and discussion

1. How does your congregation honour the seasons? Do you organise services or sessions on environmental subjects?

2. If you are vegetarian, or even vegan, what benefits have you experienced? If you are not already vegetarian, or even vegan, what is stopping you?

3. What do you think we can learn from pre-Christian Pagan and Indigenous people about their relationship with the Earth?

The author

Penelope Quest was a member and worship leader at Kendal Unitarian Chapel for 10 years, and has been a member and worship leader with Cheltenham & Gloucester Unitarians for 16 years. She is the author of seven books on Mind, Body, Spirit, Health, and Healing, published in the UK and USA.

Tread Gently – A Meditative Gathering

Sarah Tinker

Tread gently on the earth
Breathe gently of the air
Lie gently in the water
Touch gently to the fire
(from a chant by Carolyn Hillyer)

In our Unitarian communities we can encourage one another to live lives more connected with our home planet Earth, to which we are inextricably bound. We are formed of its very elements, and to those elements we return when our lives are completed.

This meditation can become a regular practice for us individually, helping us to remain awake to life itself. As a group activity it can help to bring us 'back down to earth'.

Invite a small group to gather, in person or online. Prepare a space with access to the four elements. Begin with the Unitarian ritual of lighting a chalice flame and opening a sharing circle where people have a chance to share something of their lives. To begin, use the chant quoted above, or another reading.

This guided meditation will focus attention on the elements of earth, air, fire, and water. It can be adapted to suit the particular circumstances. In each part of the meditation, ensure that participants have time to go deeper in silence.

If the weather allows your group to be outside, encourage members to take off their shoes or spend time touching a tree or rock. Indoors you might sit with a living plant or leaf, or a photograph that evokes 'Earth' for you.

What sensations, smells, and sounds do we notice when we slow down and pay attention?

Turning our attention to the air, let us take time to feel the breeze on our skin. How do you feel as the air enters and leaves your body?

Invite people to take a conscious sip of water, or sit awhile with a bowl of water in their hands. *What aspects of our complex reliance on water have come to the fore?*

Humanity's relationship with the element of fire brings both gift and danger. *As we sit quietly near a candle flame, let us consider our experiences with fire.*

Bring the meditative time to a close with an opportunity for participants to share their feelings and thoughts. Complete the gathering with a reading or blessing, and extinguish the chalice flame.

We are living in times that urgently require us to 'tread more gently' upon the earth. A shared meditation such as this can awaken us to what that means in our own lives.

The author
Sarah Tinker is now retired, having ministered for 15 years with Kensington Unitarians. She recommends readers to explore the Unitarian Earth Spirit Network, the Findhorn Unitarian Network, and the national GreenSpirit group as sources of inspiration and activities for deepening our relatedness with the Earth, with one another, and with ourselves.

6 Exploring Ecofeminist Theologies

Ann Peart

Looking back at *Growing Together*, the report of the Unitarian working party on feminist theology published in 1984, I am horrified to find that, although I was a member of that working party, there is no overt mention of ecological concerns.[1] Perhaps the most relevant pointer to a more ecological way of thinking was offered by Joy Croft:

> We are brought up to <u>analyse</u> our world by looking for the distinctions, differences, limits, divisions. There is a complementary perspective, sometimes called <u>holistic</u>, which is familiar to many women but we are encouraged to think of as 'woolly-mindedness'. It seeks out the connections, the common and unifying factors. The cultivation of such a mode of thinking will help heal the divisions among us.[2]

When Unitarian women began to explore feminist theology in the early 1980s, we were clearly aware of the importance of the natural world. In a service on Midsummer's Day at Golders Green Unitarians in 1981, we, as members of the recently formed local Unitarian Women's Group, led a solstice service which began with these words: "*Together we take a journey back to that time when Mother Earth was revered as the sacred giver of life, loved and worshipped by all who understood her. Her rhythms were sacred, and her abundantly life-giving force was in each woman.*"[3] But the feminist

---

1   Joy Croft (ed.), *Growing Together: The Report of the Unitarian Working Party on Feminist Theology* (London: General Assembly of Unitarian and Free Christian Churches, 1984).
2   Croft (1984), 5.2 2.
3   Hillary Johnson, 'Women's Worship', *Unitarian Women's Group Newsletter* no 3, August 1982.

theology working party, which included three members of the newly formed UWG, clearly failed to integrate the desire for a women-centred/ Nature-centred spirituality with the search for a feminist theology.

As someone with a degree in geography, and half a lifetime's experience of making connections with factors influencing the physical and human features of our world, I am disturbed, to say the least, by the absence of any reference to ecological understanding in the report. My geographical training came well before my feminist consciousness was raised in the early 1980s, but as one of the small minority of women students in Cambridge University in the 1960s (when only about ten per cent of the undergraduates were female), I was aware of at least some of the disadvantages relating to gender, and I remember reading Simone de Beauvoir's *The Second Sex* at that time. In recent years my geographical experience has been a helpful resource when trying to develop some coherent thoughts on Unitarian approaches to ecofeminist theologies. Both my geographical experience and my time with the ecumenical Partnership for Theological Education at Luther King House, as Principal of Unitarian College Manchester, have led me to take a contextual approach, in which individual experience is valued as a prime theological resource. Although I can speak only from my own experience, I think it is imperative to extend this approach to value the experience of others, to try to understand their alterity (otherness), and maybe even to include the natural world in this appreciation. After all, the context in which all humans live is the physical Earth, our much-troubled planet. I see ecofeminist theology as a branch of liberation theology, which has the aim of not only describing a scheme of thought and belief, but of changing the world in order to reduce injustice and bring about a fairer and more sustainable planet.

This chapter begins with an exploration of what the term 'ecofeminist theology' might encompass, followed by an exploration of the possibilities that arise from a consideration of a rejection of hierarchical, dualistic thinking; this not only divides things into two categories but values one polarity rather than the other. Exploring the age-old connection between women and Nature, I will then touch on aspects of justice which are an essential part of any feminist theology.

Ecofeminist theologies exist at the intersection of ecofeminism and theology. Most of the reference works that I have consulted concentrate on exploring the nature of ecofeminism, and rather assume that theology needs no similar treatment. I, on the other hand, am fairly clear what I mean by ecofeminism, but I still have trouble explaining what I mean by theology! The literal meaning of 'god talk' is not helpful. I much prefer David Jenkins' definition, "*disciplined and responsible reflection and argument on the beliefs and traditions of a faith considered from within*", quoted by Nicola Slee.[4] This definition may seem too broad for some, but – as I am happy with Unitarianism as a 'faith' – it works for me. Ecofeminism is obviously an intersection of feminism with ecology, but it covers many different approaches.

Heather Eaton describes four main entry points or pathways into what I think of as a traffic roundabout.[5] Firstly there is the route of local activism, where often quite specific events have provoked a response; one example that she presents is the Greenham Common Women's Peace Camp, established in 1981 with a march to a nuclear weapons airbase near Newbury by a group of 36 women from south Wales, calling themselves 'Women for Life on Earth'. Like many other Unitarian women, I visited the camp a number of times until it closed in 2000, and it was a significant inspiration for me.

The second entry point is via more academic work in an interdisciplinary fashion, including religion, ethics, women's studies, sociology, psychology, and philosophy. This attracted me because geography is also

---

4   Nicola Slee, 'Theology' in *An A to Z of Feminist Theology*, ed. Lisa Isherwood and Dorothea McEwan (Sheffield Academic Press, 1996), p.225.
5   Heather Eaton, *Introducing Feminist Theologies* (London, T&T Clark International, 2005), pp. 11–27).

an interdisciplinary subject, bridging the gap between the arts, such as history, and science, such as geology.

The third entry point, that of religion and spirituality, uncovers both the way in which religion has consigned women, often with Nature, to a subordinate status, and the growing use of female/Nature imagery in some aspects of women's worship.

Last comes the global stretch of feminist ecological work, with awareness of the unequal impact on women of ecological disasters and stresses. This was recognised as early as 1989, when the United Nations reported: "*It is now a universally established fact that it is the woman who is the worst victim of environmental destruction. The poorer she is, the greater the burden.*"[6]

Having described four routes into the roundabout, Eaton indicates some possible ways out, offering a wide variety of definitions, depending largely on the primary approach taken. I like her own version, which is "*ecofeminism as a lens through which all disciplines are examined and refocused*".[7] She ends with this statement:

> In general, ecofeminism is about the desire to heal the wounds
> caused by the splits between nature and culture, mind and body,
> women and men, reason and emotion, spirit and matter, theory and
> action, and ultimately between humans and the earth.

So the most important task is to explore and expose the dualistic hierarchical assumptions that underlie Western thought and give rise to the devaluation and abuse of both women and Nature/the Earth. Not that this is an easy task, as such thinking is embedded in our culture, and it is always very difficult to see our own cultural bias. For me it is an ongoing process, as I keep on discovering new layers of dualistic

---

6   Quoted in Eaton (2005) p.24.
7   Eaton (2005) p.35.

assumptions in my own understanding. Several ecofeminist theorists, such as Val Plumwood and Heather Eaton, trace such divisions back to ancient Greek thought.[8] The Greek emphasis on logical thinking, rational categorising, and the classification of life became the dominant way of thinking about the world in the following centuries, particularly in the medieval period, when the Christian church adopted classical Greek ideas. The pre-modern list of such dualisms included the following:

reason – emotion
mind – body
culture – nature
heaven – earth
spirit – matter
divine – demonic
man – woman

But Heather Eaton writes that the mechanistic world view added many more such binary opposites, including human nature / non-human nature; rationality / animality; public / private; subject / object; logic / chaos; production / reproduction; powerful / powerless; father (male) / other; civilised / primitive (savage, animal); enlightened / unenlightened; master / slave; universal / particular.[9] This way of thinking categorises people and views as being one or the other – without the possibility of fluidity, overlap, or a middle ground. These dualisms permeated Western society, enabling a world view which allowed slavery, colonial expansion, and a disregard for the natural world, among other evils. Coupled with the promotion of progress and economic growth, they permitted industrial capitalism, with Earth viewed primarily as a resource to be exploited for monetary gain. Many of these assumptions are still in operation. Enlightenment thinking from the eighteenth century is linked to these developments, as well as to that of Unitarianism. Yet I

8   Eaton (2005) pp.54ff, 65.
9   Eaton (2005) p.57.

do not think that the Unitarian movement is essentially joined to the world view that espouses hierarchical dualisms. There is also a healthy strand which insists that ultimately all knowledge (and life) is one, not to be divided against Itself. This is evident even in the late eighteenth century, when Anna Laetitia Barbauld argued with Joseph Priestley that controversy and the rational pursuit of truth were not the whole story of rational dissenting worship or thought. She considered that worship was, partly, a matter of taste, including elements of both aesthetics and feelings. In a letter of 1776 to Nicholas Clayton she wrote the following:

> Are Philosophy and Devotion then inconsistent? No, they are different views of the same subject, they require to be corrected by each other. The devotion of a mere philosopher will be cold, the religion of a mere pietist will be superstitious. But is it not owing to our imperfect natures that these two voices do not coalesce? I believe that it is & that in another world Philosophy and Devotion will be entirely the same thing.[10]

In pleading for the reconciliation of rationality and emotion, Barbauld was attempting to dismantle at least one aspect of the hierarchical dualistic culture, but although she is said to have done more for the status of women than her better-known contemporary, Mary Wollstonecraft, Barbauld cannot be regarded as an ecofeminist in the current sense.

Dualistic thinking, often posed as 'either/or' assumptions, still permeates much of Western thought in the twenty-first century. It is exemplified for me in the seating plan of the House of Commons chamber, which consists of two opposing sets of benches facing each other, two sword lengths apart. The much more wholesome layout of the Scottish parliament, with a semi-circular arrangement of seats, suggests that truth is better served when there can be a spectrum of

10   Ann Peart, 'Forgotten Prophets: The Lives of Unitarian Women 1760–1904' (unpublished doctoral thesis, University of Newcastle, 2006), p.64.

views, allowing much middle ground. I find that quite often if I am asked an *either/or* question I want to respond with a *both/and* answer. Both humans and the world that we inhabit are complex organisms, not describable in dualistic terms.

The linking of woman and Nature as inferior clearly contributes to the oppression and exploitation of both, but in other ways I find the association problematic. In spiritual terms, Nature has often been portrayed as female, in expressions such as 'Mother Nature' and 'Earth Goddess'. I would not want to devalue this as a way of counteracting male bias in religion, and it still contains powerful imagery for me. However, I wonder if on some level it still perpetuates some of the assumptions concerning male dominance. Like other feminists, I struggle to find a way between the essentialist argument that biological differences such as the possibility of child bearing apply to all women and the conviction that gender is largely a matter of social construction and personal experience. Not all women bear or raise children, and different cultures place a variety of values on this, while sexual preference, race, and class also affect the status of women.[11] Are not men as equally embodied and close to Nature as women, and as equally the product of evolution? Essentialist linking of women and Nature certainly does nothing to dismantle the dualistic way of thinking which is so damaging to both women and the planet.

One approach to deconstructing hierarchical dualisms can be found in some of the thinking on embodiment, incarnation, and body theology. There is not space in this chapter to spell out in detail the work done by feminist theologians in reclaiming the body as a site of sacredness and revelation. To those who want to know more, I recommend *Introducing Body Theology* by Lisa Isherwood and Elizabeth Stuart.[12] There are glimmerings

---

11   Letty M. Russell and J. Shannon Clarkson (eds), *Dictionary of Feminist Theologies* (London, Westminster, John Knox Press, 1996).

12   Lisa Isherwood and Elizabeth Stuart, *Introducing Body Theology* (Sheffield, Sheffield Academic Press, 1998).

of work towards an embodied monist theology within Unitarian thought. (Monism is a philosophical approach which maintains that there is only one 'substance', and a theory that mind–body relations are not dualistic.[13]) However, they are not developed in any way that could be described as feminist. This is exemplified by the materialism of Joseph Priestley, who eliminated the distinction between matter and spirit, considering that what might be called the soul was a 'system of intelligence' organising the matter, and that it was possessed by animals as well as by humans, though in a lesser degree. However, Priestley never developed this concept in a consistent way, although it caused considerable controversy and objection in his lifetime.[14] About a century later, James Martineau opposed Priestley's materialism, but developed an incarnational theology which went some way towards developing a means of incorporating the divine into the material: *"The incarnation is true, not of Christ exclusively, but of Man universally and God everlastingly"*.[15]

But for a developed feminist ecotheology, we need to turn to the late twentieth century. Two writers who have been particularly influential are Grace Jantzen and Sallie MacFague. Jantzen published *God's World, God's Body* in 1984.[16] Using careful theological argument to give a monist view of reality which considers the world as God's body, just as the human body embodies the self, this work thereby heals the split between the material and the spiritual. In her later development of this argument, Jantzen explicitly challenges hierarchical dualism and promotes a feminist pantheist symbolic viewpoint which dethrones masculinist thinking.[17] MacFague uses the model of the universe as God's body in order to address the ecological crisis.[18]

---

13   Antony Flew (ed.), *A Dictionary of Philosophy* (London, Pan Books, 1979), p. 237.

14   John Ruskin Clark, *Joseph Priestley; A Comet in the System* (San Diego, CA: John Ruskin Clark, 1990).

15   Alfred Hall (ed.), *James Martineau Selections* (London, Lindsey Press, 1950), p. ix.

16   Grace Jantzen, *God's World, God's Body* (Philadelphia, Westminster Press, 1984).

17   Grace M. Janzen, 'Feminism and Pantheism' in *The Monist* vol 80 no 2, 1997, pp. 266–285.

18   Sallie MacFague, *The Body of God: An Ecological Theology* (London, SCM Press, 1993).

By ascribing worth/divinity to matter, for example bodies, it is possible to build a liberationary theology which for me is what feminist ecotheology is all about. We value our own bodies, and place them in the context of a sacred embodied universe, where all matter matters. This is in contrast to the traditional Christian stance, which considers matter inferior to a separate 'spirit' and devalues this world in comparison with a world to come. The Object of the British Unitarian General Assembly affirms "*Respect for all creation*", but I prefer the American Unitarian-Universalist Association's seventh Principle of "*Respect for the interdependent web of all existence of which we are a part*". A feminist interpretation of this prioritises the body as a site of resistance to unjust practices such as patriarchy and desecration of the Earth, and considers the impact of issues such as climate change on those bodies that are least privileged. A true Ecotheology (such as MacFague's) decentres the human as the most valuable aspect of Creation and sites the universe as a whole as the body of worth. Each part is of value, as a subject in itself and interconnected and interdependent with all other subjects.[19] While I find to decentre the human perspective difficult in practice, I am committed to the feminist principle of avoiding dominance, and aspiring to an ethic of power *with*, rather than power *over*.

Another model that I find helpful is that of Process thought, sometimes known as Process Theology. This approach also disrupts dualistic thinking and emphasises the value of the material world. Process thought has many variations, some very technical, but it gives a picture of the universe as an ever-changing succession of events, with each organism continually reacting to both its past and its present stimuli, thus creating the possibility of novelty. This applies to the smallest particle as well as to the most complex arrangement, including human beings. While humans may have the most developed consciousness, all particles have subjectivity, and respond to their environment. Nothing is wasted, as all experience feeds into the possibility of future expressions of being.

---

19   Isherwood and Stuart, op. cit, p. 124.

Valerie Saiving has suggested that a "feminist appropriation" of Process thought can be used which tests "every hypothesis by reference to the immediate experience of women".[20] It can also provide a theological underpinning to the values of mutuality and openness so necessary to any exploration of Ecotheology.[21]

"*I knew that if I cut a tree, my arm would bleed*", said Shug Avery in Alice Walker's *The Color Purple*. Notions of context, radical connection, and mutuality are essential to any reading of Ecotheology. Any person or action can be understood properly only if their circumstances are known and considered. Radical connection is a feeling (which can be cultivated) rather than an academic quality, while mutuality refers to a sense of sharing in each other's welfare. Value is found in both the individual subject and its relationship to the wider world. This implies a respect for diversity, and demands that both the individual and the whole are taken into account. What is specific to a feminist interpretation is the need to take account of women's experience, and in particular the requirement for women to be treated fairly and justly. This is not at the expense of other demands for justice, but should be considered in the context of a global ecological situation which now is in crisis, particularly with regard to climate change and global warming. It is now clearly established that global warming, with rising sea levels and increasingly extreme weather, leading to droughts as well as both fires and flooding, adversely affects many poor communities dependent on fishing and subsistence farming. Within these communities the women suffer most, with the challenge of caring for children and providing food when crops fail. The Western model of development aid has exacerbated the problem, as it has often tried to impose a cash-crop monoculture and actually reduced local food supplies. At the same time it has frequently resulted in a debt

20   Valerie Saiving, 'A Feminist Appropriation of Process Thought' in *Feminism and Process Thought: The Harvard Divinity School/Claremont Center for Process Studies Symposium Papers*, ed. Sheila Greeve Davaney (Lewiston, NY, USA, Edwin Mellen Press, 1981), p. 14.
21   Marjorie Suchocki, 'Openness and Mutuality in Process Thought', in Davaney, op. cit., 1981, pp 62–82.

to pay for new seeds and infrastructure, the interest on which is now preventing expenditure on necessities such as education and health care. For feminist ecotheological values to be put into practice, a technical understanding of these sorts of injustice is needed so that they can be exposed and addressed. The first step is to make sure that the local women are listened to in places where decisions are taken.

Another aspect of feminist Ecotheology concerns issues of peace and war. Warfare results in loss of life and injury to humans; increasingly civilians rather than military personnel are killed and injured. Women are particularly at risk of rape, which has become increasingly recognised as a weapon of war. Military spending diverts resources from other areas, and results in much environmental destruction. Pollution from weapons and fires and the laying waste of land and buildings all add to global warming, as well as to people's misery. In the past I have resented the fact that peace is often seen as a women's issue, thinking that it should be a priority for all people, but I have become aware that war affects women disproportionately, so it has a place in any work that seeks justice for women.

Put briefly, ecofeminist theology aims to make the world a more just and sustainable home for all who live in it. It can do this by dismantling hierarchical dualisms which devalue women and Nature, and by creating systems of thought which prioritise relationality and mutuality, based on a respect for our diverse material and embodied existence. But it is not enough only to transform our ways of thinking. Thought must lead to engagement of our emotions, our passion, and so bring a commitment to action.

As Anna Laetitia Barbauld reminded us, what we need is both clear informed thought and engaged emotion. In the words of Rita Brock and Rebecca Parker, *"Our hearts and souls are reborn through the tender task of living rightly with one another and the earth ... It begins with love."* [22]

....

22   Rita Nakashima Brock and Rebecca Ann Parker, *Saving Paradise; Recovering Christianity's Forgotten Love for this Earth* (Norwich, Canterbury Press, 2012), p. 409.

Questions for reflection and discussion

1. Women are disproportionately affected by climate change. How might an ecofeminist perspective change our perception of the problem?

2. Is an identification of the Female with Nature helpful or not?

3. How can an ecofeminist theology change the way we worship (in form and in content)?

The author

Ann Peart is a retired Unitarian minister and former Principal of Unitarian College, Manchester. She has written extensively about Unitarian women, including her book *Unitarian Women: A Legacy of Dissent* (Lindsey Press, 2019). A life-long Unitarian, she has served as President of the General Assembly, the Women's League, the Historical Society, and the Manchester District. A founder member of the Unitarian Women's Group, she considers herself an ecofeminist.

PART THREE:
Changing Hearts and Minds

Changing Hearts and Minds: Prologue

Maria Curtis

If we are to avoid widespread ecological disaster for ourselves and other animal and plant species on the planet, we need a widespread change of consciousness. We need to take a long, hard, unflinching look at the scientific data, and not turn away in denial or give up in despair.

At the end of *The Climate Book*,[1] Greta Thunberg claims that "*Hope is something you have to earn ... Hope is taking action.*" It is warming to read that she has faith in human nature; she believes that if we had been made fully aware of our situation – the destruction of the biosphere and its consequences for the future of life on Earth – we would have acted sooner. A similarly hopeful note was struck by the anthropologist Margaret Mead, who said that we should "*Never doubt that a small group of thoughtful, committed citizens can change the world; indeed it's the only thing that ever has.*"[2]

But in considering how to go about changing the consciousness of a critical mass to avoid the dire consequences of untrammelled carbon emissions, I would argue that we need to harness both *hearts* and *minds*. We can look at cold scientific facts, graphs, statistics, and percentages and remain indifferent; it is in response to a story or an image that our feelings kick in. We need to *care* as well as to understand. So how can we nurture our own species to produce individuals who can both think and feel?

---

1   Greta Thunberg, *The Climate Book* (Allen Lane, London, 2022).
2   Quoted in *Singing the Living Tradition*, Unitarian Universalist Association, 1993 (Item 561).

Nurturing young hearts and minds

The good news is that we are expert learners. The human infant has one of the longest childhoods of any creature, so as a species we have plenty of opportunity for learning. During this long period of dependency, nature and nurture work together in a social context to shape the developing child. As Sue Gerhardt[3] says in *Why Love Matters*:

> Both our physiological systems and our mental systems are
> developed in relationship with other people ... The human baby
> is the most socially influenced creature on earth, open to learning
> what his or her own emotions are and how to manage them ... It is
> as babies that we first feel and learn what to do with our feelings,
> when we start to organise our experience in a way that will affect
> our later behaviour and thinking capacities.

It is during this critical time that the essential capacity for empathy develops.

The bad news is that because culture is socially mediated, there is an inherent vulnerability in the system, which can be both a strength and a weakness. Much learning depends on the social environment: the child's caregivers, other social contacts, and the wider social context. What is learned will depend on the people who nurture and teach us, and the 'hidden curriculum', the shared assumptions that may never be explicitly stated, but are, as it were, breathed in with the air. Our job as caregivers is to provide positive learning experiences.

We need to do all that we can to allow young children to flourish so that they can become confident and compassionate adults. Children deserve an early life that is secure and predictable – not dominated

---

3 Sue Gerhardt, *Why Love Matters: How Affection Shapes a Baby's Brain* (Routledge, London, 2004).

by trauma (caused by war, for instance). The scourge of poverty can also prevent healthy physical and emotional development. Poverty is a relative concept. In our affluent culture here in the UK, there is at the time of writing a cost-of-living crisis that is affecting the development of growing numbers of children: a child cannot learn on an empty stomach. Nor can children learn in an atmosphere of stress and anxiety, in cold or damp or cramped accommodation. They will not flourish. If we are to become a caring and compassionate society, capable of understanding the ecological crisis and doing something about it, we need to begin by nurturing the young.

Opening hearts and minds

Unitarianism has historically set a high value on Reason, our capacity to think. It was our desire to be free thinkers – exercising freedom of conscience – that set us apart from the established Church. Early Unitarians were willing to sacrifice their livelihoods for precious freedom of thought. They wanted the freedom to interpret the Bible and worship in their own way, unconstrained by dogma imposed by the Anglican Church. Integral to our "living tradition" is the commitment "to promote a free and responsible search for truth and meaning".[4] This is a courageous stance to take, as it implies a willingness to look at the evidence dispassionately and change our minds if necessary. Such flexibility in thinking is essential if we are to absorb the scientific data relating to climate change and loss of biodiversity, and reform our ways of living.

In Enlightenment thought, rationality was seen as one of the characteristics that set us apart from other animals. We saw in Part Two of this book that the more we learn about animals, the more we can see lively intelligences at work, uniquely evolved for certain

---

4   *The Seven Principles of the Unitarian Universalist Association,* The Seven Principles | UUA.org.

niche environments. We are not the only thinking creatures. By the late twentieth century, psychologists such as Stuart Sutherland[5] were discovering that we are not so very rational either – not necessarily a bad thing, as long as we are aware of our 'cognitive biases'. As a species we are not actually very good at the *deductive* reasoning that is essential to mathematics and logic. We are more geared up to use *induction*, a mental process based on experience.

It turns out that reasoning is not the main function of the brain. Enlightenment thought elevated the role of reason in morality. But the idea that our brains evolved primarily for thinking has been the source of profound misconceptions about human nature. The brain's most important job is to control the body. As neuroscientist Lisa Feldman Barrett shows in her book *Seven and a Half Lessons About the Brain,*[6] reason and emotion are not at war; they do not inhabit different areas of the brain, as previously thought. Moreover, rational behaviour does not come about in a context devoid of emotion, and thinking is not always rational. Thought and feeling, reason and emotion, mind and heart work together to help us decide on a course of action.

The world is a construction by the brain based on memory; it predicts from previous experience, rather than perceiving every situation afresh; perception is a top–down rather than bottom–up process. We expect things (and people) to be as they always have been. We *project* our expectations on to the world, based on our previous experience; if those acquired beliefs go unchallenged, we are likely to stick with them. Hence we are all prejudiced in the way we look at the world.

Predicting from the familiar will affect our attitude to the unfamiliar or to difference, but it is possible to change the predictions that we make. Because of the *plasticity* of the brain, we can carry on learning (and

5   Stuart Sutherland, *Irrationality: The Enemy Within* (Pinter & Martin, 1992).
6   Lisa Feldman Barrett, *Seven and a Half Lessons About the Brain* (Picador, London, 2021).

unlearning) throughout our lives. We can choose to put ourselves in learning situations where our prejudices are challenged, for example, and cultivate empathy for people from backgrounds different from our own. This requires an effort of will, and you would need to be feeling fairly secure in yourself to be able to adopt a curious, open outlook. Disenfranchised people who may have lost a sense of agency or self-worth, and who may feel threatened as a result, are vulnerable to persuasion to find scapegoats for their condition. We who can need to exercise the virtue of curiosity.

Bringing together groups of people with opposing views can promote understanding and lead to reconciliation. People whom you may have been brought up to see as the enemy, or as evil, can come to be seen as essentially like you. For example, movements like Seeds of Peace mix groups of young people from cultures in serious conflict, such as Palestinians and Israelis, or Indians and Pakistanis. Through engaging in activities together they come to realise that they are all just human beings. Breaking down such barriers opens up possibilities of empathy and compassion, and ultimately leads to a more peaceful world. In our efforts to combat climate change and protect biodiversity, we must take into account the experiences of those whose lives are most at risk, those who are disproportionately affected by the historical excesses of industrialised countries. We need to see them not as 'Other' but as human beings like us. What we have in common is greater than what divides us.

Unlearning can be hard (and it gets harder the older we get!). Unlearning may mean abandoning cherished or comfortable beliefs. For example, a relatively insignificant prejudice may be challenged upon meeting a red-haired person who did not have a fiery temper. More serious prejudices might include beliefs in white supremacy; male superiority; and homosexuality as a disease. An honest look at the issues implicit in the ecological crisis may mean questioning what we take for granted: for example, a blind acceptance of the economic-growth agenda. We may need to accept a lower standard of living. We may need to give up the myth of meritocracy:[7] the idea that the wealthy attained their position because they deserved it (through hard work and talent) and its corollary: that the poor are where they are because they are undeserving, lazy, or inferior in some way. Unfair advantage is prevalent both within our own society and throughout the world; there is no level playing field. We in the Global North will need to acknowledge our privilege. We may need to confess that inequities across much of the Global South are the result of colonialism from which we still benefit. We may need to lament our collective selfishness and our unfounded prejudices, acknowledging our own shadow.

Carl Jung called the dark side of our nature the "shadow", a part of ourselves that we would rather not acknowledge. However, unless we do become conscious of our shadow – a process that takes considerable effort – we are likely to project negativity on those around us. Unacknowledged, the shadow can be destructive; it is at the core of xenophobia and racism, reinforcing the establishment of "out-groups", minorities and scapegoats. Owning our shadow can be the first step towards developing our "ecological intelligence".[8]

Pursuing the truth

We have to be vigilant in our pursuit of truth. While there has always been propaganda to persuade us to adopt certain beliefs, it has become harder, with the advent of the internet and social media, to discern what is true (even though, ironically, we have never had greater access to information). Falsehoods can be circulated around the world in seconds, so the issue of where we place our trust is crucial. If we remain in our silos or echo-chambers, communicating only with those whose views we share, this closes our hearts and minds to the lives and experience of others.

---

7   Michael J. Sandel, *The Tyranny of Merit; What's Become of the Common Good?* (Allen Lane, London, 2020).

8   Ian McCallum, *Ecological Intelligence: Rediscovering Ourselves in Nature*, Africa Geographic, 2005).

During the mid-term elections in the USA in November 2022, I was much exercised by thinking about conspiracy theories. We faced the nightmare of the possible return of the 45th President (still under investigation for inciting riots that resulted in the storming of the Capitol building in January 2021). Climate-change denier, white supremacist, enemy of democracy, purveyor of fake news: why would anyone trust such a person to run the most powerful democracy in the world? Two thirds of Republican voters believe his claim that the election of 2020 was "stolen". Why? Other conspiracy theories prevail: Alex Jones (Info Wars) claiming that the Sandy Hook school shootings were a hoax, set up by the anti-gun lobby; here in the UK, disaster trolls sending hate messages to survivors of terrorist atrocities, claiming that they were actors. These examples of manipulation of the truth represent a very worrying phenomenon; there are people who are trying to control hearts and minds so that truth does not prevail. FBI investigator Kenneth V Lanning,[9] having examined allegations of satanic paedophilia against the Democrats, found no evidence, but large numbers of US citizens believed the allegations. He concluded that "People believe what they want to believe." It is of paramount importance that we understand the mindset of those willing to ignore evidence if it does not accord with their beliefs, or accept as truth what is patently false. Without a consensus on the facts of global warming and ecological degradation, the future looks bleak indeed.

We need to ask what motivates ordinary people to want to believe in extremist theories. Cognitive scientist Stephen Pinker claims that rationality at the "top end", among the scientific community, for example, is alive and well, concerned as it is with the acquisition of knowledge to attain shared goals in the world. However, this goes on alongside "the proliferation of nonsense" in other domains. He asks[10] "how sane people

---

9   Kenneth Lanning, *Love, Bombs, and Molesters: An FBI Agent's Journey* (Kenneth Lanning, 2018).
10   BBC Radio 4, *All in the Mind*, November 2022.

can hold insane beliefs". He concludes that in some areas of life, where community identity is important, the shared narrative of the group wins over the need for truth. Extreme views can be licensed by the anonymity of the internet. This is an area that demands more extensive research. Taking the long view, it points to the need for education that places a high value on critical thinking. And, perhaps, a need for better stories.

Things can change

On the positive side, there are some grounds for hope. We can look to past successes where change for the better has happened overnight. I remember as a non-smoking teacher in 1980s coming home reeking of smoke from the staff room. Now smoking is banned in public places. The introduction of compulsory car-seat belts is another example of an innovation that has improved public health. Sulphur dioxide emissions from coal-fired power plants in the USA were causing air pollution and acid rain, prompting the passing of the 1990 Clean Air Act, which established a system whereby polluters were penalised and were thus incentivised to make cheaper, greener choices. Sulphur emissions declined faster than predicted, and at a quarter of the projected cost. But we are not decarbonising fast enough; the solutions to cap warming at 1.5 degrees are all more expensive than business-as-usual. If the major polluters are indifferent to moral pressure, governments need to appeal to their self-interest by introducing laws that make it cheaper for them to do the right thing.

The ecological crisis is multi-faceted and it requires us to open our hearts and minds to hear the cry of the Earth, but also to hear the cry of those of our fellow human beings who are most affected by it: those who struggle every day ... just to survive.

Rather than closing off defensively from others, we need to open our hearts and minds to the plight of other human beings, and the flora and fauna of the planet. It is a spiritual stance to maintain a curiosity and openness towards the experience of others. We need to create opportunities for the most vulnerable to have a voice, and cultivate a listening ear to enable us to empathise with their life experience. Crossing the artificial boundaries of race, gender, class, and nationality, let us work together on life-enhancing projects that acknowledge the dignity and worth of every human being[11] and demonstrate our love of the Earth.

---

11   *The Revised Object of the General Assembly of Unitarian and Free Christian Churches* 2001

7 Owning the Shadow, Becoming Conscious

Sheena Gabriel

A skilful man reads his dreams for... self-knowledge. ... However monstrous and grotesque their apparitions, they have a substantial truth.
(Ralph Waldo Emerson[1])

Dreams are the touch-stones of our characters ... Our truest life is when we are in dreams awake ... [I]n dreams we never deceive ourselves, nor are deceived.
(Henry David Thoreau[2])

12 April 2019: *I dream I'm in a hotel at our General Assembly meetings. I see a lift shaft full of rubbish – things that people have discarded – including a fold-up metal bed and card folders from a filing cabinet. I'm shocked at the waste and wonder if it will be recycled. I feel consternation that Unitarians are implicated, and I think about reusing the card in my workshop.*

12 July 2019: *In my dream I'm with a vicar and his wife. The vicar is feeding birds – putting seeds into holes in clifftops. The seeds are in plastic packets. He's putting plastic into the earth! I protest: "You need to stop using plastic. This undoes any good in feeding birds!" I bewail how even our best intentions may have a flipside that harms the planet. The vicar seems defensive in response.*

10 October 2021: *I dream of a husband and wife – spiritual teachers – who have invited people to join them at their home in the USA for food*

---

1   Ralph Waldo Emerson, *The Complete Works of Emerson, Vol 10 Lectures & Biographical Sketches* (1904).
2   Henry David Thoreau, *A Week on the Concord and Merrimack Rivers* (1849).

and fellowship. I'm there with other guests. They teach about 'Christa': the feminine manifestation of Christ. I animatedly say how the concept of Christa has transformed my understanding of Christianity. I plaintively add that, as I finally grasp the reality of a loving deity and heal the wounds of childhood, I am overcome with grief at the climate crisis and demise of planet Earth. I voice guilt at my complicity and tearfully say how, despite my best intentions, every day I 'sin' against the Earth.

9 January 2022: *I dream that a supportive female doctor is helping me to manage stress. After exploring self-care and work patterns, she asks me if climate change is affecting my well-being on a subconscious level. In trying to ascertain where extra stress comes from in my life, she suggests that environmental concerns have more impact than I realise. I animatedly agree: "Yes. I think you're right! Though part of me is in denial, at a deeper level I feel the burden of grief at the planetary devastation we are causing."*

These four dreams illustrate the impact of the climate crisis on my psyche. I have long kept a record of night dreams, because I believe that they offer profound insights into the nature of things. The ecological emergency is harming not only our physical health, but also our mental health. The impact is especially felt by young people living with climate anxiety, as their future is snatched away by the decisions and behaviours of the older generation who wanted 'the good life' whatever the cost: people like me who will not live to see the worst of climate devastation (although I am open to the possibility of reincarnation: perhaps we *will* reap the consequences of what we have sown?).

I believe that by becoming more conscious, by paying attention to dreams and nightmares, we stand a better chance of dealing with the consequences of our collective shadow. Carl G. Jung in 1957 offered words that are chillingly prescient:

> The world hangs on a thin thread, and that is the psyche of man ...
> There is no such thing [in nature] as an H-bomb; that is all man's
> doing. WE are the great danger ... and so it is demonstrated to us

in our days what the power of the psyche is ... how important it is to know something about it ... Nobody would give credit to the idea that the psychical processes of the ordinary man have any importance whatever ... And that's the great mistake.[3]

The environmental activist and author Joanna Macy suggests that three things are needed in response to the ecological crisis: *holding actions to slow down or stop the damage; a radical change of lifestyles and structures; and a change of consciousness.*[4] The first two steps are crucial, but positive action can be sustained only as we undergo *inner* transformation. This means owning up to and taking responsibility for the mess we are in. Becoming conscious is hard work. On rare days I can face it head on; more frequently I slip into denial. My response aligns loosely with the Grief Cycle[5] that people are said to experience after the death of a loved one:

- Shock and denial
- Pain and guilt
- Anger and bargaining
- Depression, loneliness, and reflection
- Upward turn
- Reconstruction
- Acceptance and hope

Some days I can forget the burning forests and rising waters. In my privileged life, in the garden among spring blossom and flowers, I kid myself that things are not that bad. Other days, reality hits me like a body blow, as I see on the news the suffering caused to humans and

---

3   Carl G. Jung, from an Interview with Richard I. Evans (University of Houston, August 1957), extract from film: www.youtube.com/watch?v=ppFIVoug-Mc.

4   Joanna Macy, *Stories of the Great Turning* (Foreword), edited by Peter Reason and Melanie Newman (Jessica Kingsley Publishers, London, 2017, p.7).

5   The 'Seven Stages' model is adapted from the 'Five Stages' developed by Elizabeth Kübler-Ross in 1969.

animals by loss of habitat and home. Sometimes I rage at those who put greed before human flourishing – the shadowy leaders of governments, industries, and oil companies: "*I'll change my behaviour, if you clean up your act!*" Or I bargain with God: "*If you let it be OK, I'll never doubt you again.*" Then there are grey days when I feel apathetic, helpless, in response to climate deniers. When I read about new technology to repair coral reefs, or microbes that eat plastic, I have moments of uplift. When I see the courageous actions of Greta Thunberg and other eco-campaigners, I feel glimmers of hope. As with the loss of a loved one, I don't cycle neatly through the stages of grief; as I lament the degradation of planet Earth, I stagger back and forth between denial and guilt, anger and apathy, hope and despair. Early on, the Covid pandemic offered a window of possibility; in the months of lockdown we enjoyed clean air and reduced carbon emissions. But on the return to 'business as usual', in 2021 CO_2 emissions jumped by 6 per cent, to 36.3 billion tonnes – their highest ever level.[6] In 2021 COP 26 (the UN Climate Change Conference in Glasgow) offered another window of hope – but it came and went without concrete promises of real change. And since Russia's invasion of Ukraine in 2022, our attention is understandably turned elsewhere. Perhaps it is pointless to worry about climate change if nuclear annihilation is imminent? And as fuel prices surge, our government seeks a deal with Saudi Arabia, instead of using the crisis as a spur to serious investment in clean energy.

I understand the desire to carry on with one's life as usual, and I am certainly no paragon of virtue. As I contemplate a house move with my husband Rob, the desire for a quaint cottage with oak beams (however draughty!) competes with our commitment to the cause of eco-friendly homes. We don't eat meat but can't resist cod (an endangered species) and chips. We don't fly, but we own two cars. We have changed to a greener energy supplier, but have not installed solar panels. My

---

6   'Climate War puts 1.5C goal at risk', Fiona Harvey and Matthew Taylor, *The Guardian*, 22 March 2022.

ministerial pension was invested in fossil fuels ... The litany of errors goes on. Almost all of us are caught up in lifestyles which mean that it is all but impossible to avoid harming the planet. To choose eco products, invest in eco-friendly pension funds, and insulate homes costs money, time, and energy. As a church minister, I found that environmental concerns inevitably slipped aside, caught up as I was in the immediate needs of my congregation. Even now, after my retirement from that ministry, I am still busy within our denomination, being useful, I hope. But that means that I have less capacity to stand alongside climate activists making a last-ditch stand for the survival of the planet. My temperament and constitution render me more of a contemplative than an activist – although for the last few years I have tried to support my husband's involvement in Extinction Rebellion (XR), have woven ecological concerns into Sunday worship, and chaired interfaith events on environmental issues. More 'pastor' than 'prophet', I am discovering the hard truth: alongside *'comforting the afflicted'*, we are called to *'afflict the comfortable'* (which includes myself!). I want to offer solace, but the Covid pandemic cannot be an excuse to ignore the ecological crisis, especially as some scientists suggest that the two things are inextricably linked. So I do what I can, knowing that I should do more – and it still won't be enough. Oil magnates, governments, and global corporations, seeking to cover up their own dirty behaviour, put the onus on us little people to recycle and watch our carbon footprint. XR exposes this web of deceit and calls on ordinary people to take back power. Those whose wealth depends on exploiting the planet should know that a divided house cannot stand. If XR can be demonised, then the energy for change is dissipated. XR is not perfect, but as a grassroots movement it has been effective in highlighting the climate crisis and calling for real change.

I don't want my comfortable life to be disturbed, but just as Adam and Eve ate from the Tree of Knowledge and were kicked out of Paradise, so too, for me, the way back to the Garden of Innocence is barred. Talking of Adam and Eve, of course it must be admitted that religion contributed to the mess that we are in:

> God created humankind in his image ... God blessed them ... and
> said to them, "Be fruitful and multiply, and fill the earth and subdue
> it; and have dominion over the fish of the sea ... the birds of the air
> and over every living thing that moves upon the earth."[7]

Scripture taken too literally created a mindset of domination, giving
rise to the Protestant work ethic and the Industrial Revolution, and
encouraging wealthy factory owners (some of them Unitarians) to pollute
the skies, rivers, and soil in the name of progress. Industry conferred
many benefits, but we have not learned when to stop. As wild fires rage,
world leaders still insist that it is their God-given right to drill for oil and
gas. My own family includes good people who think that climate change
is fake news, and that freak weather is a punishment imposed by God,
rather than the consequence of human behaviour. It breaks my heart.

But if religion is part of the problem, secularism has not served us any
better: our shrines are now shopping malls, and our gods are celebrity
icons. We have disconnected from nature, and until we learn to see Earth
as a living being, as indigenous peoples do, we will continue to exploit
her. People have talked about the ecological crisis for decades. Despite
paying subs to Greenpeace, I have been slow to listen. The theologian
Augustine of Hippo, 1,500 years ago, lamented his slow awakening
to God's love: "*Late have I loved you, O Beauty ever ancient, ever new!
You called, you shouted, and you broke through my deafness. You flashed,
you shone, and you dispelled my blindness.*"[8] That lament is my own as
I belatedly awaken to the beauty of the Earth, and the consolation that
nature provides is marred by my awareness of its suffering. I find myself
weeping at film footage of a scrawny polar bear rummaging for scraps
of food in a town miles from his melting home, and at images of the
last two white Northern Rhinos on the planet – mother and daughter.

---

7   Genesis, Ch. 1 vv 27–28, *The Bible* NRSV Catholic Edition (Darton, Longman &
      Todd, London, 2005).

8   Augustine of Hippo, *The Confessions*, Book 10, chapter 27.

Thich Nhat Hanh, instead of identifying strategies when asked what we most need to do to save our world, replied, "*What we most need to do is to hear within us the sounds of the Earth crying.*" [9]

Christopher Bache, in his extraordinary book *Dark Night, Early Dawn*, describes a visionary experience in which he encounters what he perceives to be the Intelligence behind the universe. This Intelligence seemed to delight in having someone able to appreciate its work, having waited billions of years for human consciousness to evolve sufficiently to recognise the magnitude of its creation. Bache weeps at the isolation of this Intelligence, which in its extraordinary love has remained hidden, as part of some larger plan. Bache is in no doubt that LOVE is at the heart of creation, and everything that exists is an outward expression of this love. [10] This idea of loving Intelligence resonates with my own concept of 'God', and as I realise my complicity in trashing the work of a most prodigious artist, I weep. I dispose of non-recyclable plastic knowing that it may end up in the stomach of a beautiful sea creature, I eat biscuits made from palm-oil and see the face of an orphaned orangutan. I sin daily, caught up in economies, duplicities, and systems beyond my control.

I grew up with the idea of 'original sin' drummed into me. In adulthood I rejected such doctrines as oppressive, and eventually I became a Unitarian. I now accept that there is something in me that sins, not so much against Father God in Heaven, but against our Mother the Earth. Unitarians don't like the word 'sin'; but perhaps we should reclaim it in recognition of our tendency to err from the straight way. Two world wars put an end to the old Unitarian motto, "*Human progress onwards and upwards for ever*". Human 'progress', untrammelled, got us into this mess. Some would say that I am naïve, but I am looking to something larger than myself to save me from myself. Not 'Jesus the saviour' who will wash away my sins with his blood, but rather 'Jesus the shower of

---

9   Joanna Macy, *Stories of the Great Turning* (foreword) p.7.
10 Christopher M. Bache, *Dark Night, Early Dawn* (State University of New York Press, 2000) p.70.

the way' who can remind us of our divinity and restore us to the original goodness that is humanity's birth-right. And so I find myself calling on the name of the Christ that I thought I had outgrown. Others will feel more comfortable calling on another spiritual teacher, or the God of their understanding, or their Higher Self. Who we call on is not so important as getting down on our knees and praying in all sincerity: "*Please help us!*" An old joke observes that Universalists believe that God is too good to damn, while Unitarians believe that we are too good to be damned. I think that we Unitarians should reclaim the notion of grace and admit that we cannot solve all planetary ills by ourselves. Of course, we can't simply look to the heavens to rescue us: we must take full responsibility for our actions. But I do believe that there is a power for good working in the universe with which we can align ourselves, as Jung writes:

> Everything now depends on man; immense power of destruction is given into his hands, and the question is whether he can resist the will to use it and can temper his will with the spirit of love and wisdom. He will hardly be able to do so on his own resources. He needs the help of an 'advocate' in heaven.[11]

Pelagius, the Celtic Christian deemed to be a heretic and silenced by St Augustine, rejected the doctrine of original sin but has been misinterpreted as saying that we do not need grace. Rather, he stressed the need for divine grace to bring us to our senses, so that we remember our original capacity for goodness. We sin by forgetting our connection to the Source of all creation. Eco-theologian Thomas Berry stresses that only a deep change in consciousness can cure the 'cultural pathology' which manifests in our harmful behaviour against the planet; only by awakening to the beauty and abundance of nature can we align ourselves with the 'spiritual energies' needed for the task ahead.[12] We need the

---

11   Quoted in Claire Dunne, *Carl Jung: Wounded Healer of the Soul* (Continuum, Parabola Books, London, 2000), pp.197–9.

12   Thomas Berry, 'Alienation' in *The Sacred Universe*, ed. Mary Evelyn Tucker (Columbia University, 2009), p. 48.

humility to remember our place in the universe (humility – '*humus*' – 'of the earth'), but Berry claims that through human intelligence the universe has, as far as we are aware, found its most complex expression: "*The human is that being in whom the universe reflects on and celebrates itself ... the universe ... thinks itself, in us and through us.*"[13] What an awesome responsibility is given to us creatures of dust! It is said that Rabbi Simcha Bunim of Peshischa (1765–1827) carried two slips of paper, one in each pocket. On one was written "*For my sake the world was created*", and on the other: "*I am but dust and ashes*". True humility asks us to hold these two perspectives in creative tension.

I am greatly inspired by the twelfth-century German mystic Hildegard of Bingen, who is heralded as a 'green prophet' for our age. Her writings are scattered with '*viriditas*' – translated as 'greening power' – the divine attribute working in creation. She wrote:

> The earth is our mother ... mother of all that is natural, all that is human. She is the mother of us all, for she contains within herself the seeds of all. The earth ... contains all moisture, all verdancy, all germinating power. It is fruitful in so many ways.[14]

Over 800 years ago the seeds of environmental destruction were perhaps already visible in the felling of forests in the Rhineland, for she warned: "*God has directed for humanity's benefit all of creation. If we abuse our position to commit evil deeds, God's judgement will permit other creatures to punish us.*"[15] Hildegard saw sin as the drying up of all that is natural, and she described the Fall of Adam and Eve in ecological terms:

13 Thomas Berry, *Meditations with Thomas Berry*, Selected by June Raymond (GreenSpirit, London, 2010), p. 64.

14 Quoted by Jean Moore, 'Hildegard's Story', in June Boyce-Tillman, *The Creative Spirit: Harmonious Living with Hildegard of Bingen* (The Canterbury Press, Norwich, 2000), p.1.

15 June Boyce-Tillman, p.108.

Now in the people that were meant to be green there is no more
life of any kind. There is only shrivelled barrenness. The winds are
burdened by the utterly awful stink of evil, selfish goings-on ... The
air belches out the filthy uncleanliness of the peoples.[16]

Hildegard foretold a time of judgement: "*The earth should not be injured,
should not be destroyed. As often as the elements ... of the world are violated by
ill treatment, so God will cleanse them ... thru the sufferings ... the hardships
of humankind.*"[17] She foresaw a sabbath age of rest for the planet – but
first a time of purification.

Many spiritual teachers warn of the suffering that must come before we
collectively give birth to a new age. Christian scripture talks of all creation
in "*bondage to decay ... groaning in labour pains*" as it awaits the "*freedom
of glory*".[18] Surely our world is in the throes of birth pangs right now?
And the pain may get far worse before it gets better. Christopher Bache
recognises the perils that we have unleashed as a species, but he offers
hope based on a principle within physics. If a system enters sufficiently
into a state of non-equilibrium, it comes to a fork called a 'bifurcation
point', where many possible futures exist. Chaos theory posits that at this
point the slightest fluctuation in temperature, or the flap of a butterfly's
wings, allows the system to take off in a new direction. Bache suggests
that the eco-crisis may drive humanity to a bifurcation point in history,
whereby small changes could be amplified and have far greater impacts
than expected under usual circumstances. Thus the 'spiritual practices'
and 'right action' of a minority might disproportionately influence
the whole human species, as the severity of the crisis precipitates an
evolutionary shift.[19] Bache predicts that the escalating crisis may bring
about the 'ego' death of our species, after which humanity may awaken

16   Quoted in Gabriele Uhlein, *Meditations with Hildegard of Bingen* (Bear and
      Company, Santa Fe, 1983), p.77.
17   Ibid., p.79.
18   Letter to The Romans, Ch. 8 vv 21, 22, *The Bible* (NRSV).
19   Christopher M. Bache, *Dark Night, Early Dawn*, p.243.

from a state of disconnection to realise oneness with the web of all life. He envisages the rise of the feminine – '*the Cosmic Goddess*' – uniting with the masculine, suggesting a marriage of opposites.[20] Many claim that only a return to the feminine within religion and society can save our planet. According to Andrew Harvey, the Hopi Native Americans prophesied that if humans do not turn to the Mother, we will be shaken off planet Earth "*as a dog shakes off fleas*". And the mystic, Sri Aurobindo, claimed at the end of his life, "*if there is to be a future it must wear the crown of feminine design*".[21] My dream of 'Christa' (a concept developed by feminist theologians) suggests to me a second coming of Christ-consciousness mediated by the feminine – for the old patriarchal ways have surely failed.

I began this chapter by suggesting that night dreams can help to bring us to consciousness. I have been inspired by the books of Jeremy Taylor – Unitarian minister and dream-worker – who urges us to awaken both to the impact of our technologies and to the energies that motivate us towards creativity or destruction. Taylor claims that dream-work, and other activities which increase self-awareness, are no longer optional extras for creative people, but an "absolute necessity" for the survival of the planet.[22] Ecologist Derrick Jensen, likewise, draws on the wisdom of dreams to highlight the planetary crisis. Some may say his dreams – filled with polluted rivers, extinct species, and powerful men controlling the world – are paranoid expressions of his own dis-ease, but I think that he is bringing to consciousness what the rest of us cannot bear to acknowledge. Perhaps he is the canary sent down the coal mine, warning us of the dangers that we face unless we clean up our act fast. Jensen ends his book with a dream of hope. As he weeps over the murder of the planet, an old Native American man hugs him and says, "*The worst*

---

20   Ibid., p. 256.
21   Andrew Harvey, *Radical Passion: Sacred Love and Wisdom in Action* (North Atlantic Books, Berkeley, California, 2012), p.3.
22   Jeremy Taylor, *The Wisdom of Your Dreams* (Jeremy P. Tarcher/Penguin, New York, 2009), p.110.

will not happen. The world will recover." [23] But Jensen reminds us that whatever consolation is offered by the dream, we cannot be complacent. The future is not set: we create it each moment. The choice is ours. Words from ancient scripture still have power: *"I have set before you life and death, blessings and curses. Choose life so that you and your descendants may live."* [24]

The conservationist Rachel Carson, using imagery from Robert Frost's famous poem, 'The Road Not Taken', warned us in 1962 that humanity stands where two roads diverge. But unlike the roads in Frost's poem, Carson's are not equally fair. The "smooth superhighway" on which we have travelled for too long ends in disaster. The other road offers our only chance of survival. Will we get off the "superhighway" and take the "road less travelled by" before it's too late?[25] As the Christian Gospels tell us, it is the narrow road, not the broad road, that leads to life. I don't know if it is already too late to save planet Earth. The signs are not hopeful. But we must try. Even as we feel powerless, we should not underestimate our influence. Jung reminds us:

> The whole future, the whole history of the world, ultimately springs as a gigantic summation from these hidden sources in individuals. In our most private and subjective lives we are not only the passive witnesses of our age, and its sufferers, but also its makers. We make our own epoch.[26]

We may not feel up to the task – but thus it is in every age. In Tolkien's *The Fellowship of the Ring*, Gandalf describes to Frodo the terrible threat that they face. Frodo says, *"I wish it need not have happened in my time."* Gandalf replies, *"So do I, and so do all who live to see such times. But that*

23   Derrick Jensen, *Dreams* (Seven Stories Press, New York, 2011), p.551.
24   Deuteronomy, Ch. 30 v. 19, *The Bible* (NRSV).
25   Rachel Carson, *Silent Spring* (Houghton Mifflin, 1962), p.277.
26   Quoted in Claire Dunne, *Carl Jung: Wounded Healer of the Soul* (Continuum, Parabola Books, London, 2000), p. 196.

is not for them to decide. All we have to decide is what to do with the time that is given us." [27] I wish with all my heart that climate change was not a reality in my time. But all I have to decide – all each of us has to decide – is what to do with this time that is given. We can draw strength from the men and women throughout history, and in this present age, who have faced the darkness within humanity and within themselves, doing the necessary inner work to become more conscious and bringing the shadow into Light.

As we face up to the greatest challenge that humanity has ever known, however tempted we are to despair – and even if we *do* end up destroying ourselves as a species – I take some comfort in the hope that life on Earth will continue to manifest in new forms. In the words of the nineteenth-century naturalist John Muir:

> One is constantly reminded of the infinite lavishness and fertility
> of Nature – inexhaustible abundance amid what seems enormous
> waste ... when we look into any of her operations that lie within
> reach of our minds, we learn that no particle of her material
> is wasted or worn out. It is eternally flowing from use to use,
> beauty to yet higher beauty ... [Let us] exult in the imperishable,
> unspendable wealth of the universe, and faithfully watch and wait
> the reappearance of everything that melts and fades and dies about
> us, feeling sure that its next appearance will be better and more
> beautiful than the last. [28]

---

27 J.R.R. Tolkien, *The Fellowship of the Ring* (Unwin Paperbacks, London, 1974), p.78.
28 John Muir, *My First Summer in the Sierra* (The Riverside Press, Cambridge, 1911), Ch.10.

Questions for reflection and discussion

1. What has been the impact of the climate crisis in your own life (physically, mentally, or spiritually), and the lives of people close to you? Can you identify with the seven-stage model of grief in relation to your own feelings?

2. What importance do you ascribe to the 'shadow' (that which we deny in ourselves)? Might facing up to the destructive side of our human nature enable us, as individuals and communities, to better respond to the planetary crisis?

3. Has Unitarian theology been too positive in its view of human nature? Do concepts such as 'sin', 'repentance', 'grace', and 'salvation' have a place within our evolving faith community, as we respond to the climate crisis?

4. What is your response to the suggestion that transformation may come about for our species only after global catastrophe and suffering precipitate a collective evolutionary shift in consciousness?

The author

Raised in the Pentecostal Church, Sheena Gabriel first attended a Unitarian service at Meadrow Chapel, Godalming, in 1996 – which she describes as "a life-changing moment". Having found there a spiritual home, she became the lay leader at Meadrow Chapel in 2009, and after training at Harris Manchester College Oxford she was appointed as their minister in 2012. Sheena stepped down from this post in 2022, but is still active at national and district levels as a Unitarian worship leader, tutor, and group facilitator.

Before her ministry Sheena worked as a creative-therapies group facilitator in psychiatric and palliative care settings, and as a counsellor within the NHS. This developed her interest in the ideas of Carl G. Jung, depth psychology, and the importance of attending to night dreams – not just for personal growth and well-being, but for the greater good of society and the world.

Transforming Ourselves, Enabling Others
Peter Hawkins

Much of my recent work has focused on how to enable leaders and mentors to address the human-created ecological and climate crisis. This crisis, resulting from the deep split between humans and the 'more-than-human' world of the wider ecology, requires us individually and collectively to undertake a fundamental and spiritual shift in human consciousness.

To enable another on this journey of growing ecological consciousness, we have to go on our own transformational journey. We need to start by deepening and broadening our own awareness – connecting with ourselves and also with our wider purpose. Only when we have done the work for ourselves can we then facilitate the work in others.

Mapping the transformational journey

We need to be constantly 'eco-curious' about the wider environment and the changes taking place in all aspects of Earth's ecology, in order to become more and more 'eco-informed'. With this learning process come waves of emotional responses, which we need to work through in order to become 'eco-aware' and realise that the ecological crisis is not a problem 'out there', but deeply rooted in each of us and in our ways of perceiving and being in the world. Only then are we ready to enable others in a way that is 'eco-engaged', where the ecology becomes a partner in every conversation. However, merely changing our conversations is not enough, and the final stage is to become 'eco-active': helping to transform our congregations, communities, professional bodies, and organisations. The journey is not a linear process but a cycle; it requires constantly revisiting stages in the cycle, so that we are continually healing the split within us and helping to heal the split between the human and 'more-than-human' worlds.

Mentoring in an eco-engaged way will require us to be curious, to be open to exploration, and to own our own feelings about what is going on in the world, to be connected to ourselves and to others. Just by being, and encouraging a breadth of dialogue, free of judgement or expectation, we may allow wider perspectives to emerge.

The author
Peter Hawkins, a Unitarian for 46 years, hosts the Bath Unitarian Fellowship. He also trains inter-faith celebrants for the Sufi Way, an international universalist Sufi community. As a professor of Leadership he has published many books, most recently contributing to *Ecological and Climate-Conscious Coaching* (Routledge, 2022).

8 Privilege and Climate Change
Judy Ryde

The truth that anything that affects one of us affects all of us is no longer just an esoteric idea: it is a fact that is becoming more and more evident as we witness the climate of our planet change more quickly than even experts had expected.[1] When I say 'us', I do not mean human beings exclusively, but everything that exists on Earth. Everything is interconnected, and therefore every action that we take must affect every other living thing. The activity of human beings is having an increasingly negative effect on the planet, and these effects, such as alterations in weather patterns, mean that we cannot escape an awareness of this state of affairs.[2]

For me as a Unitarian, that concept of basic interconnectedness was originally hard to accept, constructed as Unitarianism is on the essential tenet of the Enlightenment that the rights of individuals are paramount, as is the importance of the individual human conscience (Smith 2008).[3] I understood myself to be a separate individual with a separate mind and my own separate conscience. However, an even more fundamental idea in Unitarianism is the encouragement to be thoughtful and open to truth wherever it can be found. This has helped to deepen my understanding of the place of the individual within this one world, and thus to develop an understanding of the issues of the climate crisis as complex and deeply interrelated.

Through making this shift in my consciousness, I gradually came to understand that those mostly responsible for this threat to the planet

1   F. Capra and P. L. Luisi, *The Systems View of Life: A Unifying Vision* (Cambridge, UK: Cambridge University Press, 2016).
2   R. Leakey and R. Lewin, *The Sixth Extinction: Patterns of Life and the Future of Humankind* (Crux Publishing, 2020).
3   L. Smith, *Unitarians: A Short History* (Toronto: Blackstone Editions, 2008).

are my own kind: white people. By 'white' I mean mostly Western Europeans and their diaspora in other parts of the world such as North America and Australasia. I have written elsewhere about white privilege[4] and the way that white people have disadvantaged those who are not white by making them 'other' and lesser. Unitarians were not exempt from this way of thinking, and it behoves us to acknowledge that our own forebears were guilty of assuming their own superiority over non-white peoples. In *White Privilege Unmasked* I have discussed the ways in which white people have become powerful through exploiting the planet and thus causing global warming. The wealth that was created through the exploitation of the colonies endowed upper-class and middle-class white people with the resources to develop technologies that were highly ingenious and needed more and more energy to maximise their potential. (I say 'middle-class' white people, as class privilege is also a factor here, and the wealth that accrued at that time has not been shared among all white people equally. This is still true today, as has become starkly obvious in the current cost-of-living crisis.) As success built on success, huge quantities of coal were extracted from the earth to drive the industrial revolution, emitting huge quantities of harmful particles and carbon dioxide into the atmosphere.

Of course, Victorians did not understand the knock-on effects of the use of coal (and oil and gas) in such quantities, or the exponential growth of their use in the future. From their perspective, the discovery that it is possible to harness the power of fossil fuels was progress, and they were sure that the benefits of that progress would be enjoyed all over the world, in the colonies as well as at home. It is clear that many Victorians thought that they were bestowing a blessing on humankind. And this is true not only of Victorians. More recently, the bringing of electricity to all parts of the world was considered to be helping 'under-developed' countries to join the 'modern age', and those that did not do so were thought of as 'backward' and in need of 'developing'. But many

---

4   J. Ryde, *White Privilege Unmasked* (London: Jessica Kingsley Publishers, 2019).

communities in Africa and Asia, for instance, had a sophisticated culture that was sustainable for all their inhabitants, both human and 'more than human'[5] – a culture that they now struggle to keep alive.

The white, Western European diaspora still comprises the dominant culture world-wide, and those who are part of it remain privileged. Being white, speaking English, and living in a country that provides free health care and education confers huge advantages in life. Colonisation and industrialisation have allowed white people access to financial, social, and cultural capital[6] that has built up over the decades and centuries. They/We are privileged indeed. As this wealth was built on the on-going exploitation of other parts of the world, we in the richer nations must shoulder the greatest responsibility for intervening to alleviate the environmental crisis, both by making the necessary changes ourselves and by supporting poorer countries to do so.

Although each one of us has to understand the need to live more ecologically, it is, as I have indicated, the special responsibility of white people to make these changes. There are several reasons for this.

It was white Anglo-Saxons who set the world on this path. It is often said that those who are not part of the white, Anglo-Saxon diaspora – those who live in what used to be called the 'third world' – are big polluters. Insofar as poorer nations do pollute the world, they are doing so in an effort to achieve the same standard of living as those who live in richer countries. To do this they need the easiest and cheapest forms of energy. In addition to their own use of this polluting energy, much of their pollution is generated in the course of providing cheap manufactured goods bound for richer countries. The energy used in this manufacture is counted in their tally of pollution. But the responsibility for that pollution should, by rights, be laid at the door of the countries where the goods are consumed.

----

5   D. Abram, *The Spell of the Sensuous* (New York: Random House, 1996).
6   J. Ryde, *White Privilege Unmasked* (London: Jessica Kingsley Publishers, 2019).

White Anglo-Saxons have spread their culture throughout the world. The aggressive acquisition and marketing of manufactured goods and services throughout the world have created a monoculture in which the same chains of hotels and shops can be found all over the globe. This has been called 'McDonaldization',[7] and it is a culture that requires and expects a certain standard of living in order to sustain itself. Ancient cultures with rich traditions but low carbon footprints tend to be excluded and forgotten.

We are still living off the wealth that was created centuries ago. In *White Privilege Unmasked*, I argue that the wealth obtained by white people in their exploitation of non-white peoples is something from which our culture still benefits. Those who object to the word *privilege* in this context say that colonisation and slavery no longer exist in the way that they once did, and we cannot therefore be held responsible for the consequences. This might have had some credibility if white people did not still benefit from the privilege and wealth that were accumulated over the centuries, along with the domination and exploitation of non-white peoples. In the same way, the wealth that was built up decades ago by our use of the fossil fuels that put the world on course for global warming is still with us. We therefore have a responsibility to put this right.

We have the wealth to develop alternative technologies. Wealthy countries are in a better position to develop sustainable alternatives to fossil fuels, and we could help poorer countries to put those alternatives in place.

Robin Wall Kimmerer, mother, scientist, and enrolled member of the Citizen Potawatomi Nation, in her book *Braiding Sweetgrass*,[8] points out that *Homo sapiens* is the youngest child of creation. This idea is in contrast to the more familiar concept of human beings being the pinnacle, the

---

7   G. Ritzer, *The McDonaldization of Society: Into the Digital Age* (London: Sage, 1993).
8   R. W. Kimmerer, *Braiding Sweetgrass: Indigenous Wisdom, Scientific Knowledge and the Teachings of Plants* (London: Penguin Random House, 2020).

crowning glory, of creation. It behoves us therefore to learn from our older brothers and sisters how we might live within our means, in a sustainable way, so that those who share this planet with us may thrive. We might then be able to pass on the world in a better state than we found it, to those who come after us, both the human and the 'more than human'.

One idea that has been promulgated in white, Western cultures is the mindset that 'more is better'.[9] That makes it difficult to change our behaviour and adopt an eco-friendlier way of life. This mindset is hard to reverse, as it is, by now, an unquestioned assumption in our culture. As early as 1992, A. T. Durning argued that the economic model of continual growth is untenable,[10] but it is still espoused by all major economies. They find it imperative to try to do better, be better, and build on their strengths. This would be fine if it did not lead to greater and greater consumption.

So how can we privileged Westerners break away from this habitual way of thinking, and really make the kinds of change that will lead to our descendants inheriting a world that can be lived in? Our existence on this planet is, in itself, a privilege which has come to us by grace, rather than because we have worked for or deserved it. How can we ensure that the beautiful planet that we have, by grace, come to inhabit can continue to sustain its wonderful diversity of interconnected and interwoven lives? If we cannot deeply understand how our one life is, in fact, completely dependent on the continuing health of all the creatures and habitats that exist around us, then we "don't have a snowball's chance in hell" of surviving as a species.[11] We are likely to take most of life on Earth into an ecological collapse with us.

9   Y. N. Harari, *Homo Deus. A Brief History of Tomorrow* (London: Penguin Random House, 2016).

10 A. T. Durning, *How Much is Enough?: The Consumer Society and the Future of the Earth* (New York: Norton, 1992).

11 G. Bateson, *Steps to an Ecology of the Mind* (San Francisco, CA: Chandler, 1979, p.436).

Not all human beings are so arrogant and lacking in the knowledge of how to live sustainably. Those from indigenous communities (which survive in many parts of the world, though often under threat) tend to live harmoniously with the 'more than human world'.[12] In the past it has been thought that indigenous peoples are something of an inconvenience to the smooth running of society, as they work by different rules. Often indigenous peoples, such as those who live in what we now call America and Australia, would wander over the land with no notion of 'owning' it. They lived in harmony with all the living things in their environment. Colonising governments often made great efforts to get rid of the people who originally lived on the land, or they found ways to integrate them into the wider population. In Australia, for instance, this has involved the kidnapping of indigenous children and giving them to white people to bring up.[13] Many methods of what amounts to ethnic cleansing have been used in shameful and wanton acts of destruction by colonisers, to rid themselves of indigenous peoples and take possession of their traditional land. It is only more recently that it has become clear that their way of living, far from being something that should disappear, is one that we can all learn from. Indigenous peoples should become our teachers, and not be seen as children who need to grow up. There are many examples of indigenous people who try to provide us with their wisdom.[14, 15] Their attempts are a blessing for those outside their communities, and those on the receiving end of their wisdom should have the humility to learn from them. White peoples have tended to see themselves as more intelligent and more capable than others,[16] and thus deserving of their greater wealth. As the world suffers from the effects of such hubris, we can see that the holistic approach of indigenous peoples

---

12   D. Abram, *The Spell of the Sensuous* (New York: Random House, 1996).
13   S. Corry, *Tribal Peoples for Tomorrow's World* (London: Freeman Press, 2011).
14   I. X. Kendi, *Stamped from the Beginning: The Definitive History of Racist Ideas in America* (Boston: Harvard University Press, 2016).
15   R. W. Kimmerer, *Braiding Sweetgrass: Indigenous Wisdom, Scientific Knowledge and the Teachings of Plants* (London: Penguin Random House, 2020).
16   N. Irvin Painter, *The History of White People* (New York and London: W. W. Norton & Company, 2012).

is the one that will ensure the continued existence of humans on this planet for millennia to come.

The lessons that we need to learn are so profound that it seems almost impossible to expect people to take them to heart over the short period of time that we have left. So is there any hope of our making these changes? Berating people is not going to work. It is more likely to cause antipathy and have the opposite effect to the one intended. It is, nevertheless, necessary to make people aware of the scientific evidence which shows that change is needed, and how it might be tackled. But this appeal to the rational mind, although necessary, is not sufficient. The problems that we solve with our rational mind tend to be addressed in a rather blinkered way. For instance, if the world needs more food, and genetically modified crops deliver this need, it seems rational to grow them. We forget to take into account the impact that the subsequent lack of diversity has on the whole planet.[17]

Peter Hawkins and I have shown the need for ecological understanding to be central to a new psychotherapy of integration.[18] We should no longer perceive ecological health as a 'special interest' but as a factor that needs to underpin our understanding of psychological distress. Peter Hawkins developed a model based on my 'White Awareness Model',[19] called the 'Ecological Awareness Cycle'. This model (Figure 1, below) shows what a process could look like which would develop the shift in consciousness that is needed to ensure that global temperatures do not rise by more than 1.5°C, in order to reduce the worst impacts of climate change.

----

17   S. Corry, *Tribal Peoples for Tomorrow's World* (London: Freeman Press, 2011).
18   P. A. Hawkins and J. Ryde, *Integrative Psychotherapy in Theory and Practice: A Relational, Systemic and Ecological Approach* (London: Jessica Kingsley Publishers, 2020).
19   J. Ryde, *Being White in the Helping Professions* (London: Jessica Kingsley Publishers, 2009).

Figure 1: Ecological Awareness Cycle

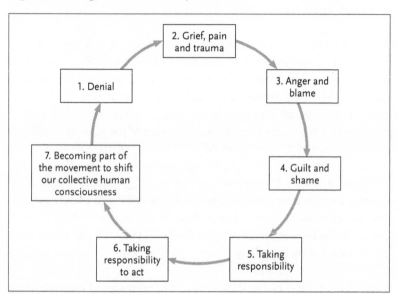

Readers might like to think about where they are themselves on this cycle. The model can be used as a tool to help members of engagement and study groups to think about their own levels of ecological awareness. The model is presented as a cycle rather than an upward path, as it is all too possible to fall back to an earlier level of awareness when our busy lives demand more of our attention, and other priorities seem to take precedence.

As with the White Awareness Model, this model starts with *denial*. Over the last fifty or so years, the number of people who cognitively deny the existence of climate change has declined. Nevertheless, those who earn their living via the production of carbon-emitting substances will often, through understandable self-interest, play down or deny the fact that our climate is warming due to man-made activity. This is true of most other people whose comfortable life styles are guaranteed by the use of fossil fuels. Those who do not deny that the planet is warming nevertheless often deny that the problem is caused by human actions. Conspiracy theorists tend to think that climate change is a myth, promoted by people with vested interests. Some think that the danger is exaggerated and that human beings are ingenious enough to find technological solutions. These ideas are being discredited daily by fresh evidence that climate change has already happened, and that it very urgently needs to be addressed in order to avoid catastrophe.

Once we understand enough to let go of our denial, we advance to the second phase in the Ecological Awareness Model. Here we may be overcome by *grief and pain* at the loss of thousands of creatures and the habitats that sustained them. So many have already become, and will become, extinct even in the best-case scenario of the future. In the worst case we could be facing the sixth mass extinction since Earth came into being.[20]

It is tempting, in our distress, to blame others for this state of affairs (the third phase of the model): we blame our government, other governments, global corporations, and the unthinking consumerism of ordinary people. *Blaming others* can lead to the hardening of attitudes and polarisation. In blaming others we are not taking responsibility for our own part in the whole.

As we see in the Ecological Awareness Model, a sense of guilt can prompt us towards taking more responsibility, and deepen our commitment to making the necessary changes. These changes start with individual acts, such as making a commitment not to use single-use plastic, or to transfer to a sustainable form of energy. We may feel a sense of *shame and guilt* about the consumer choices that we make, such as deciding to travel round the globe by air, or to put off acquiring an electric car. A sense of guilt can be a motivator to find other ways of living (phase 5). This can lead to a gradual change in consciousness and can help us to live in a constant state of ecological awareness that becomes more and

---

20   R. Leakey and R. Lewin, *The Sixth Extinction: Patterns of Life and the Future of Humankind* (Crux Publishing, 2020).

more natural (phases 6 and 7). If we are from a privileged culture, we can learn to acknowledge our particular responsibility for our unsustainable life style, built on decades and centuries of exploitation.

As argued above, all lives are interconnected, and so this change in consciousness can be spread to others. Just as the idea that 'more is better' spread into human consciousness, so can eco-awareness. We may need to do more to ensure the speed of this spread, but the aggressive blaming of others is more likely to cause resistance than change. Working through the Ecological Awareness Model is one way forward which may help to develop compassion for the Earth, resulting in the fundamental changes that are urgently needed.

To live on a healthy planet, we not only have to take the necessary steps to reverse the global rise in temperatures by reducing our carbon emissions: we also need to respect the diversity and interdependent nature of all that exists in this world. We are only now beginning to understand the symbiotic relationships that exist among plants and animals in natural, biodiverse environments, as well as the risks incurred when humans intervene, upsetting the balance by destruction of habitats for agricultural monocultures, for example. The biosphere is an interconnected, interdependent web with which we tamper at our peril.

The oneness of all that lives is something that the mystics of all faiths have understood for millennia. They understood this through direct experience, and they taught meditation and other spiritual practices in order that we might experience this too. Besides the lessons to be learned from indigenous peoples, we can also go back to visionaries such as Lao Tsu and Rumi, who instinctively understood the beauty of the paradox that there is, on Earth, a multitude of diverse but interconnected organisms alive and dying in a natural and benign process. These are not separate, discrete organisms but one whole, one living organism. Some might call this oneness God. Unitarians are open to wise teaching wherever it is to be found, and this openness has been a foundational principle for me in learning and responding to the truth of climate change.

Whatever we call it, this oneness sustains our lives. We are privileged to have been born and to live on this breathtakingly beautiful planet. Let us do so with grace and humility and help it to heal, rather than persisting in its destruction.

Questions for reflection and discussion

1. Would you accept a reduction in your standard of living if it meant that resources would be more equitably distributed (a) in this country and (b) throughout the world?

2. What privileges do you experience in your life? Who is underprivileged in your society?

3. Is it only the privileged who can afford to live sustainably in our culture? (For example, organic food, green energy, and electric cars are expensive; cheap clothes are often produced by exploited workers and leave a large carbon footprint; ready meals are less nutritious but cheaper than cooking from scratch.)

4. What might we learn from the values and ways of life of some Indigenous peoples about living in harmony with the Earth?

The author

Judy Ryde is a psychotherapist and has worked for many years with asylum seekers and refugees. Following doctoral research at the University of Bath, she published two books, *Being White in the Helping Professions* and *White Privilege Unmasked*. She is a life-time Unitarian, and is currently a member of the Bath Unitarian Fellowship.

Opening the Seven Levels: a practice
Peter Hawkins

It is my privilege, as an inter-faith spiritual celebrant, to facilitate weddings, child blessings, funerals, and other rites of passage. I also train other spiritual celebrants in this important work. One core practice requires celebrants to prepare themselves by opening to seven levels of awareness.

1. First, be open to the individuals involved in the rite of passage, and picture them with love and compassion.

2. Then refocus on the relational connections. In the case of a wedding, the relationship between those marrying; for a child blessing, that between the parents, siblings, and new arrival; and for a funeral, that between the family and the deceased.

3. Thirdly, be open to the wider community of family, friends, and neighbours who will shortly gather.

4. Then move the focus to those who will not be present, because they are ill or have died, or have not been invited: the ex-wife or ex-husband, the estranged sibling, the dementing parent.

5. Then to the whole interconnected human family, all 8 billion of us who share this planet.

6. And then to all the sentient beings that surround us, and the elements that support and flow through us.

7. Finally, we open the door to the mystery of oneness – that which connects everything, beyond time and space, beyond words, and certainly beyond our own limited comprehension.

Every meeting with another, and every congregational service, is, in some way, a rite of passage, so we can do this practice as fellow travellers before every meeting. Picture the individual, his or her important relationships, the family, friends, and community that they talk about, and the community that they leave out and ignore. Then the one human family, the more-than-human-ecology, and the mystery of oneness.

We know from the experience of many practitioners that when you are open to some new awareness within you, even though you never mention it, the other person starts talking to that same level, as though they had only been awaiting your readiness.

9 Consumerism is Bad for Your Health (and the Planet's)

Bob Janis

Admit it: shopping can be fun.

Back in the days before Coronavirus, I would often go to the High Street and nip into a Boots store, or a Waterstones book shop. Even though, like many others, I bemoan the fact that every British High Street now looks exactly the same as all the others – thanks to brand capitalism – there is something reassuring about being able to get whatever I want, from a duvet cover to a collection of 14th-century poetry. And it's so convenient: I simply stroll past the sliding glass doors, pick up an item, flash some paper or card at the anonymous assistant at the counter, and *voilà*, just like that, I have what I want. Or – if that's too much effort – I can push a few buttons in my living room, and the items will show up on my doorstep the next day.

There is, of course, a price to be paid for all this convenience. In the ten generations since the Industrial Revolution, we have utterly defaced the surface of the Earth, and filled the skies with pollution. There are 5.25 trillion micro pieces of plastic in our oceans, right now – and more filling the seas every day.[1] At our current rate of deforestation, the world's rainforests are on target to vanish in 100 years.[2] Thanks to climate change, the sea levels are rising: large sections of cities, including Ho Chi Minh, Mumbai, and London, are projected to be under water by 2050.[3]

---

1 https://www.condorferries.co.uk/plastic-in-the-ocean-statistics
2 https://www.theworldcounts.com/challenges/planet-earth/forests-and-deserts/rate-of-deforestation/story
3 https://www.loveexploring.com/gallerylist/91927/incredible-places-that-will-be-underwater-by-2050

Climate change is real. In Lancashire, where I used to live, older people remember regular snowfalls each year – and a lot more green space, which has now been 'developed'. Science and technology have improved our existence in ways too numerous to measure. Few of us would want to go back to a tenuous existence of living in caves. But science has also given us the means to melt the polar ice caps, increase our planet's temperature by 0.2°C per decade (a rate roughly one thousand times faster than natural temperature fluctuations), extract all the world's oil by 2065,[4] and destroy 50 per cent of the world's species by 2150.

Thanks to human ingenuity and the scientific method, humanity has become immensely powerful. We are becoming aware, however, that this hubris has the potential to be our downfall as a species. We depend upon our ecosystem to survive. If the bees and insects disappear, we will surely go with them. The food we eat, and the air we breathe, are the results of millions of years of co-evolution.

We know we have to change our ways. If we do, science is likely to be part of the solution, just as it has been part of the problem. Science is morally neutral. It can be used for good or ill, to create the polio vaccine or the atomic bomb. Science paired with capitalism has been, literally and figuratively, a toxic mix. Industrial facilities pump out 310 kg of toxic chemicals into our air, land, and water *every second*.[5] That's 10 million tons a year. These toxic chemicals are a by-product of all the items that clutter our homes and our cupboards. We have a disposable economy – in other words, we have far more stuff than we really need. Economists devised the concept of 'planned obsolescence' in the 1930s. This was a feature of product design, whereby products were intended to last only a given number of years, at which point they would need to be replaced by a new model. Ever noticed that the operating system on

---

4   https://rentar.com/much-oil-used-whats-left-using/
5   https://www.worldometers.info/view/toxchem/, based on data from the United Nations Environment Program.

your computer is out of date nearly as soon as you purchase it? That's planned obsolescence. The attractiveness of planned obsolescence for companies is obvious: when consumers need to buy a replacement every few years, it nets the company lots of money. It's not such a great deal for consumers, though. And it's terrible for the planet.

Want, find, purchase, consume. This simple little cycle is repeated billions of times every day on our planet. Meanwhile the rivers are dying, the air grows carcinogenic, and the future of the human race becomes ever more tenuous.

Impellers of a growing civilisation

Unitarianism has been heavily involved with the growth and promotion of capitalism over the last three centuries. Here in Britain, wealthy industrialists like the Courtaulds and the Tates helped to promote Unitarianism and other forms of dissenting religion. The freedoms and new social structures promised by dissenting religion were of great appeal to the growing middle classes and entrepreneurs of the Industrial Revolution. In the words of the dissenting poet and writer Anna Laetitia Barbauld:

> In the great manufacturing towns dissenting families were at the head of many of those vast establishments which have given our fabrics their worldwide reputation, and which are the great aliment [sustenance] of commerce abroad, the means of employment to busy millions at home, the source of enormous wealth, and the impellers of a growing civilization ... we are a mercantile people.[6]

---

6   Anna Laetitia Barbauld, 'Address to the Opposers of the Repeal of the Corporation and Test Acts', cited in William McCarthy, *Anna Laetitia Barbauld: Voice of the Enlightenment* (Baltimore: John Hopkins University Press, 2008), p. 2.

Unitarians were, and are, keenly interested in social justice and the betterment of humankind. Countless sermons, from the eighteenth century through to the twenty-first, have affirmed a belief in the positive potential of human progress in this world. We have championed the rights of the individual: freedom of conscience, freedom of speech, and civil rights. But at times this general interest in a better society clashed with the opportunities offered by a new global capitalism. Quite a few Unitarians owned slaves; many more invested in companies that profited from slave labour. Unitarian abolitionists railed against the abomination of kidnapping and enslaving fellow human beings. But many preferred abolition to be a theoretical discussion in the parlour, rather than an immediate strain on their bank accounts. There was a reason why cotton, tobacco, railways, shipbuilding, and sugar were typically such good investments: everything connected to unpaid slave labour was immensely profitable.

Today, slavery is still connected with many of the products that we buy, as well as many of the companies that we as individuals invest in – although uncovering slavery in labyrinthine corporate supply chains is difficult, even within companies themselves. But nowadays, planetary destruction is a much more profitable capitalist temptation than slavery. In our parlour discussions, everybody wants to save the planet. But when it comes down to our bank accounts, we mutter about viability and being realistic.

Few Unitarians believe in the concept of Original Sin – so we can't blame Adam and Eve for our own unwillingness to be fully honest about the price of our comfort. Each of us has a responsibility to take a closer look at how our actions, purchases, and investments affect the planet. These decisions have direct impacts on the future of our planet, and the quality of our grandchildren's lives.

Individualism reconsidered

Unitarianism's focus on creating a better world is as vital now as it ever was. However, one widespread Unitarian religious principle that we may need to rethink is the upholding of the individual as the primary unit of value. We seldom question individualism – it is a bedrock principle of both capitalism and democracy. Every person is important. This is very true. Every person is uniquely beautiful, and entirely worthy. But every animal is important, too. So is life in general, and the world which gives us life. We have begun to realise that an exclusive focus on human beings as the principal units of worth is detrimental to the survival chances of our planet. Not only is it unfair to our sisters and brothers the animals: it belies the chain of life, our deep connections to one another and to our world. Without numerous other species, human beings simply cannot exist.

There is still a need to assert individual dignity and individual human rights, worldwide. Transgender folx, and women, and people of every background other than white Caucasian are often denied their full humanity by a system that casually asserts that "all lives matter", while in actual practice prioritising certain lives over others. Individual dignity – the fierce insistence on a human being's fundamental importance – is a crucial and necessary corrective to a society of indifference and injustice.

At the same time, competitive individualism is not only killing the planet: it is also making us deeply unhappy. From an early age we are separated into grades, and told that individual success is what really matters. Many adults still have nightmares about their school days: rushing from one class to the next, feeling that they were never good enough, trying to measure up. But it gets worse: when we grow to adulthood, we are told that we are on our own, it's up to us to secure a salary that puts food on the table and makes our family proud. While the UK has a social safety net (albeit an ever-eroding one), there is enormous stigma attached to the failure to "pay our own way". Plus, it's not just about necessities: endless advertisements tell us what our houses ought to look like, what car we should drive, which products signify that we really are living the good life. Make money, buy stuff, be happy. *Want, find, purchase, consume.* Again, again, again.

Practised by billions of people at the rate of many times a day, this is an accelerating cycle that could very easily lead to temperatures and oceans drastically rising, culminating in a series of events that cause the extinction of the human race – and many other species besides.

Plus, let's be honest: although the cycle of *want, find, purchase, consume* can be fun, it's not *that much* fun. There has to be a better way to live.

Six trade-offs towards ecological living

Environmentalism can feel like a chore. We know that our current way of life is unsustainable. But our spirits groan at the immensity of the task ahead. Change our whole life around? Who has time for that? And we each feel powerless, the collective task too daunting.

I want to suggest that living in a more sustainable way can be an exciting adventure. Yes, on an ethical level it is something that we *should* do – but, far from being a chore, it also might prove to be a more fulfilling, much more enjoyable way of life. Yes, it involves sacrifice, giving up some aspects of our current lives – but perhaps the sacrifices are not quite as dire as we were expecting. Here are six trade-offs that could be involved if you and I lived in a more environmentally responsible way.

1. A sustainable life means trading convenience for happiness

One of the first things that many of us dread about living more sustainably is that it will inconvenience us terribly. No surprise there: convenience is one of the main selling points of consumerism. In a throwaway society, we get what we need quickly and easily (at least in theory). But sustainable living invites us to trade some of that convenience for something else: happiness.

As I admitted at the start of this chapter, I actually enjoy shopping malls, in small doses. A mall is a bustling sort of place, full of activity and people

– and delicious junk food. But shopping malls often fail to provide us with lasting happiness. We bring home the plastic thingamajig that we were looking for, flushed with a mild sense of accomplishment. But then it's gone. The next day, the sought-after thingamajig is promptly forgotten about.

There are so many situations where the environmental choice, while moderately less convenient, is the happier choice. If I cycle to work, it will take me longer, I shall have to figure out the best route as I go along, and it'll make me sweaty – but the endorphins will roll all the while, elevating my mood far more than driving a car would. If I wash out these jars, I will waste valuable time, and these week-old leftovers at the bottom of them are yucky. But it is still the happier choice – especially if I choose to enjoy the experience of washing them, feeling the water against my skin, the sense of satisfaction in putting them back on the shelf.

Sustainable living is about spurning convenience – the rush to get to the next activity – to truly enjoy the present moment. As Thich Nhat Hanh says, "*The present moment is filled with joy and happiness. If you are attentive, you will see it.*" [7]

2. A sustainable life means trading stuff for story

I would not say that stuff can never make us happy, because when I was about 8 I got a He-Man Castle Grayskull Playset for Christmas, and it was *awesome*. I was ridiculously happy playing with that thing, for a whole month. The material world can be beautiful. However, more stuff does not always equal more happiness. Sustainable living invites us to trade some of the stuff that we love for something that we might end up loving even more: story.

---

7   Thich Nhat Hanh, *Peace is Every Step: The Path of Mindfulness in Everyday Life* (Random House, 1995).

Generally, in consumerism, stuff enters our lives with very little story attached. I can go to the store and pick up a new coat, a new microwave oven, or a new computer without even a single thought about where these items come from, or who made them. One way in which we might slow down the flow of stuff through our lives is to love what we already have a little more carefully. Rather than buy a new, anonymous item of clothing, wearing a second-hand shirt reminds me about the person who wore it before me – a stranger, or the friend who gave it to me. Before I run to the store to satisfy some consumerist craving, I ask myself if I've really fully appreciated the stuff that's kicking around my house. I am not saying that this eliminates every urge in me to accumulate useless junk (I am a one-man-hoarder-TV-special waiting to happen), but it definitely is a more meaningful, and more sustainable, way of life.

Of course, another way in which we are invited to trade stuff for story is to tell stories instead of shopping. By 'stories' I don't just mean formal storytelling in circles around a fire – although those are great – but also just chitchatting with the people around us. Shooting the breeze – talking to people – is environmentally responsible, and costs nothing. What will give me more satisfaction: a new microwave oven or friendly chats with my next-door neighbours? They both have their pull, but deep down I know it's the latter that will make me happier in the long run.

3. A sustainable life means trading constant information for peace

When was the last time you shut off all your electronic devices – including your mobile phone – for an entire day? If you shudder at the very thought, I feel your pain. I am always checking the latest news, whether anyone has emailed me, and my 12 phone notifications. But if I put away my devices, even for an hour or two, I feel a sense of peace that no amount of web-surfing can bring. This morning I woke up to the birds chirping, ate a little oatmeal, read a few pages of a novel. I didn't know who had emailed me last night, or if there was any pressing global news that I should know about. And you know what? It felt fine.

Sustainable living invites us to trade being constantly bombarded with information for enjoying the peace of the natural world.

Our digital world wants us to believe that everything is urgent all the time, that every notification needs to be checked, that every email needs to be answered right away. It's not true. We can live in the world, pay attention to the clouds, hear subtle sounds of the river running in the background, notice the changing of the seasons. This is qualitatively different from watching a screen. The contents presented on our screens are designed to be direct encounters with a curated piece of information. They are always (supposedly) urgent and important, always demanding our attention. Nature is not like that. When we return to Nature, we notice the beauty of a world that isn't trying to sell us something: a world that exists because of the relationship between thousands of wonderful lives, existing in concert. This experience of Nature might – just might – inspire us to take better care of it.

Seeking the peace of Nature doesn't mean living in total ignorance of the digital world. We can still check the news once a day. The email will still be there in our inbox when we want to read it. And if we check our phones a little less, we will have spent a lot less 'battery' – both the literal battery on our phone, and the charge of our inner spirits. The world will feel less urgent – but much more meaningful.

4. A sustainable life means trading purposeful nihilism for meaningful chaos

A lot of people seem to be very driven, without having the foggiest idea of where they are going. In our society today you can get top school marks, then get a high-paying job, collect the best toys, buy the biggest house, save up and buy the farm – all the while not doing any real good for anybody, just moving money around. Most of us have come to the realisation that a nihilistic existence is not for us. While I would love to take a yacht out for a spin some time, it's hard to envy multi-millionaires who are so lost in their hedge funds that they need to take cocaine just to take the edge off their stress.

Sustainable living invites us to trade a purposeful nihilism for a meaningful chaos.

This era of constant change bewilders us all sometimes. The old systems are falling apart. It's not at all clear what is coming to replace them. In this rudderless age, I can appreciate how some turn to a fundamentalist religious or philosophical outlook, one that claims to provide, in stark black and white, all the answers to life's great questions. As challenging as true faith is (and faith in a religion or system demands much of us), it can be a great comfort to believe that the Bible or the Qur'an or libertarianism or Marxism has all the answers to every question that life poses. I don't belittle people who do believe that. I just don't believe it myself. My own faith involves doubt, uncertainty, wonder, and questioning.

If you, like me, are not certain that one belief system has all the answers to life's questions, I would suggest that we might learn, gradually, to be a little more comfortable with chaos and uncertainty. By that I don't mean our lives falling totally apart – merely a sense that we don't have all the answers, and that that's OK. Chaos is the place from which possibilities emerge. Chaos is a healthy place to be. Our lives don't always have to make perfect sense. Rather than trying to figure everything out all at once, why don't we recognise how meaningful it is to live in an ecologically responsible way? When we are connected with the Earth, living in right relationship with other lives, we have a felt sense of harmony and meaning. This is not the same as having all the answers. But wisdom is about much more than the ideas in our heads.

5. A sustainable life means trading personal success for community enrichment

I don't want to be in a rat race with you, because I am not a rat. While we human beings have a competitive drive of our own, the wisdom-advanced civilisations, from the Bantu to the Iroquois, all recognised that a life of 'we' is much more fulfilling than a life of 'I, me, mine'. We are social creatures. We may rightly laud individual geniuses like Marie Curie or Kendrick Lamar, but individual achievements – from the arts to the sciences – all happen in a context of mutual inspiration, societal planning, and teamwork.

Sustainable living invites us to trade the cult of individual success for community enrichment.

Consumerism and Enlightenment individualism have isolated us to the extent that we tend to think of our lives as our own story, more or less separate from the stories around us. As well as being a false narrative, this outlook on life tends to exacerbate environmental problems. There simply are not enough resources on Earth for everyone to have a 200-acre manicured lawn and a four-car garage. Thus, our personal success can hinder the personal success of others.

"*I am because we are*" – the philosophy known as *Ubuntu* – is the Bantu explanation of what it means to be human. At the end of the day, a happy neighbourhood is more important than an impressive CV.

6. A sustainable life means trading sainthood for Robin Hood

"If Al Gore cares so much about the environment, why is he flying about in jets?" ... "So many environmentalists are hypocrites – they drive cars and have children." ... "You say you're an environmentalist, but yesterday I saw you use a plastic bag at the supermarket."

For goodness' sake, give it a rest. Trying to live into a new way of life is not easy. And we are human. Lobbing puritanical hand grenades at one another will not accomplish very much. If you want to vie for environmentalist sainthood, go ahead. But I am just trying to live a little better every day. We can't all be saints. Maybe we can be a bit more like Robin Hood. He didn't claim to be perfect, but he took from the rich and gave to the poor. He was a good guy. Mostly. I mean, he probably didn't give every last penny to the poor. He may have given Maid Marian a filched brooch every once in a while. Or even pocketed a few pennies for a drink at the ale house. The media probably would have splashed a big headline, "Robin Hood: Corrupt!". But over the course of his (probably fictitious) life, Robin Hood found a way to improve the lives of hundreds of people. The same can be said of our real heroes: they are not perfect, but by and large they improve the lives of others. They live their lives in the right direction, in other words – giving more to those who have the least.

When it comes to environmentalism, let's not bother asking each other to be saints. Let's forgive each other. With each day, let's try to do a little more to help the Earth, and a little less to destroy it.

Conclusion

Capitalism tells us to want more, to do more, to be more. We have more, we do more, we consume more than we ever have before. But it's not making us any happier or healthier. We keep striving for more and more and more – and in the process we forget to be grateful for what we have.

Rather than trying to achieve and get everything on Earth, and instead of constantly striving to be more successful than anybody else, an ecological lifestyle embraces a simple life. The taste of honey on a piece of wholegrain bread. Sunshine on our backs. A good life. That's what we want. Not being the greatest. Not being #1. Not beating all the competition. Just a good life.

I am not a Biblical literalist, as I said, but I do like the question that Jesus poses: "*What does it profit someone if they acquire the whole world, but lose their true self?*" We absolutely need to adjust to the massive changes that are happening in our world due to climate change. The good news is: the change in our lifestyle, though hard, may be a change for the better.

Questions for reflection and discussion

1. How, in your view, has capitalism contributed to the ecological crisis? Can we have both global capitalism and a sustainable world?

2. Do you agree with the author that modern individualism is not only killing the planet, but making us deeply unhappy?

3. The author proposes six 'trade-offs', or changes to our way of life, to help us live more sustainably. What do you think about these propositions? What changes are you willing to make for a sustainable world?

The author

Bob Janis has been a Unitarian – and Unitarian Universalist – minister for 17 years. He currently lives in Connecticut, USA, and serves as the minister of the Unitarian Universalist Congregation of the Catskills. Before that, he lived in north-west England and served Unitarian chapels in Wigan, Warrington, and Chester, in addition to serving as the Congregational Connections Lead for the denomination. Father of two amazing children, Bob is an amateur poet, Saturday footballer, and three-chord guitar wonder.

Earth Mother, Our Fragile, Floating Home

Kate Dean

Earth Mother,
Our fragile, floating home,
We hear your weeping.

As we sit in our comfort,
Help us to see how changes – large and small –
Can make a difference to our suffering siblings.

Let us put the natural world
At the heart of every action,
At the centre of every decision,
Choosing to tread lightly on the earth
So that we may be good ancestors
To those not yet born
And good stewards
Of that which is yet to grow.

May we not be bowed down
By our despair for the future,
But use our anger as potent fuel
To energise our actions
For a fairer world
For all.

The author
Kate Dean is the Unitarian minister serving Rosslyn Hill Chapel in
London. Her diverse spiritual practices are grounded in her reverence
for nature. She leads pagan Wheel of the Year ceremonies eight times a
year at the Chapel.

10 Learning to Cherish the Earth
Michael Allured

The problem

The ways in which we disrespect our home planet Earth have led many eminent scientists to argue that we face an ecological crisis. We are beginning to experience the devastating effects of global warming: melting icecaps and glaciers, floods, drought, famine, and wildfires. The monsoon season in Pakistan in 2022 resulted in rainfall ten times heavier than usual. Temperatures reaching 40°C degrees in July 2022 in the United Kingdom were the hottest on record. We cut down forests that provide life-sustaining oxygen and we use harmful pesticides that pollute the soil, our rivers, and our seas, as well as threatening the viability of pollinating insects on which we depend. We burn fossil fuels and find it impossible to live without the plastic that revolutionised modern living but is now a major source of pollution. The convenient plastic carrier bag, which takes up to 20 years to decompose when consigned to landfill, is but one example of human ingenuity gone wrong with devastating consequences to wildlife. Human beings are responsible for creating this ecological crisis to accommodate our needs. It is our duty to halt that harm in order to save our planet Earth.

We know what we should do, but we have little inclination to take the drastic action needed to achieve it, because the sacrifice is too great. However, education gives us grounds for hope. But what do we mean by education? For the Dalai Lama it is about hearts as well as minds: "*I have always had this view about the modern education system: we pay attention to brain development, but the development of warm-heartedness we take for granted.*" The crisis of the current education system, he believes, is that it is orientated towards materialistic goals and neglects the emotions. For the Dalai Lama an education of the heart is needed to transform us from being individuals who put ourselves at the mercy of an industrialised culture and a global consumerist economy. We need to re-learn how to be empathetic and respectful guests of planet Earth who are determined to heal the wounds inflicted on what Panentheists consider to be 'God's Body'. The Dalai Lama offers humanity this reflection:

> We have to think and see how we can fundamentally change our education system so that we can train people to develop warm-heartedness early on in order to create a healthier society ... This is not just the concern of religious people; it is the concern of humanity as a whole.[1]

Confronting our disconnection from Nature

The Dalai Lama's words can be applied when we consider what kind of education we need in order to foster a healthier relationship with the planet. Not only do we humans lack warm-hearted care for the ecosystem that gives us life: we are actively abusing it. In the past century the physical and emotional disconnection between humanity and the natural world has grown. For example, the days of hop-picking holidays, a regular opportunity for children of working-class families up to the 1950s to spend all six weeks of the school holiday in fields, are gone. One boy's recollection of his sense of awe at seeing a cow for the first time reveals what children have lost. His sense of wonder was expressed from the heart:

> I saw stars for the first time in clear skies away from the industry of our area. Falling asleep on a hay-smelling mattress under a gently flickering oil lamp as the adults sang songs round a campfire was

---

1   https://educationoftheheartdialogue.org/dalai-lama-education-of-the-heart/#:~:text=%E2%80%9COur%20work%20is%20to%20educate,of%20humanity%20as%20a%20whole.%E2%80%9D.

magical ... My mum and nan did most of the work, leaving me to climb trees and go wild in the country, including one high jump over a fence to avoid a charging bull.[2]

A brief visit to a city farm, however enjoyable and educative, does not offer quite the same experience of 'communing with Nature'. I am not surprised that *The Economics of Biodiversity: The Dasgupta Review* reported that our "connection with nature declines in childhood to an overall low in mid-teens".[3] Nor am I surprised to read in a report based on market research published in 2020 that the majority of children own a mobile phone by the age of seven. *"Many admit that they are fearful of being without their phone, and more than half sleep with it by their bed. Overall, children spend about three hours and 20 minutes each day messaging, playing games and being online, the report by Childwise found ...".*[4]

Technology is wonderfully liberating and makes possible things that our recent ancestors could only have dreamed about. Yet it has taken away our capacity to recognise and respect the workings and significance of the natural world: its amazing beauty and complex intricacy, as well as its capacity to be 'red in tooth and claw'.

The hop-pickers learned about Nature without any formalised programme of education. As a child in the 1960s I loved the inviting aromas of the unpackaged fruits and vegetables on display at the greengrocer's – potatoes covered in soil, for example, leaving no doubt about where they came from. In the butcher's shop children had a more authentic experience of the food chain, compared with today's experience

---

2   https://londonsroyaldocks.com/forgotten-stories-hop-picking-fields-kent/.
3   Final Report of the Independent Review on the Economics of Biodiversity led by Professor Sir Partha Dasgupta, quoted from *Sustainability and Climate Change: A Strategy for the Education and Children's Services System*: https://www.gov.uk/government/publications/sustainability-and-climate-change-strategy/sustainability-and-climate-change-a-strategy-for-the-education-and-childrens-services-systems.
4   https://www.theguardian.com/society/2020/jan/30/most-children-own-mobile-phone-by-age-of-seven-study-finds.

of shopping, when meat purchased from supermarkets is hermetically sealed in plastic.[5]

It is time to rebuild the connection between *Homo sapiens* and the natural world before it is too late. Undoubtedly education is the way to do this. But it has to be about more than filling our brains with facts and the ability to investigate and test theories, important though these are. As well as encouraging clear thinking, we need to find again our feelings: our warm-heartedness and emotional connection with Nature. We need to reimagine and rethink how we all see the purpose of education.

Rethinking the purpose of education

The main driver of educational systems in industrial societies is acquiring skills linked to economic productivity. In England schools are ranked by the examination performance of their pupils, and the inspection system requires measurement of quantifiable outcomes. These factors have created a competitive system whereby schools have little choice but to 'teach to the test'. Success in life and earning a 'good' salary depend on the grades that young people are awarded in public examinations – and so we 'learn more only to earn more'. There is little time to embrace learning for its intrinsic value or for pure pleasure.

After more than 150 years of universal education, and now living in the shadow of pandemics and global warming, we should wonder if our philosophy of education has moved much beyond that of Mr Gradgrind, the school-board superintendent in Charles Dickens's *Hard Times*, who uttered these infamous words:

> "Teach these boys and girls nothing but Facts. Facts alone are
> wanted in life. Plant nothing else, and root out everything else. You

---

5   https://www.farminguk.com/news/british-children-lack-basic-food-knowledge-survey-shows_46677.html.

can only form the minds of reasoning animals upon Facts: nothing else will ever be of any service to them."

There is no place in such a system for learning anything that cannot be measured by economic value. Kenan Malik, writing for *The Observer*, draws our attention to the number of universities no longer offering degrees in the arts and humanities, in order to concentrate on more 'career focused' learning.[6] But for us to flourish and grow, our education throughout our whole lifetime must embrace heart as well as mind. Such an education extends beyond utilitarian needs, to connect with what is intangible and unmeasurable: the awakening of our soul's thirst for knowledge and experience for its own sake.

In the nineteenth century the benefits of arts education for working people were expounded as a means of social improvement. Modern research suggests that young people who studied arts subjects were more likely to volunteer for community projects, because they felt a stronger sense of connection to their social environment. Why is this so? The arts and humanities enable us to witness the lives of others who are different from us and who live in different environments; we come to understand feelings that take us beyond our own narrow experience. Through the power of imagination the arts encourage empathy and compassion, binding us together in our common humanity. The Greeks understood this. Annual drama festivals were a spiritual exercise and a form of civic meditation where audiences wept together in empathy with the characters struggling with impossible decisions and facing up to the disastrous consequences of their actions.

Beneath the surface of what passes for education there lies buried the potential for another kind of knowledge with an altogether different texture, more akin to awareness and empathy. The scene in *Hard Times* in which Sissy Jupe and Bitzer are asked to define a horse illustrates

---

6   https://www.theguardian.com/commentisfree/2022/jul/31/education-frees-working-class-not-getting-better-job.

this powerfully. Bitzer gives the facts: number of legs and teeth, diet, the season for shedding coat, when hooves are shed, the means of telling a horse's age. Sissy does not speak. But as a child of travelling circus parents, she might have spoken, had she not been terrified, about horses' personalities, the texture of their skin, the warmth of their bodies and the smell of their breath. Dickens, a Unitarian before he reverted to Anglicanism, contrasts the warm tone of her skin in the sunlight with Bitzer's, which was *"so unwholesomely deficient in the natural tinge, that he looked as though, if he were cut, he would bleed white".*[7] Sissy is firmly embedded in the sensory world, a world of feeling and imagination (condemned by Gradgrind as "fancy"), a world from which Bitzer is detached.

Another Unitarian, the author, artist, farmer, and conservationist Beatrix Potter, observed: *"Thank goodness I was never sent to school; it would have rubbed off some of the originality".* That originality, inspired by close observation of the natural world, reflected Potter's respect for and love of Nature. One of her biographers, Linda Lear, wrote that she *"brought nature back into the English imagination"* at a time *"when the plunder of nature was more popular than its preservation".*[8] If she were alive today, Potter, a practical woman of action, would have been sceptical about whether the national curriculum in its current form was enough to spark the reverence for Nature found in her books and illustrations.

The scale of the challenge

There is no easy answer to ecological problems. Solving them is more complex than each of us just 'doing our bit' to put things right. If she were alive today, I would like to think that Potter, with her desire to leave the world a better place, would not have been daunted. I like to

---

7   Charles Dickens, *Hard Times*, Book 1, Chapter 2 ('Murdering the Innocents').
8   Linda Lear, *Beatrix Potter: A Life in Nature* (Penguin Random House UK, 2007).

imagine the woman whose passion for conservation drove her to protect large areas of the Lake District for future generations joining forces with Sir David Attenborough as an influential presence at the 2021 COP26 international climate conference. I wonder if she would have agreed with evidence presented to the UK Parliament's Environmental Audit Committee by Archie Young, the UK lead negotiator, that "across the board, we achieved what we set out to achieve"? Or would she have shared the view of the UN Secretary-General António Guterres that the approved COP26 agreements were a compromise that reflected "the interests, the conditions, the contradictions and the state of political will in the world today"?

Guterres has identified the very essence of the global challenge: a preoccupation with making ever-bigger profits; the idea that expanding economic markets is good regardless of the environmental cost; the arrogance of human beings; and the ever-growing power of corporate culture that sees Earth's resources as capital to be exploited for profit. In spite of its commitment to doubling climate-adaptation schemes, there are those who believe that COP26 once again failed "to provide vulnerable nations with the money to rebuild and respond to the unavoidable impacts of climate change". Instead we remain at the mercy of a global economy in which multinational corporations, under pressure from governments and pressure groups, are keen to display their green credentials – with varying degrees of authenticity. Economic globalisation is a strategy now firmly embedded in the business world. We should not be surprised if profit margins rather than feelings of reverence for and stewardship of the planet are paramount.

If as a species we are serious about stemming and reversing the damage that we are inflicting on the natural world, what are we called to do? Cherishing the Earth means that we cannot continue acting as though human beings are the measure of all things. As a first step we need to be brutally honest with ourselves and stop pretending that we can have our cake and eat it. Sacrifices are required, and we may have to accept a drop in our standard of living. The question is whether we as individuals and the global companies and governments that control our lives are willing to make such sacrifices in order to honour the Earth and hold it in trust for future generations. What needs to change if we are to live in right relationship with the planet? And how can we Unitarians, who embrace the ethic of seeing ourselves as part of the interdependent web of life, help to bring in those changes? For the headline response to both questions I echo the Dalai Lama's philosophy: the need to educate the heart as well as the mind. But how do we begin?

Education of the heart

Since Roger W. Sperry developed the 'right brain/left brain' theory in the 1980s, modern neuroscientists have concluded that, generally speaking, we in the West depend more on the left hemisphere of the brain, the source of logic and rational thought, language, and numbers. People for whom the right hemisphere is more dominant are said to be more creative and intuitive, stirred by poetry and music, more open to religion, and sensitive to the beauty of Nature. More recent research, however, has revealed the brain to be more complex than that and has shown that its two hemispheres can work together by communicating through the corpus callosum.[9] What is needed is for us to reassess the value that we place on the branches of learning that feed the soul rather than the bank balances of multinational corporations. This way leads towards healing our own spirit, starved by our alienation from the natural world, and our relationship with Nature itself. We need more right-brain thinking or, at least, we need to engage in more activities that encourage the two hemispheres to talk to each other.

---

9   https://www.verywellmind.com/left-brain-vs-right-brain-2795005 quoting J. Liederman, 'The dynamics of interhemispheric collaboration and hemispheric control', *Brain Cogn.* 1998;36 (2): 193-208. doi: 10.1006/brcg.1997.0952.

Experiencing awe and wonder in the natural world

In her recent book *Sacred Nature*,[10] Karen Armstrong writes that we need to think differently about the natural world, and that acting differently is not enough. She writes that we *"need to recover the veneration of nature that human beings carefully cultivated for millennia"*, and that if we fail in this responsibility *"our concern for the natural environment will be superficial"*. When using the word 'thinking', she means more than getting the rational left brain into gear: she is talking about the re-education of our hearts. We need to allow ourselves time to be fully present in the sensory world; only then will we encounter a sense of awe and wonder that leads us to a state of reverence and gratitude.

This was my experience when I reached the top of Kinder Scout, the highest point in the Peak District, standing at 636 metres above sea level and visible from miles around. I took in gulps of fresh air and looked around as I felt the wind against my body. On another occasion, walking alone along the beach in Broadstairs and pausing to look far out to sea, tasting the salt in the air, looking across Viking Bay to the house where Dickens stayed, I wondered about the lives of those who had done the same over the centuries, and the souls who will do so when I am long returned to dust. These experiences were brief moments when body and soul had connection with Earth's mystery and grandeur, a sense of being part of that which is greater than humankind.

Without these feelings of reverence and awe, we put ourselves and future generations in peril. My companions and I were told not to embark on our Kinder Scout pilgrimage in poor weather or without proper boots, suitable maps, warm clothes, and an awareness of the terrain. In other words: be respectful in your encounter, especially by taking your discarded food packaging home with you. As to the sea, even

---

10   Karen Armstrong, *Sacred Nature: How We Can Recover Our Bond with the Natural World* (Bodley Head, 2022).

when looking in wonder at the beauty of the water reflecting the sun's rays, we must not underestimate its strength – as I did when, aged seven, I was knocked off balance by a wave and swept under the current. Our life-giving planet deserves our respect. We are not showing respect by filling the sea with sewage, pesticides, and plastic.

Getting close to the Earth

A deeper respect for the living Earth beyond a superficial nod is urgently needed. We shall rediscover a healthier relationship with the Earth by re-learning mindful gratitude towards our planet and treating with reverence the life that it sustains. We can only hope that UK government initiatives like the green education strategy published in 2022 will provide the catalyst to awaken curiosity about the natural environment.[11] To nurture warm-heartedness towards the planet, the curriculum will need to do more than simply provide *"opportunities to develop a broad knowledge and understanding of the importance of the nature, sustainability, causes and impact of climate change"*. The translation of empirical knowledge into positive actions and solutions requires 'heart knowledge' too: the sense of connection that we experience by getting our hands dirty growing our own fruit and veg and picking it fresh to use in creating a nutritious meal from scratch, rather than relying on unhealthy ready meals in plastic containers. Empathy with the Earth is found by spending more time outdoors, walking in woodlands and parks, paying attention to birdsong, and stopping to notice the grandeur of trees through the changing seasons.

In modern life we are so driven by time-related demands and relentless activity that it can be almost impossible to be fully present in the moment, to pay attention to the environment around us and enjoy the

---

11 'Sustainability and Climate Change: A Strategy for the Education and Children's Services Systems', April 2022. https://www.gov.uk/government/publications/sustainability-and-climate-change-strategy/sustainability-and-climate-change-a-strategy-for-the-education-and-childrens-services-systems.

quiet that brings forth birdsong. We walk in Nature and yet we do not see or stop to listen: we are too preoccupied with taking photographs of flowers and birds on our phones, rather than standing still to experience their beauty with our senses.

Feeling reverence as well as respecting reason

As a minister of religion I feel the need to consider what our response as Unitarians should be to the plight of our planet Earth, and how we can draw strength and courage from our dissenting roots to help us find our way. From earlier times our faith called us to stand for religious liberty and social justice. Unitarians and Unitarian Universalists campaigned for women's suffrage and equality for lesbian and gay people, including equal marriage. We need to ask if caring for the planet and promoting holistic education about environmental concerns are the pressing theological and ethical problems in the present century to which Unitarians should turn.

With heart and mind I believe this to be so. Society 'educates' for economic achievement and so places greater value on competitiveness over connectedness in a way that *"dehumanizes its participants by seeking to 'impose a social discipline on the non-rational passions of human nature'"*.[12] We are left spiritually poorer because this *"is a major source of spiritual alienation"*, leading to a *"materialist urge to control nature"*.[13] Rooted in reverence as well as reason, each of us reading this book is called to challenge the reductionist approach to education. It processes meaning only through the dualism of body and mind, when what we need for wholeness is to recognise the central place of spirituality in our lives, and our soul connection with that which is greater than ourselves. The deeper calling of education is surely to break through the limitations of valuing

12   R. Miller (1997), *What Are Schools For? Holistic Education in American Culture* (Holistic Education Press, 1997, p. 41).

13   Ibid., p. 19.

only the human knowledge and skills that create wealth, and instead to connect with our deeper purpose: finding the 'soul wisdom' to set us free to live in harmony and not conflict with Nature. Therein lies our hope.

Hope, of course, can be empty if there is an emotional disconnection between understanding the facts with our rational minds and realising what they mean in our hearts. If we plant seeds in the expectation of growing food but then do not tend the soil by watering it, the seeds do not grow. Greed, power, competition, ignorance, and all manner of vested interests prevent meaningful and effective action. Surely with our love for the Earth, and guided by what we understand to be matters of ultimate concern, our mission as people of reason and reverence is to acknowledge the ecological disaster that we are witnessing and to confess our complicity in causing it. We need to help the world see the disconnection between targets agreed at international summits and action that comes from the humility of realising that human beings are not the apex of life on Earth and should no longer be regarded as the fundamental unit of value. The needs of other species must be paramount; we are mutually dependent, but only we humans are capable of making the decisions that will restore the balance in our relationship with the Earth.

For each of us the journey will be different. If we are to care for this magnificent planet that we call our home, we must begin the journey – although 'pilgrimage' might be a more fitting description – using our heart as well as our head for orientation. On the way to our destination – the redemption of our relationship with the natural world – there will be many hours of what Karen Armstrong calls "quiet sitting" in contemplation. In the end the heart of the matter is this: whether we view Earth's eco-system in wholly secular terms or are also influenced by religion and spirituality, it is time for humanity to rediscover empathy for the Earth and its interconnected web of life, in order to find solutions to ease its suffering. On this all our lives depend.

Questions for reflection and discussion

1. The Dalai Lama tells us: *We have to think and see how we can fundamentally change our education system so that we can train people to develop warm-heartedness early on in order to create a healthier society ... This is not just the concern of religious people; it is the concern of humanity as a whole.* What do you understand by this idea? What does 'education of the heart' mean to you?

2. Where do you find your moments for 'quiet sitting' with Nature? How do those moments influence your thoughts and feelings about your relationship with the Earth?

3. What responsibilities do faith communities have towards caring for the planet through the education of our hearts and minds, and how do we honour Earth in our everyday lives?

4. The Unitarian minister Edward Everett Hale said this: *I am only one, but still I am one. I cannot do everything, but still I can do something, and because I cannot do everything, I will not refuse to do the something that I can do.* What continuing gift to the planet will you make to the Earth today?

The author

Michael Allured is the minister with Golders Green Unitarians. He has been an active Unitarian for over twenty years, leading worship in Unitarian congregations across the London and South East District and beyond. Michael has a particular interest in pastoral ministry, meditation, the power of storytelling, and 'deep listening' as a spiritual practice. Alongside Unitarian ministry Michael continues to work part-time for the Civil Service. From the beginning of the pandemic he led half-hour daily meditations (*"a tea break for the mind"*) for his office colleagues.

Incantation

Linden McMahon

I cut my forearm
on the Shard;
let the blood fall
into my garden.
I take a seed I found
in the cemetery-turned-woodland
with its uncountable textures
and clearings floored in leaves
turning to humus turning to mushrooms:
I take that seed and plant it
in the clotted earth.

I breathe in outbreath CO_2
on the crowded Tube
like leaves. I know my cells
are floating through the tunnels.

I eat what I am given:
canal-side blackberries
enclosing pollution that drifted
into flowers like stardust.
Know that you are not a cancer,
they say. *Know that you are a cell*
which is plotting to overhaul the city
by becoming it.
Let the black snot and smog cough
be your communion.

I speak to the thin fox regarding me
from the garden wall. She is not afraid.
She says, *This is land.*
This is what we have made of it.
I tell her, I cannot bring back the holy grove
that some say London was named for.
But I can be it, I can take my hands
and make them into trees.

The author
Linden McMahon is a poet, performer, and member of the wider
Lewisham Unity community. This poem was first published in *Finished
Creatures* in 2019. The copyright remains with the author.

PART FOUR:
Active Hope

Active Hope: Prologue
Claire MacDonald

> *We need to recognise that we live in the world as it is, but not let go of*
> *our expectations of the world as it should be.*
> (Keith Hebden[1])

The alchemy of modern Unitarianism brings together a commitment to reason and a passion for social justice with an increasing interest in care for the environment and the spirituality that attends it. I say 'alchemy' because that deep attention to the Earth itself, and the wisdom traditions that celebrate the sacred nature of the human bond with the Earth, may, potentially, transform what it means to be a Unitarian today. At this global tipping point, Unitarians are among those contributing to a green-spirited theology of change in which we understand ourselves as fully participant in an ecosystem that we do not control but for which we are responsible.

This section of the book has been entitled 'Active Hope' because the contributors share experiences that connect personal and spiritual transformation to environmental care. The essence of active hope lies in that connection. Some of us might say that active hope is essential to our well-being. It has certainly been so with human beings since ancient times as an emblem of faith that contributes to the common good, even when that good seems buried or even impossible to find. In more recent times this connective practice has developed into a community toolbox and training network called Active Hope.

Founded by the poet and ecologist Joanna Macy, Active Hope is a compassionate and spiritually open form of eco-social activism. The

---

1   Keith Hebden, *Re-Enchanting the Activist: Spirituality and Social Change* (London: Jessica Kingsley Publishers, 2017).

training sessions begin by expressing gratitude for the gift of life, and acknowledging the critical state of our endangered planet. We are invited to become participants in a spiritually rich approach to climate justice which changes who we are, as well as acting for the common good. As Macy has written, working to change ourselves as well as our Earth enables us to "*discover new strengths, open to a wider network of allies, and experience a deepening of our aliveness*".[2] Macy is now in her nineties. Thirty years ago she took her recognition of the rising ecological crisis and its effects on personal and spiritual well-being and developed it into an eco-philosophy. The urgent cry of those times (and these) is that if we fail to act now, we are doomed. Macy's philosophy approaches human destiny differently. In her world view, "*hope becomes something we do rather than have*".

I first encountered Joanna Macy about ten years ago when she was interviewed by the theologian and presenter Krista Tippett for American National Public Radio's programme *On Being*. Macy said something that struck me deeply: " *(T)here's absolutely no excuse for making our passionate love for our world dependent on what we think of its degree of health, whether we think it's going to go on for ever*".[3] In other words, however despairing we may feel about the future of the planet, our passionate love for the world is innate. In the 1960s, James Baldwin defined that love in his book of prophetic essays, *The Fire Next Time*:

> Love takes off the masks that we fear we cannot live without and know we cannot live within. I use the word 'love' here not merely in the personal sense but as a state of being, or a state of grace – not in the infantile American sense of being made happy but in the tough and universal sense of quest and daring and growth.[4]

2   Joanna Macy and Chris Johnstone, *Active Hope: How to Face the Mess We're In with Unexpected Resilience and Creative Power* (San Francisco: New World Library, 2022).

3   Joanna Macy (2010), *A Wild Love for the World*, https://onbeing.org/programs/joanna-macy-a-wild-love-for-the-world/.

4   James Baldwin, *The Fire Next Time* (London: Penguin Books, 1964).

We cannot do the work of change without honouring our grief for our losses, both those that environmental devastation has brought – the loss of species, of habitats, of seasons, even of the future – and the discomfort and pain of human-made injustice. But our future flourishing will not come from our anger and despair: it will be powered by love "*as a state of being, or a state of grace*".

That commitment to a transformational, universal love suggests a connection between James Baldwin and Joanna Macy, and between racial justice and environmental justice. Baldwin's advocacy of a questing and daring love called for oppression and racial injustice to change under love's power, releasing the "*untapped and dormant force of the previously subjugated, in order to survive as a human, moving, moral weight in the world*". Macy's advocacy for a better world is also committed to facing injustice and fuelling change with love. For each of them (and the many other writers, thinkers, sages, and ordinary people for whom change is an urgent demand), our love of where we are and who we are can transform our day-to-day encounters with one another and nourish the Earth for which we are called to care. It is here that we can find the sacred as a counter to despair.

At Lewisham Unity,[5] where we brought Active Hope workshops into the local community in 2020, Macy's philosophy of "*discovering new strengths, open to a wider network of allies and experiencing a deepening of our aliveness*" has been a crucial part of our own change, asking us to engage with hope as practice, and connecting ecological activism to the possibility of other kinds of much-needed activism for justice. Our workshops were led by a queer gardener and poet and a writer who is a woman of colour. Poet Linden McMahon and writer activist Yaz Autwal trained as leaders with Active Hope London, and they brought with them an attention to the power of collective and personal transformations and transitions of many kinds, actively addressing the fluidity of identity and understanding the vulnerability that injustice and marginalisation produce.

---

5   A Unitarian community in south London.

We began working with Active Hope in the middle of the Covid pandemic. As the Minister, I was searching for a practical green theology that addressed our need for hope in hard times. Like everyone else I had my own 'hope history', my personal times of searching for hope, and my own history as a member of campaigning groups. I too had experienced the burn-out that comes from acknowledging the urgency of what faces us, and the connections between racial, social, and climate justice. I too needed to find space for that 'deepening sense of aliveness'. In services and talks I had cited Barak Obama's commitment to hope as the *"thing inside us that insists, despite all evidence to the contrary, that something better awaits us if we have the courage to reach for it"*.[6] I had found resources for hope in Lynne Segal's writing on *Radical Happiness,*[7] in which she invites us to co-create our imagined future not by scrolling down a To-Do list of jobs to make a more equal world, but by creatively imagining ourselves into a world that we want to be in — a world not dominated by economic rules but made in imagination and love. These and other writers and activists insist that, despite all evidence to the contrary, as James Baldwin wrote in the 1960s, *"Everything now, we must assume, is in our hands; we have no right to assume otherwise"*. But these were (and are and continue to be) hard times for hope. Change takes a long, long time.

We often perceive our own times as particularly tough. We imagine that our own hard times are uniquely special – but we know that they are not. They are merely *our times*. Yet we also know that we inherit a degraded world that we are called upon to heal; that we face an ecological crisis of almost unimaginable proportions; and that we are in the midst of continuous warfare fuelled by extractivist economies which exacerbate the likelihood of destructive climate change. No other human population at any other time has lived so precariously close to the precipice. Even those who have no truck with the Judaeo-Christian narrative of end

---

6   *Barak Obama's Caucus Speech*, 2008, https://www.nytimes.com/2008/01/03/us/politics/03obama-transcript.html.

7   Lynne Segal, *Radical Happiness: Moments of Collective Joy* (London: Verso, 2017).

times, redemption, or messiahs may feel that we might just be coming to the end of a world in which it is possible to thrive.

In these times, to imagine that hope is something we can *do* rather than *have* is in itself an act of faith. Yet we can 'do' hope – through the ways in which we care for, love, and honour the world as we find it in the unfolding present – shot through as it is with extreme polarities and anger – and still make space for beauty and possibility. That is why I think that Macy's words about our passionate love for the world in which we live ring true, and why I think they are important enough for us to carry them into the shaping of the Unitarianism of the future.

The new ecology of hope is informing an approach to contemporary spirituality that I now find in many and varied places. There is a rising commitment among spiritual thinkers, artists, and others across all faiths and none to the idea that, as Karen Armstrong says in her new book *Sacred Nature*,[8] the natural world itself is *"imbued with sacrality"*. The holy is not somewhere out there, but is, as the Unitarian Universalist minister Kendyl Gibbons reminds us, among us at all times. At Lewisham Unity her words are often used as the chalice candle is lit:

> The holy is nothing but the ordinary, held up to the light and profoundly seen. It is the awareness of a creativity and a connection that we do not control, in a universe that is always larger, more intricate, and more astonishing than we imagine.[9]

Karen Armstrong suggests that in order to treat the world as sacred we need to do two things. The first is to understand God differently, to perceive divinity within the entirety of the material world, both animate and inanimate, and to understand ourselves as participants in

8   Karen Armstrong, *Sacred Nature: How We Can Recover our Bond with the Natural World* (London: The Bodley Head, 2022).
9   Kendyl Gibbons (2006) *Human Reverence*, UU World, https://www.uuworld.org/articles/need-language-reverence.

a connected ecology that we do not and should not control. Thirty years ago, the anthropologist Cedric Robinson wrote that we are, all of us, agents of the divine, and if we think of ourselves as divine agents we move away from any idea of being in control or dominion over this world and become instead "guarantors" of our world and our imaginations, *"measuring freedom instead by what we are capable of divining"*.[10] The second thing that we need to do is to renew the rituals and collective imaginings – drawing as they will from past wisdom traditions – that enable us to practise our commitment to the sacrality of Earth.

Active Hope can guide us in developing practices that are not based in creedal commitments, but in an ongoing and unfolding journey of what some recent writers call 'enchanted' activism. The activist Anglican minister Keith Hebden says of enchanted activism that it takes place when we allow ourselves to engage with the full reality of our lives, acknowledging our mortality and learning to *"lose and find ourselves in the broken world around us and participate with it, for the common good"*.[11] Enchanted activism embraces the spiritual work that Joanna Macy calls a "deepening of our aliveness". For writers such as Karen Armstrong and others, the ecologist and story-teller Sharon Blackie[12] and the nature writer and activist scholar Robert Macfarlane[13] among them, story telling, art making, and music are integral to this. Along with practices drawn from ancient religious teachings, these arts draw us into creative connections beyond logic and science and into a deeper knowledge of the hidden realities of the material world. They encourage us to become enchanted activists. Far from being out of touch with the ordinariness of life, enchanted activism is based in an acknowledgement of our mortality, and our responsibility for Earth care and people care within

10   Cedric Robinson, *An Anthropology of Marxism* (London: Pluto Press, 2019).
11   Keith Hebden (op. cit.).
12   Sharon Blackie, *The Enchanted Life: Reclaiming the Magic and Wisdom of the Natural World* (Tewkesbury: September Publishing, 2021).
13   Robert Macfarlane, *Underland: A Deep Time Journey* (London: Penguin, 2020).

what the Lutheran sociologist Peter Berger calls the "sacred canopy" within which we make our lives as humans.[14]

I call this "taking to the edge", after the theologian Howard Thurman. In the 1950s, Thurman used the phrase "the growing edge"[15] to name the place that we occupy in full recognition of the danger that we are in as a species, of our finite lives, and of the beauty and joy of our existence. At the growing edge we dance, play, build for the future, love, and die, knowing that, as the writer Ursula K. Le Guin wrote in her novel *The Farthest Shore*, "*We need the darkness to see the stars. The dance is always danced above the hollow place, above the terrible abyss.*"[16] At the growing edge we dance the dance of active hope.

These strands of creative response and new purpose share much with Unitarian values and ethics as I understand them: that there is a spiritual dimension to our lives; that it is in a continuous process of revelation, unfinished and always changing; that symbols give us the capacity to make meaning; that the world that we inhabit is sacred at its heart because we make it so; that what we do together is more than what we do apart; that our relationships with one another are founded in free consent; that a better way is possible; that freedom is grounded in the connection between individual and community. As Unitarians we know that our ethics, principles, and commitments are necessarily in a continuous process of collective re-visioning which emerges from interrogating the values of the past that we inherit. As the twentieth-century theologian James Luther Adams said, we must put our trust in a creative narrative that is also re-creative, each generation finding "*insight into the nature of human existence and spiritual values*".[17]

---

14   Peter Berger, *Sacred Canopy: Elements of a Sociological Theory of Religion* (Anchor Books, 1990).
15   Howard Thurman, *The Growing Edge* (Richmond, Illinois: Friends United Press, 2014).
16   Ursula K. Le Guin, *The Farthest Shore* (New York: Bantam Press, 1977).
17   James Luther Adams, *On Being Human Religiously: Selected Essays on Religion and Society* (Boston: Beacon Press, 1976).

In the essays that follow in this section the contributors offer threads of connection between hope as an ideal and the practice of cultivating joy, abundance, and creativity at the growing edge. To be actively hopeful requires a practice of being human differently. It requires us, while allowing the terrible fact of the planet's degradation to inform us, still to dance, dig, and hope. That's soul work. The implication is that it is only when we face the edge with love that we understand our true potential, and, I suggest, our divinity. We live at the growing edge, and the edge is a space of joy and wonder, an understanding expressed in Ursula Le Guin's perception that we always dance above the abyss.

In Catherine Robinson's account of the transformation of "*a scruffy piece of waste land in my home town of Oxford*" into a collective project for urban eco-renewal, a lively spirit of connection runs between reflecting on the small, detailed commitments needed for real change to happen and an awareness of the wider implications of rewilding and environmental projects. Some of Unitarianism's foundational writings express active hope in the healing power of our connection with nature. Catherine reminds readers of Ralph Waldo Emerson's perception of the Universal Being as a current circulating through him – a theology closely connected to Karen Armstrong's call to reconnect the ancient bond between humanity and the Earth. Whatever we call God is here with us, and we exist alongside the 'current' that circulates through all things.

Rebecca Daley and Elizabeth Bergeron each write on gardens, community, and personal journeys. Emerson's deep feeling of connection with nature is echoed in Elizabeth's meditation on encountering nature in a time of grief, learning from her early childhood sowing of pansy seeds, guided by her mother, and remembering "*the patting down of the earth, a little water, a bit of hope, and together we'd created something. We'd created life.*" In Elizabeth's essay, Earth care and people care intertwine in her own journey through loss, into love, and onwards into community-orchard stewardship. Through all of this, the understanding that it is in co-creation, in seeding new growing projects, and learning to let go and let others pick up the threads, that gratitude becomes part of the sacred social mix. The world is sacred for us because we make it so, and the future practice of making sacred caring rituals – from the ancient Blossom Day to the newer Apple Day, founded by Common Ground in 1991 – is in our hands.

Rebecca Daley's essay is about her first garden, the patch that she still gardens and that used to be an orchard. She proposes that gardening prepares us to accept the uncertainty at the heart of human experience and to understand that in the process it teaches us trust and even grace. A garden is material; things fail and die; we work hard only for it to go wrong; we become tired – and yet: *"As a spiritual practice, gardening has taught me how to fail, and how to be patient. It has reminded me again and again that my contribution is needed, even though it is imperfect and never really feels like enough. Put more simply, I realise, gardening has taught me how to hope."*

#Blessed are a group of young bilingual and bi-cultural Welsh-based Unitarians whose response to what they call in their collectively written essay this *"crazy, chaotic, and beautiful world, during these worrying and uncertain times in which we are living"* is to join the dance and make things happen. Their essay takes a ground–up, activist approach to change making that embraces spirituality and social justice and that digs deep into the fun of mutual self-care while doing it, from collective beach cleaning to their audacious creative piece of land art called Sally the Rock Snake, in which rocks from the local river formed the body of a snake, shaped, drawn, and painted on and continually rearranged by local children. *"We want to make an impact on the world and its inhabitants; we want a hand in shaping it into a better place,"* the group says. #Blessed are now reaching out virtually to young Unitarians across the globe, part of a conversation that links them with activism and activists across generations through projects that connect Earth care and people care in mutual care.

Each of these essays is in itself a kind of journey, fuelled by trust that the journey itself matters, and that in undertaking it we nourish ourselves and serve the future of the planet. And the writers are witnesses to the transformative alchemy of active hope. As Catherine Robinson says, *"Our planet is sick. On that, I think, we can all agree. But I believe that on a small and local scale, at least, we can heal it ... and in the process we can heal ourselves."*

Questions for reflection and discussion

1. What does 'active hope' mean to you as a Unitarian?

2. How might acknowledging the pain, grief, and discomfort of our current environmental crisis grow into hopeful action?

3. How important are rituals and practices in deepening your own sense of sacred nature?

The author

Claire MacDonald is a Unitarian minister and writer working in social change and art contexts to explore new ways of doing, being, and meaning through conversation and collective practice. As an activist for change, she is committed to the idea that change originates in culture; and that religion, like art, operates at the moving edge of experience, always edging into what is just beyond what we think we know. She was the minister with Lewisham Unity from 2017 to 2022 and is currently the Chaplain and Ministry Tutor at Harris Manchester College Oxford.

11 Redeeming a Rubbish Dump: some lessons learned

Catherine Robinson

Our planet is sick. On that, I think, we can all agree. But I believe that on a small and local scale, at least, we can heal it ... and in the process we can heal ourselves. I know this from my own experience of working to save the Trap Grounds, a scruffy piece of waste land in my home town of Oxford. Reclaiming this site for wildlife and community well-being has taught me the healing power of doing constructive manual work in the open air, in a green space, as part of a team of like-minded people. As someone who is prone to occasional bouts of depression, I have found that such work is essential for my mental and physical health. In the words of Stephan Harding in his book *Animate Earth*, by making peace with planet Earth, we make peace with ourselves.[1]

Squeezed between a canal and a railway line, with housing estates on the other two sides, the Trap Grounds consist of nine acres of reed bed, woodland, and meadow, forming a rich mosaic of wildlife habitats. The land had been used as a rubbish dump for many years until it was acquired by the city council for development in 1975 – and even then it was neglected for another 20 years. Although drug dealers and rough sleepers moved in, so did a wealth of wildlife: badgers and bats, water voles and lizards, foxes and kingfishers, slow-worms and glow worms, reed warblers and cuckoos, orchids and butterflies. Local people walked their dogs and picked blackberries there.

But the site was squalid and overgrown, so in 1995, inspired by the Unitarian principle of *"respect for the interdependent web of all existence of*

---

1   Stephan Harding, *Animate Earth: Science, Intuition, and Gaia* (Green Books, 2007).

which we are a part" (and desperate for relief from my desk job), I mustered a group of local volunteers to start reclaiming the land in a campaign of 'guerrilla gardening' that (although I didn't know it at the time) would change my life in the process. In the past 25 years we have dragged tons of rubbish from a filthy swamp; created a lake and five ponds; cleared invasive willows from the reed bed; installed a boardwalk for wheelchairs and pushchairs along the bank of the stream; built a bird hide and an insect hotel; and planted hundreds of trees (fifty shades of green!), not to mention snowdrops, primroses, and bluebells. The work never ends.

Now formally constituted as the Friends of the Trap Grounds, we manage the site for wildlife, recreation, and education. There are regular work parties, with tasks for all ages and abilities. Expert ecologists lead bird-song walks at dawn, and glow-worm expeditions at dusk. From the very start, we had a vision of the site being used for educational purposes. Now the local primary school uses the glades for storytelling and nature study. Students from Oxford University conduct research here. Teenagers come to do photography projects and litter-picking tasks for their Duke of Edinburgh award.

Sometimes at community events we invite visitors to write their thoughts on scraps of paper and tie them to trees. One visitor wrote: *"This place is a patch of Paradise"*. In a creative-writing project with the local school, a class of seven-year-olds were invited to sit quietly and note what they could see, hear, and smell. One wrote:

If you are quiet for just a moment you can hear the water trickling down the freezing waterfall. I tasted the sour wind with my tongue.

And another:

If you are quiet for just a moment you might see the swans making ripples along the water. You will feel calmer or you may thank God.

On another occasion, nine-year-old Noa wrote:

The snowdrops are the very first flowers to break through the snow at the end of the winter. They are the encouragement for all flowers through the whole year, as one of the most beautiful of all. So be the encouragement for the people around you, and you will be the most beautiful of all as well.

What better motto for a group of volunteers up to their knees in mud, dragging rusty car parts and broken lavatory cisterns out of a smelly swamp?

Lessons learned: working with volunteers

There is nothing like tackling a manual task together as a team to create a sense of purpose and solidarity. In the process of organising countless work parties on the Trap Grounds, I have learned some useful lessons about motivating volunteers and maximising their impact.

For example, although it may seem obvious, don't forget to *introduce the volunteers to each other*. Don't just assume that they will know each other, or have the confidence to introduce themselves. ... *Explain the purpose of the task.* ("We're clearing this swamp to encourage the return of water voles"). ... Try to *make it fun*, and if it isn't fun, find some other way to reward the volunteers and make them feel appreciated. Tea and biscuits round a big bonfire work wonders! ... *Set realistic goals*, with easy targets that can be reached in small steps within an identified deadline. A deadline is good because it reassures volunteers that they are not signing their whole lives away. ... Once people have been introduced to each other, and the target has been set, *leave them to organise themselves*. For example, one group devised an efficient system of transporting rubbish to a skip in relays, without any prompting from me. ... *Get to know each volunteer as an individual, and discover their particular skills.* In another group I identified a keen photographer, a book-keeper, a web designer, a graphic artist, an expert botanist, and a musician who had contacts with performers all over the city. All of them eventually contributed their specialist skills to an epic judicial campaign to save the Trap Grounds from destruction. Finally, don't just thank your volunteers: *report back to them afterwards* with a summary of what they have achieved.

Lessons learned: raising money

Volunteers have always been our greatest asset, but money is also essential: there is no getting away from it. Reclaiming the Trap Grounds has cost money – lots of it. The boardwalk alone cost £25,000 in materials and labour. Paying contractors to dredge the stream and create the lake and the ponds cost £15,000. The city council, which nominally owns the land, has no funds to spare for its conservation. So we raise all the money ourselves, and in the process I have learned some useful lessons.

For example, there is actually plenty of big money out there to fund community-run environmental projects, but you have to prove your worth before you can win support from the likes of the National Lottery. So *start small.* Once you've adopted a simple constitution and set up a bank account with at least two signatories, look around for potential local allies. Organise *concerts in community centres* and invite local musicians to play for expenses only (or split the profits with you); we made £4,000 from a single concert in the local church which the vicar allowed us to use free of charge. ... Organise *sales of arts and crafts* on street stalls: invite local artists to sell their work and share the profits. We asked artists to design postcards and greetings cards for sale – these are high-value, easily stored items. ... *Involve local businesses*: many have budgets for charitable donations which they can set against tax. Offer to use their logos on publicity materials. Of course you have to be careful to choose commercial partners whose activities or reputation won't conflict with your group's objectives.

Once you have proved that you can raise lots of small sums, the larger donations (from trusts and big businesses and wealthy individuals) are easier to obtain. But these potential benefactors want proof that you are serious before they will give you money. You should never neglect your local support base. We invite people to contribute a minimum annual sum (£5) plus whatever they can afford; from experience we have learned that this produces better results than charging a fixed membership fee. It is essential to motivate supporters to keep on giving, so I issue an emailed update every two or three weeks, with news of forthcoming events, and members' reports and photographs of wildlife sightings. We have considered applying for charitable status, but are deterred by all the paperwork that is entailed; however, we do of course observe the dreaded GDPR regulations designed to protect supporters' personal data.

What's it worth?

Actually our biggest single expenditure (£50,000) has involved a judicial campaign to register the Trap Grounds as a Town Green under the 1965 Commons Registration Act. It went all the way from a public inquiry in Oxford to the High Court in London, thence to the Court of Appeal, and ultimately to a landmark victory in the House of Lords in 2006. But that's another story, told on our website (www.trap-grounds.org.uk), and anyone rash enough to attempt something similar under the Tory government's subsequently amended legislation is strongly advised to consult the Open Spaces Society for expert advice first.

Cynics might question whether the conservation of nine acres of suburban wilderness actually merits an expenditure of £90,000. In reply I could try to calculate the volumes of carbon dioxide absorbed by the hundreds of trees that we have planted, or the risks of flooding that they have mitigated. But how do you put a price on people's mental health (particularly during the anxious months of pandemic lockdown in 2020/2021)? Studies show that exposure to green spaces can significantly reduce stress and improve people's mood. What price the lasting impact on local children of their regular visits to watch Ethel and Ernest, our resident swans, building a nest, incubating their eggs, guarding their newly hatched cygnets, and then teaching them to fly? How can you monetise the presence of Brown Hairstreak butterflies and Willow Emerald damselflies, two rare invertebrate species that are breeding on our site against all the odds?

For the future, the Trap Grounds, and similar suburban sites easily accessible by public transport, have the potential to host 'Green Gym' schemes. Instead of prescribing medication, in suitable cases GP surgeries prescribe conservation work in the open air for patients who are suffering from depression or who need more physical exercise. This is my ultimate aim; but whether or not it succeeds, the Trap Grounds will always offer fresh air, peace and quiet, and wild beauty to anyone whose spirits need uplifting.

Acting Unitarianly

Throughout the campaign to save the Trap Grounds, I have been influenced by Unitarian values. In the gruelling judicial battle that ended in the House of Lords, I decided right from the start that I had to tell the truth and act transparently – or Unitarianly, if you like. To register the land as a Town Green, I had to provide evidence that it had been used by the local community for lawful recreation, as of right, for at least 20 years. Mustering witnesses to be cross-examined by a leading QC before a government inspector, I warned them that the barrister would try to catch them out with rigorous and tricky questioning, and that the only advisable response would be to tell the truth in every minute detail, even if it seemed contrary to our case. They did – and the inspector accepted every single piece of testimony as valid, and praised the witnesses for their integrity.

Spiritually my inspiration is the Unitarian Transcendentalist Ralph Waldo Emerson, who wrote (in 1836, in his essay entitled *Nature*):

> In the woods, we return to reason and faith. ... Standing on the bare ground, my head bathed by the blithe air, and uplifted into infinite space ... the currents of the Universal Being circulate through me; I am part or particle of God.

It's a thought echoed – whether consciously or unconsciously – in a hymn written by the British Unitarian June Bell: "Wide Green World", in *Sing Your Faith*.

> Wide green world, we know and love you:
> clear blue skies that arch above you,
> moon-tugged oceans rising, falling,
> summer rain and cuckoo calling ...
> If with careless greed we use you,
> inch by extinct inch we lose you. ...
> We are part and parcel of you.
> Wide green world, we share and love you.

Questions for reflection and discussion

1. Do you have personal experience of 'guerrilla gardening'? If so, what were the results? If not, can you think of a patch of wilderness in your neighbourhood that would benefit from some unofficial love and attention?

2. For the benefit of our planet, is it better to devote one's energies to small-scale local conservation projects, or to national and international campaigning initiatives?

The author

Catherine Robinson has been a member of the Oxford Unitarian congregation since 1992, and the Secretary of the Friends of the Trap Grounds Town Green & Local Wildlife Site since 1995. She co-ordinates regular work parties involving members of the local community; nature study and creative-writing projects with local schools; and bat hunts and glow-worm expeditions led by expert environmentalists. Details can be found at www.trap-grounds.org.uk.

12 Growing Together: from pansies to apple trees

Elizabeth Bergeron

People care and Earth care: the twin aspects of active hope. In my own life and work, in love and in grief, I have seen how communities can come together in a commitment to care for others, and I have seen how spiritual communities and eco-projects can help people to feel connected and purposeful, and even to find something called home in unsettled lives and unsettling times. For me, it all began with pansies.

My mother loved to garden and to cook. I grew up in Gloucester, Massachusetts, and, for an American garden, ours was pretty small, but Mom transformed every single inch of it. She would spend hours and hours working out there in her Birkenstocks, tan lines on her feet. Sometimes, she would get the whole family involved for the bigger projects, but mostly it was just her. The first flowers that I remember growing with her were pansies. My mother began by making deep holes in the soil with her thumb, then she let me sprinkle the seeds in. We covered them together, patting down the earth, the soil getting under our fingernails. She was most probably singing too, or humming some kind of tune. It would have been Spring. In the days that followed, I took daily trips to the garden to check on the pansies' progress, enchanted and in awe as the beginnings of the green delicate stems began to peep through, and then – as if in a real-life magic trick – I watched this unassuming stalk suddenly burst into a mass of vibrant colours, overwhelming my senses – but in the best possible kind of way. The flowers became our secret, one that I didn't have to share with my three brothers, a secret over which I had complete ownership. Everyone could enjoy the pansies, but only my mother and I knew how they had begun. I was so proud of them, our pansies – the tiny cut that we had made into the soil, the patting down of the earth, with a little water, a bit of hope – and together we had created something. We had created life.

By the time Mom was admitted into the hospital for the last time, that garden was so beautiful. I wish she had had more time to teach me more about gardening, but in the end there was so little time left. We needed to prioritise. We spent hours on the phone while she was having treatment, and she would talk me through her favourite recipes. I refused to have that taken away from me as well. That would have been a travesty.

After she died, things unravelled. My post-college plans, so full of possibility and opportunity, morphed into a series of minimum-wage jobs and the task of raising a younger sibling while trying not to be a child myself. There were final demands and a poorly heated summer house, the only place that we could afford to live in during the brutal, freezing Massachusetts winters. There was no time to think about gardens or growing.

And then there was the Unitarian Universalist church.

We were brought up Catholic. When our Dad became the choir director at the local UU church, my brothers and I made fun of it because we didn't believe it was 'a proper church'. But when we began to attend regularly and sing in the choir, it really got under our skin. We soon changed from making fun of it to understanding and embracing everything that it stood for. The church community felt like an inclusive space that was incredibly accepting, welcoming, and celebrating of difference – especially important for us as a family with three queer siblings out of four. It made both our parents more tolerant, and they officially joined the church, signing the book and becoming integral, loved, and respected members of the community.

When my Mom first got sick, it was the UUs who saved us. It was a difficult time. We were still young, and our dad was emotionally shut down. Mom was in hospital for a long time. She had to have surgery and she almost died. The UU community gathered around. They organised hospital visits, and most importantly they made sure that Mom was never alone. They put together a rota, working out who would feed us, and who was going to drive us places so that we could still go to our crappy teenage jobs. I had a job working for a catering company that required me to travel up and down the North Shore, and members of the church community drove me to every one of those jobs, including one with a 5:30am start in Salem for which I had overslept. Lucy, an alto in the church choir, waited outside for me in the pouring rain, knocking on the door, calling me on my mobile until I woke up. I was a bit late, but she got me there.

After Mom died, the church established the UU Care Committee. They realised that there will always be a member of the community who needs extra support. The committee still exists, and it feels like such a poignant and touching tribute to my mother. I know that, if she were still alive, she would be a big part of it, and one of the first to volunteer. The actions of the community taught me so much about care and what it means to really support someone in a useful, helpful way. To me, the way that we were looked after, and not just abandoned, is my definition of active hope.

To lose a parent when you are on the cusp of adulthood is a cruel thing, and her loss still ricochets, even now, years later. But even during those awful years after she died, when I was still so sick and broken by the grief of it all, Nature found a way to break through to me. And that too is a sign of active hope.

People talk about dark moments in their lives, when they feel a sense of hopelessness and they wonder about the point of going on with it all. I don't remember ever feeling like that. Sometimes I think I might be the only person I know who has never felt suicidal. In those years after Mom died, I would take my dog Memphis for walks, and we would sit on the rocks by the sea in Gloucester, by the inner harbour, looking out across the water. In those brief, snatched moments away from the chaos at home and all the responsibilities that I had suddenly inherited, I knew that the world was bigger than me, and that realisation was incredibly humbling.

There is something about looking out at sea, acknowledging how infinite it is, that is grounding. Even when everything felt so helpless, those moments on the rocks reminded me that life still had the potential to be beautiful. It was a gift, something to be nurtured and treasured. And that experience, along with the support of my community, really helped to save my life. Even when everything felt as though it was falling apart, I still felt cared for; I still knew what it was to be held. The harbour was partly man-made, not some wild thing: there was a breakwater to protect the whole community when the hurricane season came through. It was unconditional in its protection.

I ended up moving to the UK for a Master's degree in Cultural Heritage & Museum Studies at the University of East Anglia, and I think that the most heartbreaking thing, among the many heartbreaking things about losing my Mom, was moving away from Massachusetts, to which I had always been so committed. It was my home. It was where I felt rooted, I knew its history and it had become embedded in my own history, but it became too difficult to stay. And in the UK it was hard to settle. Partly because of my work as an arts producer, I don't feel particularly tied to any one place, but in every place where I have lived I have always tried to make some semblance of a garden – which is difficult when you move around a lot, and when the house where you live does not belong to you.

Then I fell in love. We were lucky enough to buy a house – finally – with our very own garden. I found a job as a Community Development Officer in the charity sector: a step-change for me. I had spent most of my professional life working in the arts, but working and engaging with communities and bringing people together was something that I had always been drawn to; it made sense. I had seen at first hand how powerful it could be when communities come together: how it could unite people in positive ways. It was a no-brainer to apply these lessons to my professional life.

I feel that capitalism is all about the interests of the individual, and the emphasis on the individual can sometimes be a really dangerous thing. A person can have a home life and a work life, but there is also room for a third place: one where you can make meaningful connections with people who are not your colleagues or your family. This can happen in shops and cafés, but we can take it a step further. I believe it works best when people have a common goal, a shared purpose. Whether it happens within a spiritual community or is a self-organised local gardening project, the outcome is often positive, helping people to feel connected – not just to one another, but also to the place that they choose to call home.

In my new job I was tasked with engaging with a local community in the Fens of East Anglia to help set up a community orchard, funded by the National Lottery Heritage Fund (NLHF). This three-year project involved everything from securing the land to planting trees, working with volunteers from the local area, understanding the history of what was once described as the 'fruit basket' of the country because it was so full of orchards. There was a huge degree of biodiversity in terms of the types of fruit that were grown, including apples, pears, plums, and cherries – and nuts. These orchards, often consisting of smallholdings, had been the very ecosystem of the Fens. After World War II there was a move towards the industrialisation of farming, and these ancient orchards, with big old Bramley apple trees that had been there for decades, were ripped out, giving way to monoculture. As a consequence, there has been much more soil erosion and flooding in the area. The project's main goal was to increase biodiversity through smaller, more manageable initiatives, eventually empowering the community to take them on and manage them together. It was an attractive proposition, and it was strongly aligned with my values.

When I joined the initiative, we had only just received funding. No trees had yet been planted, but land had been secured from the local council on a long lease, and some fencing had been erected. There were plans for a car park, an outdoor classroom, and a compostable toilet, and we had obtained funding to plant a hundred fruit trees. We also discussed planting some willow trees, because willow weaving used to be a big part of the local heritage. We were going to produce events and workshops to raise awareness about the project, getting people excited, encouraging them to take ownership of the venture and invest in it. I wanted to celebrate the amazing diversity of the varieties of apple that are grown in the UK, so I planned events based on the traditional calendar: wassailing in January; Apple Day in October (which is actually a relatively new tradition, founded in 1991 by Common Ground); and my favourite, Blossom Day, dating from the years before the old orchards were destroyed, when people would come from miles around to admire the plentiful blossoms. We were going to try to recreate all these traditions, and more.

But sometimes life has other plans. My relationship with my partner broke down, and it became untenable for me to stay in the area. Again, I was on the move, leaving both my home and my job. I hope to go back to the orchard one day. At the moment it's just an idea, but one that I know will become a reality because of the people from the community whom I had met during the short time when I had been part of the project, all of whom were already committed to making it work. I had started to build the foundations, and because of that I like to think that I played a small part in it. There will always be part of me now in the Fens, in a community that I helped to build, with so many roots, all intertwining and connected, and trees that blossom like clockwork every Springtime, yielding juicy apples ripe and ready for Fall.

It's not insignificant, I think, that Mom chose pansies as the first seeds for me to sow. The most common association that people attach to them is that of love: a love for anyone who is close to your heart and occupies a special place in your life. But pansies can also reflect a person's compassion and empathy, something of which my mother had plenty. Pansies also symbolise free thinking and thoughtfulness, something that cannot help but remind me of Unitarian Universalism and the values that we hold dear. I can't wait to have my own garden again, to make it completely mine, as my Mom did, and pansies will definitely be the first flowers that I plant in it. Being in her orbit taught me that it is possible to teach yourself, that it's OK to keep making mistakes and having to start all over again: you will always get to where you need to be in the end.

Questions for reflection and discussion

1. Do you have memories of childhood gardening? What is the significance of these memories?

2. How have interactions with the natural world shaped or changed you?

3. What role does nature play in your community?

The author

Elizabeth Bergeron is an American Creative Producer, living and working in the UK in the arts and heritage sectors. Her mother church is the First Universalist Church in Gloucester, Massachusetts, but for the last five years she has been a member of Lewisham Unity in London.

In writing this chapter Elizabeth is grateful for the help she has received from Jo Kimber, a Bristol-based Creative Producer, writer, and zine maker who focuses on telling queer stories that history has often forgotten. Having shown some of her work internationally, Jo is currently working on a short film and trying to finish her first novel.

13 The Space in Between

Rebecca Daley

Our garden used to be an orchard. An ancient apple tree guards the gate, bent and twisted into an archway: gnarled twigs in winter; pink and white blossom in springtime; then fresh green leaves and abundant fruit by late summer. The orchard was partly cleared and made into gardens for a row of houses in the 1880s. Our house was divided into three flats a century later, and so the garden was split lengthways into three – like so many in suburban London. Ours is the top flat, and the last garden.

So far back from the road, and reached by a narrow path between other gardens on either side, it feels set apart. If you stand on the stone ledge at the back, you can just see the river through the elders and sycamores that line the steep bank. Birds trill and flit between the trees all around: robins and goldfinches, blue tits and wrens. Coots and moorhens call to one another against the gentle rush of the water. Occasionally there is a flash of white as an egret soars past and, even more rarely, the peregrine falcons that nest in nearby tower blocks swoop into view. The trees are what I love most. The green summer canopy, unfurling every April against a bright blue sky, is the most beautiful sight that I see all year.

It is certainly a spiritual thing – walking every day down the same path, into the same garden. I come here to rest, to feel held by the green world. Watching the bees buzz lazily from flower to flower, wondering why they choose the ones that they settle on, and how honey made from hyacinths might taste. Bright white butterflies flutter against the lime green of the ivy-clad fence. A robin lands on the handle of my spade. I feel my shoulders begin to relax, my breathing slows. I place my hands again into the soil, marvelling at how much the garden has changed since yesterday – new stems sprawling, buds unfurling. Taking a deep breath of cool morning air, face upturned towards the vibrant green – this is the closest I come to worship.

The Unitarian Universalist minister Kendyl R Gibbons writes that these moments of reverence *"[don't] need gods or angels or magical other worlds. The world we have is magical enough, holy enough, sacred enough ... The holy is nothing but the ordinary, held up to the light and profoundly seen"*.[1] And so it is. I have looked for the holy in all the usual places, and all too often I fail to find it. But I find it here in my garden. Talk to me about flowers. Take me by the hand and name every plant, every tree. Show me the rippled sand of the seashore, let me slip into the cool rush of a river at midsummer – then I can understand transcendence.

* * * * *

The garden can be a space to gaze skywards, but it is also a place for hard work – practices that root us deeply in the physical world. I find solace in the repetition: pruning and watering, kneeling and pulling, firming soil and tying in stems. It gets me out of my head. After a spring storm, as I hammer nails into a trellis shattered by fallen branches, I remember lines from the Indigo Girls' song: *"I gotta get out of bed and get a hammer and a nail / Learn how to use my hands, not just my head / I think myself into jail"*. I have thought myself into more than one jail over the years – but, to continue the song: *"Gotta tend the earth if you want a rose"*.[2]

This work cannot be hurried – and my sense of time has lengthened. I have begun to think in weeks rather than days, years rather than months. The steady turn of the seasons which once left me frantic now holds the miraculous promise of second, third, and fourth chances to try again. Victoria Adukwei Bulley writes that in gardening we find *"a mode of connection in which we understand that growth of any kind means that you must both work and wait. Water, and wait. What happens or does not happen*

---

1   K. Gibbons (2006) 'Human Reverence', www.UUworld.org, last checked by the author May 2022.
2   E. Saliers, 'Hammer and a Nail', Indigo Girls, *Nomads Indians Saints* (Denver: Epic, 1990).

next will not be entirely up to you." [3] I had to force myself to wait, to let things become what they would be at their own pace.

I also had to pay attention. Initially I tried to learn everything in advance from books and from the internet. I wanted to skip the part where I didn't know what I was doing. But the intricacies of this place could not be learned from any book: the curve of the edge of the flowerbed, the sun's pattern as it moves across the sky, how the light ripples through the leaves. How often to water in dry weather, when to prune, when the soil will be warm enough to sow seeds: I had to learn it all just by being here. And the more hours that I spent outside, the more I felt myself changing.

* * * * *

The garden can be a space for personal growth, and gardening can be a spiritual practice – but can gardens be more than a refuge? Can they support us in changing the world?

In her essay 'Revolutionary Plots', Rebecca Solnit reflects on the relationship between gardening and activism. She writes: *"A garden can be, after all, either the ground you stand on to take on the world or how you retreat from it, and the difference is not always obvious."* [4] Solnit goes on to explore the danger of gardens becoming a *"realm of quiet idealism ... that too readily slides over into disengagement or the belief that your activism can stop with the demonstration of your own purity and lack of culpability"*. Here she specifically discusses the problem of gardening as an encouragement to focus too much on individual choices – personally opting out of problematic food and farming systems, rather than pushing for the systemic change that would benefit those without access to gardens, or lacking the time to grow their own food.

---

3   V. Adukwei Bulley, 'What We Know, What We Grow at the End of the World', in *In the Garden: Essays on Nature and Growing,* by Various Authors (London: Daunt Books, 2021).
4   R. Solnit, 'Revolutionary Plots', *Orion Magazine,* Volume 31, Number 4, July/August 2012.

Perhaps – in their most functional sense as producers of fruit, vegetables, and flowers – gardens will not usher in a utopian future any time soon. But the beauty of these spaces, and the lessons that we can learn by paying close attention to the seasons and to the soil, are essential in their own way. The natural world is certainly a refuge; but often its beauty challenges just as much as it restores.

The American poet Mary Oliver wrote that *"properly attended to, delight, as well as havoc, is suggestion"*.[5] When we rest in the world, when we acknowledge our deep need for green leaves, bluebells, and bird song, when we experience the wonder of a seedling emerging from cool earth, then we acknowledge just how closely our fates are tied together. Gardening is an invitation into a relationship with the natural world: a stepping stone towards what the Norwegian environmental philosopher Arne Næss calls Deep Ecology. It underlines the idea that we are inherently part of, and interdependent with, the earth: in this way of seeing, we are all connected. Therefore, our work to protect the system that supports human life is no longer altruism, but essential to our own survival.

In all the everyday holiness of the garden, I come to understand that the delight that we experience in nature is the strongest and deepest call that we will hear to protect it.

* * * * *

How then do our gardens prepare us to return to the world better than we were before? The answer will be different for everyone. For me, it is the stubborn messiness of plants and growing: the constant need to try again. I remember reading early on that gardening is a lifelong experiment. I was horrified: I did not enjoy experimenting, there was too much room for error. But there was no success without failure. Almost everything that I planted in the first couple of years was in the wrong

---

5   M. Oliver, 'What I Have Learned So Far', *New and Selected Poems* (Boston: Beacon Press, 1992).

place; too-delicate leaves scorched in the south-facing bed, light-starved stems sprawled sadly from shady corners. Calendula and cornflower seedlings grew pale and withered as summer trees blocked out the sun.

The first spring was hot and dry – and I didn't water anything enough. The second was damper and cooler – there was less need for watering, but instead an army of slugs and snails crawled up from the river (or so I imagined) and proceeded to munch their way through most of what had survived the first year's drought.

And then, of course, there were the urban diggers: the squirrels and the foxes. They stole birdseed and dug up bulbs, throwing around the contents of pots with what felt like a vindictive glee. Once, a feather poking out of the flowerbed revealed itself to be a dead pigeon – buried whole by a fox planning to return and eat later. I wept as I loaded the unfortunate bird on to a shovel and tipped it over the back fence. At night I could hear the foxes' shrill barks in the inky blackness. I imagined them at the end of the garden, indignant at my attempt to cultivate this patch of wilderness that had been theirs for so long.

But I kept trying – and the garden was mostly forgiving. Leggy and slug-nibbled *Verbena bonariensis*, rescued from its shadowy bed and potted up on the sunny patio, recovered enough to thrust out spires of tiny purple flowers by late summer. I moved an *Erigeron karvinskianus* three times, and it rewarded my inexperience on each occasion with a reliable tumble of daisy-like flowers. Hardy geraniums which had seemed unhappy at first grew bushy and flowered profusely in their second year – making me glad that I had not dug them up in despair after just one season. For every seedling that withered, a bud unfurled with inexplicable grace. As the garden flourished, my self-confidence grew: perhaps, despite all of my mistakes, I *did* deserve beauty.

Growing is for me a vital reminder that we are called into a deeper relationship with the world even though we are flawed, even though we will make mistakes. There is value in failed endeavours; there is peace in the process. Even if the flowers never bloom, tending the seedlings can still bring calm; hoping for growth can still sustain us.

And so I find myself again in that space between retreat from the world and engagement with it. In our Unitarian community, we talk about existing in the place where sacred meets social. We feel sure that our spirituality, far from inviting us to turn inwards and away from the suffering of the world, gives us the sustenance and the deep roots that we need in order to engage more fully with it.

As a spiritual practice, gardening has taught me how to fail, and how to be patient. It has reminded me again and again that my contribution is needed, even though it is imperfect and never really feels like enough. Put more simply, I realise, gardening has taught me how to hope. In her essay *Solas, Solace*, the Northern Irish writer Kerri ní Dochartaigh writes:[6]

> I wish I'd known, long before now, that sowing is an act of trust. That the body, as it sows and plants, when it tends the land, as it hopes for growth, gives itself over to a vast and shifting future it could never, in that moment, quite imagine.

When we feel as if we are getting nowhere, when conversations end in misunderstanding and stonewalling, we say to each other: "*Well – you never know, you may have planted a seed*". Perhaps, although it felt hopeless, you said something that will resonate with that person more deeply when the conditions are right.

Hope, in the garden (or anywhere), asks us to give ourselves over repeatedly to the "vast and shifting future" that ní Dochartaigh conjures: the future that we cannot yet imagine. In *Active Hope*, Macy and Johnstone describe hope as "*a practice ... It is something we do rather than have*".[7] This practice

---

6   K. ní Dochartaigh, 'Solas, Solace', in *In the Garden: Essays on Nature and Growing*, by Various Authors (London: Daunt Books, 2021).
7   J. Macy and C. Johnstone, *Active Hope* (Novato: New World Library, 2012).

requires us to take practical steps towards a future that is neither known nor guaranteed, in the full and painful knowledge that our contributions may come to nothing in the end. To hope does not require certainty, or even optimism, but instead asks that we find the value in the in-between, in the doing *something*, when we cannot know the outcome.

And as we work here – in that space between – we need flowers. We need green leaves and the simple magic of fresh air. We need permission to sink unapologetically into joy – knowing that without it we cannot change a thing.

Questions for reflection and discussion

1. What role does the natural world play in your spiritual life? Would you like to do more to connect with nature?

2. When we are doing important work, joy can feel like a luxury – but it's often what keeps us going. What is your relationship with joy? How can you make room for more of it?

3. The ecological and social challenges that we face can often feel overwhelming. Do fears that your contribution may be too small or too imperfect stop you from getting involved in things that you care about? How can you show compassion for yourself when you feel afraid?

The author

Rebecca Daley is a writer, gardener, wild swimmer, and civil servant. She grew up in the Lake District and has a degree in History from the University of Oxford. Rebecca discovered Unitarianism in her late twenties and is currently a member of Lewisham Unity, a Unitarian community based in south-east London.

14 People Care, Earth Care
#Blessed: the Youth Group at Gellionnen Chapel

Hope shall admit no bounds, as love no limit knows;
each new-born dream made real in our commitment grows;
the possible, the yet-to-be, is now, is here, is you and me.
(Frank R Clabburn[1])

We are #Blessed, the Youth Group of Gellionnen Chapel. Our amazing ancient chapel, in the Swansea Valley, is the home of a Christian, bilingual (Welsh/English) community – one of 22 Unitarian chapels in Wales. Initially, the formation of the youth group was just a vague idea which we decided to pursue, with the Chapel's full backing. After numerous meetings and discussions, we became #Blessed. We were excited at the prospect of our new evolving space and what impact we might make. We eagerly put our minds together, and a plan for social action crystallised.

The process of finding our feet involved many meetings, hosting virtual pub clubs, and getting to know each other, Covid willing, on monthly dog walks in the mountains. We brainstormed how we wanted to start off as a group, and we were fortunate in having the full support of the congregation. While the group was starting to form, we all bonded over the problems that Covid was causing us. Not only was social isolation a common frustration within the group – we were missing our families, friends, communities – but watching news about the pandemic, the strain on the health-care sector, national and international disagreements,

---

1 Final verse, Hymn 61 in the Unitarian hymnbook *Sing Your Faith* (Lindsey Press, London, 2009).

ecological disarray, and an out-of-control climate crisis did nothing to help our state of mind. We created a safe space, free of judgement, where we felt able to share our anxieties. Despite the unprecedented circumstances, we found solidarity in each other.

As our group has grown, we meet our more distant members on Zoom, but we still look forward to face-to-face gatherings when possible. At present there are nine of us, aged between 18 and 27. #Blessed provides a space where we can get together, connect with one another, express ourselves, and make a positive impact on the world around us. Through our gatherings and our social-action work, we can live out our Unitarian values and explore what it means to be a Unitarian in this crazy, chaotic, and beautiful world, during these worrying and uncertain times in which we are living. We come with our own distinct stories, experiences, and ideas, our strengths and our weaknesses, joining together as one group under the banner of #Blessed.

We recognise that the Unitarian movement offers a place for everyone, of any age, from any background or walk of life, to gather together and grow together. As young people in the movement we are keen to learn more about our Unitarian heritage and traditions; be an active part of today's Unitarian fellowship, both nationally and internationally; and bring with us a hopeful vision for the Unitarian movement of tomorrow. A common feeling within our group is that we want to make an impact on the world and its inhabitants; we want a hand in shaping it into a better place.

As Unitarians, we are a community of people who take a liberal approach to our religion and spirituality. We encourage the freedom to believe in what your life-experience tells you is true and what your conscience tells you is right. For us, Unitarianism means connection, togetherness, trust, respect, love, and community. We believe in equality for all, regardless of sexual orientation, gender identity, race, ethnicity, or faith. We believe in God, however we choose to conceive of Her/Him/Them/It – as a Divine Being, Nature, Love, or our own Conscience. We follow the teachings of Jesus: to love our neighbours, to treat others as we would wish to be treated. Some view Jesus as the Son of God, others as a wise man alongside other inspiring spiritual figures like the Buddha or Guru Nanak.

Projects

Social projects

It became clear within the first few meetings of #Blessed that there was an intense desire among its members to accomplish something more than just pleasant social events. We wanted to acknowledge the feelings of helplessness caused by the emergence of a global pandemic and harness our energy in order to do some good in our local communities. Our first project was engineered during the first Covid lockdown in 2020, when we worked hard to organise something that would help our local communities, where goals could be achieved remotely, in line with the strict restrictions in place at the time. We took it upon ourselves to write letters to the elderly and vulnerable members of our congregation, broadening out to include other families from a wider area, in order to combat social isolation. Once restrictions were eased in the autumn, we used the opportunity to create and deliver Christmas hampers for those we had been writing to, especially those who lived alone or who did not have any family members close by to share the Christmas holidays with. Since then, we have continued to organise projects with a focus on caring for our local environment.

Beach cleans and waste removals

We have completed two successful beach cleans in Aberavon. We are also addressing the issue of fly tipping on Gellionnen mountain, where our chapel is located, by clearing waste that has been left in difficult-to-reach areas, and we have endeavoured to hold our local councillors accountable for its removal. This project was motivated by the continual disappointment of seeing fly-tipped rubbish appearing along the route that we take to and from Chapel. Our first excursion included the removal of 18 tyres; the second generated 20 bin bags full of rubbish; and our latest attempt involved the removal of 123 tyres, two TV sets, and a kitchen sink. To our great surprise, we have received masses of support in response to our teamwork and have gained a newfound confidence from what we have been able to offer our local environment. We take pride in what we have achieved.

Sally the Rock Snake

In the summer of 2022 we introduced Sally the Rock Snake into our local community. As a group, we decided to paint a large rock as a snake's head, and we invited nearby residents, groups, and schools to create and add to her body. We placed her head on the mountain, close to the Chapel, and initiated the project during our annual #Blessed Sunday Service. We asked the congregation to draw on a rock collected from the local river to help start off Sally's body. The rocks were adorned with drawings and positive words in bright colours.

We then posted pictures on social media and appealed to the local primary school for help in forming the rest of her body. We encouraged people within our local area to add to Sally's body and create an amazing piece of art. Before long, every Sunday as we passed her grassy patch on route to Chapel, her body was growing, becoming longer and longer! The local children would come and count the rocks, rearrange them, and play with the formation to make her body curvier. We are proud to say that after the six-week summer holiday Sally had reached a total of 70 stones! This project brought joy to adults and children alike within the local community, bringing new life to the beautiful area that we call home.

Our results so far show that we are making a difference, and we are having so much fun in being proactive. Actually going out and achieving something brings us together, encourages us to reconnect with nature, and gives us a much-needed boost to our mental health.

We are committed to nurturing our local area, to show the respect that our environment and its inhabitants deserve. And along the way we are showing the impact of young people leading change – collective teamwork – to reach a greater goal. The support that we have received so far in response to our environmental efforts has been a real boost to our confidence, and we hope that we are leading by example, to change the stigma associated with young people and to encourage others to join in.

International connections

We take part in monthly virtual conversations with young Unitarian and Unitarian Universalists from the UK, the Czech Republic, the USA, and Canada. This space that is slowly evolving is the perfect opportunity for us to be our goofy and wacky selves, while learning more about other young people, their interests, passions, and ambitions. Best of all is learning what it means to each individual to be a young Unitarian. We discuss the local, national, congregational, denominational, even continental similarities and differences. The energy is so different with this group, and the freedom that it gives us also gives us great hope that our connections will get stronger, and hope for what will become of this international movement of young Unitarians. Mobilising all this good will and energy will surely change the world for the better.

What does it mean to be a part of #Blessed?

We are always looking for ways to further our outreach and involve as many people as possible in these projects, particularly as we need young people in the Unitarian movement in order to maintain our faith community. The sense of responsibility and dynamism among the members of #Blessed can make a significant contribution to the movement, especially as we will collectively face so many environmental and social challenges in the coming years. Thanks to Zoom, our work now extends beyond the original area around Gellionnen Chapel, with the addition of members who have joined from further afield. The age range has become a little more flexible too, to include some older members, so we adjust as we grow, both in numbers and in age. This opens us up to wider possibilities, and we hope to do a great many things as we move forward.

Being a part of #Blessed has been a big game-changer for us all. Despite our differences in locations, interests, backgrounds, languages, and ages, we are the greatest of friends. This group is making waves, and we are having so much fun doing it! We are very excited about our next chapter: youth leading change, proving the impact of meaningful participation and teamwork, connecting with more people, demonstrating hope in action, and continuing to take pride in being young Unitarians.

The authors

Sian Evans (who also edited the piece), Gwennan Evans, Laura Davies, Joshua Davies, Steffan James, Libby Osullivan, Zac Baker, and Nicola Temple

PART FIVE:
Young Voices

Young Voices: Prologue
Maria Curtis

who were so dark of heart they might not speak,
a little innocence will make them sing:
teach them to see who could not learn to look
– from the reality of all nothing

Will actually lift a luminous whole;
turn sheer despairing to most perfect gay,
nowhere to here,never to beautiful:
a little innocence creates a day.

(e.e.cummings[1])

I feel that we – the not-so-wise elders – owe an apology to young people. We have known for over thirty years that CO_2 emissions were causing global warming, but we have, to our shame, failed to act globally to stop impending disaster from happening.

COP27, the United Nations Climate Change Conference, held in November 2022, failed to achieve a commitment to limit global warming to 1.5°C above pre-industrial levels by 2030. After a temporary reduction during the Covid-19 pandemic, emissions are on the rise again at a time when we need a cut of at least 45 per cent to stay below 1.5°C. We are facing a global problem, the most serious problem the human race has ever had to face, but we do not have global government. Our children have to witness the failure of politicians to take the long view and act now in the interests of the next generation; instead, they see them opting for short-term profits, continuing to take more coal, oil, and gas out of the ground, rather than looking to renewable energy sources for the future. The grown-ups are playing their selfish games, in denial about

---

1   e. e. cummings, *XAIPE: Seventy-One Poems* (Oxford University Press, New York, 1950).

the seriousness of the issues. We have proved ourselves to be unworthy guardians of people or planet.

I would not want to be young in today's world, although the natural world continues to be as beautiful and amazing and nourishing as ever. I do not envy the young having to live with the burden of impending disaster, knowing that the answers lie with our species, yet looking on as we fail to work in concert for the betterment of the world. Their innocent voices cry out, telling the truths that we turn away from in denial or despair. I fear for their mental health, having to live with the prospect of the annihilation of the human race by its own hand, alongside the loss of many plant and animal species that have thrived on Earth for millions of years, long before *Homo sapiens* appeared.

Young people have also witnessed the impotence of adults to stop the war in Ukraine; they are confronted daily with news of atrocities – the bombing of civilians, power stations cut off in the middle of winter – but we seem powerless to intervene, for fear of escalating the war. We cannot be trusted to protect them from danger. And yet some of us lived, as children, through the Cold War in the shadow of the nuclear threat. Our human resilience is astounding. We celebrate our capacity to go on living, forming intimate relationships, enjoying *being* in the natural world, retaining hope.

> When we look at nature, we receive a sort of permission to be alive in this world, and our ... bodies get recharged.
> (Naoki Higashida[2])
> (Naoki wrote this as a 13-year-old autistic boy with no spoken communication.)

Perhaps it is no coincidence that some of the most vociferous young people speaking out on behalf of the natural world are on the autistic

---

2   Naoki Higashida, *The Reason I Jump: One Boy's Voice from the Silence of Autism* (Sceptre, London, 2013).

spectrum or neurodivergent: Greta Thunberg, for instance, and Dara McAnulty. They are our prophets, our seers, unable to dissemble. They speak truth to power. They seem to have a direct relationship with the natural world. We would do well to pray for our innocence to be regained, so that we, too, are able to hear the cry of the Earth, to feel empathy for the creatures whose habitats we are destroying, and for all the people whose lives are being changed irreparably by global warming. Naoki Higashida again:

> Nature calms me down when I'm furious, and laughs with me when I'm happy ... Human beings are part of the animal kingdom too, and perhaps us people with autism still have some left-over awareness of this, buried somewhere deep down. I'll always cherish the part of me that thinks of nature as a friend.

Let us be encouraged by young people like Bella Lack, 18-year-old author of *Children of the Anthropocene*,[3] an inspiring collection of stories of conservation from those most affected by climate change all over the world. Bella says: "*It is the role of humanity, of you and me, to confront society's sluggish resistance to change and to imagine a different story for the future*". Young naturalist, Dara McAnulty, was interviewed by Bella for the book. As a young child growing up in Belfast, he was bullied at school for being different. He was diagnosed with Asperger's Syndrome. His life changed when the family moved to the country and his love affair with nature began. He says, "*We don't need to infuse nature with wonder, we just need to pay attention, because the wonder already exists.*" Let us give thanks to the children and young people the world over who take part in *Fridays for Future* protests, inspired by Greta Thunberg.

When I read the following contributions from young Unitarians, I have confidence that we **will** reach the critical mass of those who care for the

---

3   Bella Lack, *The Children of the Anthropocene: Stories from the Young People at the Heart of the Climate Crisis* (Penguin Life, 2022).

Earth and are determined to live in right relationship with the natural world; who put co-operation above competition; who approach the Other in a spirit of openness and curiosity; who face the truth with courage; who love the world enough to make a difference.

Thank you for your wisdom. Thank you for cherishing the Earth.

15 Children's Contributions

God Is In Every Blade of Grass

At my previous school we had an Eco Club. I'm thinking maybe I should talk to the teachers at my new school about forming one there. The Club tried to help the school environment. We planted bee-friendly flowers, like lavender, and organised litter-picks. We wanted to improve the planet little by little, starting with school.

Climate change worries me. People cut down forests so there is too much CO_2, and greenhouse gases are causing pollution and deaths. Also only 7 per cent of plastic is recycled, the rest ends up in the ocean. I care because we live in this world, the changes are impacting our lives. It won't be the same world any more.

I think religion is involved in our response. God is in everything, every blade of grass, so harming the earth is destroying God. It's His or Its Creation, and we're not following his wishes. We are here to help the world; instead we do the opposite. All religions should come together on this, to create peace with nature, like the Buddhists want, but it's all being disrupted. Our pollution, and also our wars, impact the environment.

In the future there has to be change. I'd like to see new generations help change things and fix our mistakes, to learn better ways.

Rhoslyn Millard (aged 14)

My Ecological Concerns

Here are my worries about the ecology. They are worries that infect children's lives about the world that grown-ups have left us with. Unfortunately, we are being taught to do the same as they do.

Here are some examples. Animals are becoming extinct because of lack of habitat and pollution. Forests are being cut down to collect wood and make houses. The population of the world is dangerously high. And there is not enough housing. Air conditioning is needed, but it takes too much energy.

People need energy to support their lives. Some sources of energy cause global warming, like oil, gas, and coal. Others are good for the environment like wind, solar, and water, but even solar panels use dangerous liquids and are expensive to make.

The food we consume is infected with bad chemicals and processed sugar and fat that are bad for you. Some people think those who are against this are irritating and picky.

This is what children of today have to deal with, and adults have handed us for our lives to come.

I would like to see people more aware and informed and take practical steps to save our beautiful world. Not many people realise that it needs saving. This is what we are dealing with.

Iris Jubb (aged 10)

We Need to Change

We need to change.
Plastic bags, plastic bottles, plastic straws,
Ghost nets and tyres polluting our oceans,
We need to change.
The shoes on our feet,
Flip flops, jellies, crocs, and wellies, too,
The food we eat, the water we drink,
Contains plastic, you better believe,
We need to change.
Forests are being chopped down,
Few still left but not enough
To give us all the air we breathe,
To bear what is ahead.
Not this generation, but the next
Must survive in a world
Of our mistakes.
The world is not getting better,
It is sick.
I am worried and you should be too,
We need to change.
The world as we know it is dying –
That is why
We need to change.

Lucy Ives (aged 11)

The Point of No Return

We have limited time to stop climate change before we reach the point of no return!

Countries need to start co-operating and taking action on big decisions that could affect the environment in a positive way. We need new and sustainable ways to live our lives. We need new solutions to the big problems.

Amelia Ives (aged 13)

I Feel Sad

I feel sad because we shouldn't treat the world like a sandbox where we can do what we want to it and in it.

We should recycle more and use other sources of power like solar or wind, and we should PLANT MORE TREES.

Toby Powell (aged 11)

It's Not Fair

My thoughts on the ecological crisis are that it's not fair. It's not fair that animals and ecosystems are being lost just because we want what's cheapest and easiest to make, not what's best for the environment. My concern is that even if we do manage to switch to electric vehicles and find more eco-friendly ways of doing things, the damage will have been done. You can't bring the extinct animals back. You can't unmelt the glaciers. What if it's already too late?

Sophie Emm (aged 12)

Gurgle
(A climate summit with my 8-month-old son)

John Harley

I look into your eyes.
I see a flower of browns radiating from each planetary pupil.
You stare into my interior,
unblinking,
as if all the wild and innocent life of this Earth
is demanding an answer to why our twenty-first century tribe
continues to cook the climate.

You gurgle and burble.
You speak the language of joy and curiosity.
I wonder what you make of the grown-ups'
babble about the environment?
When you grow, will you forgive your elders' refusal
to halt the exploiting and the cheating
of this spinning garden of blue and green?
Our only home in the vast velvet of the universe.

I look into your eyes.
Your gaze is so pure.
I cannot hide.
Your vision is a lit torch to my excuses and denials.
You have no time,
we have no time,
for neat targets and comfortable promises.
You are the real ambassador of nature,
along with all the babies of this sublime and troubled world.

The fragile skin of the soils and fields of the future,
all living things that simply wish to flourish, not just survive,
the songs of tomorrow's human family –
this blessed kaleidoscope of life
is stored in the geology of your eyes.

My dearest one,
you continue to stare at me,
unflinching,
with a piercing beauty that seeks out
my inadequacies and contradictions.

No doubt you will win this little staring contest,
but will we all lose our priceless foothold on existence?

The author
John Harley is the minister of the Bridport Unitarian community, and
the father of Alec (born in 2022).

APPENDIX

Who are the Unitarians?

We are a spiritual community who encourage people to think for themselves. We believe:

- that everyone has the right to seek truth and meaning for themselves;
- that the fundamental tools for doing this are one's own life experience, one's reflection upon it, one's intuitive understanding, and the promptings of one's own conscience;
- that the best setting for this is a community which welcomes people for who they are, complete with their beliefs, doubts, and questions.

We can be called 'religious liberals':

- 'religious' because we unite to celebrate and affirm values that reflect a greater reality than self;
- 'liberal' because we claim no exclusive revelation or status for ourselves; and because we afford respect for those who follow different paths of faith.

We are called 'Unitarians':

- because of our traditional insistence on divine unity, the oneness of God;
- because we affirm the essential unity of humankind and of creation.

A brief history

The roots of the Unitarian movement lie principally in the Protestant Reformation of the sixteenth century. At that time, people in many countries across Europe began to claim:

- the right to read and interpret the Bible for themselves;
- the right to have a direct relationship with God, without the mediation of priest or church;
- the right to set their own conscience against the claims of religious institutions.

Many came to question 'orthodox' Christian doctrine and to affirm beliefs of their own. These included:

- the Unity or uni-personality of God, as opposed to the doctrine of the Trinity – hence the name 'Unitarian';
- the humanity, as opposed to the deity, of Christ;
- the inherent worth of human beings, as opposed to ideas of original sin or inherited guilt;
- the universal salvation of all souls, as opposed to the doctrine that most of humanity is predestined to damnation.

The earliest organised Unitarian movements were founded in the sixteenth century in Poland and Transylvania. In Britain, a number of early radical reformers professed Unitarian beliefs in the sixteenth and seventeenth centuries, some suffering imprisonment and martyrdom. An organised Unitarian movement did not emerge until the late eighteenth century. The first avowedly Unitarian church in Britain was opened in Essex Street, London, in 1774. Denominational structures were developed during the 19th century, finally uniting in the present General Assembly in 1928.

(Based on *A Faith Worth Thinking About* (a leaflet produced by the General Assembly of Unitarian and Free Christian Churches). More information about Unitarianism can be found at www.unitarian.org.uk.)

The Object of the General Assembly of Unitarian and Free Christian Churches (UK)

Preamble

We, the constituent congregations, affiliated societies and individual members, uniting in a spirit of mutual sympathy, co-operation, tolerance, and respect; and recognising the worth and dignity of all people and their freedom to believe as their consciences dictate; and believing that truth is best served where the mind and conscience are free, acknowledge that the Object of the Assembly is:

Object

To promote a free and inquiring religion through the worship of God and the celebration of life; the service of humanity and respect for all creation; and the upholding of the liberal Christian tradition.

(An extract from the covenant adopted at the General Assembly Annual Meetings, April 2001)

The Seven Principles of the Unitarian Universalist Association (USA)

1. The inherent worth and dignity of every person;

2. Justice, equity, and compassion in human relations;

3. Acceptance of one another and encouragement to spiritual growth in our congregations;

4. A free and responsible search for truth and meaning;

5. The right of conscience and the use of the democratic process within our congregations and in society at large;

6. The goal of world community with peace, liberty, and justice for all;

7. Respect for the interdependent web of all existence of which we are a part.

The living tradition which we share draws from many sources:

- Direct experience of that transcending mystery and wonder, affirmed in all cultures, which moves us to a renewal of the spirit and an openness to the forces which create and uphold life;

- Words and deeds of prophetic women and men which challenge us to confront powers and structures of evil with justice, compassion, and the transforming power of love;

- Wisdom from the world's religions which inspires us in our ethical and spiritual life;

- Jewish and Christian teachings which call us to respond to God's love by loving our neighbors as ourselves;

- Humanist teachings which counsel us to heed the guidance of reason and the results of science, and warn us against idolatries of the mind and spirit.

- Spiritual teachings of earth-centered traditions which celebrate the sacred circle of life and instruct us to live in harmony with the rhythms of nature.

Grateful for the religious pluralism which enriches and ennobles our faith, we are inspired to deepen our understanding and expand our vision. As free congregations we enter into this covenant, promising to one another our mutual trust and support.

(Reprinted with the permission of the Unitarian Universalist Association)

ACKNOWLEDGEMENTS

This book was commissioned by the Lindsey Press in response to a Zoom workshop held in mid-pandemic which identified a need for a Unitarian book with an eco-spirituality focus. So my first thanks go to the Lindsey Press Panel for entrusting me with the role of commissioning editor. It has been a daunting task in organisational terms, but what a privilege to engage at such a deep level with thoughtful and gifted Unitarians, as we shared our hopes and concerns for the Earth! Thank you to all the writers who showed humility and commitment during the editing process, often producing several revisions before submitting their final drafts. I am also grateful to Quaker activist Alastair McIntosh for his profound, challenging, and erudite Foreword – he is a true friend of Unitarianism. I think we have all done a grand job in co-creating a substantial body of work.

None of this would have been possible without the unstinting work of copy-editor Catherine Robinson. She has helped me through the process every step of the way, latterly becoming the editor for my pieces. She has a gift with language, sniffing out any vagueness or ambiguity, with clarity of expression as her prime goal. In doing so, she identified some of my stylistic quirks (although I still haven't worked out when to use *that* or *which*!). It has been a pleasure working with her.

Midway through the commissioning process I asked Claire MacDonald to take over the editing role for the Active Hope section. I am grateful for her excellent introduction and her editing of the contributions in Part Four.

I would like to thank my *Horizons* friends and colleagues, Elizabeth Birtles, Michaela von Britzke, Lindy Latham, Ann Peart, and Isabel Pebody – sources of endless support and encouragement, fun and seriousness.

Finally, a big *Thank you* to my dear companion, Ray Ramsden, for his patient reading of my contributions to the book and his gentle suggestions for improvements; his emotional support was invaluable as deadlines approached.

Maria Curtis
January 2023